For Manfred Edwin Schubert

Preface

The present work was greatly aided by the invaluable guidance and the excellent suggestions of Professor Kurt Müller-Vollmer of Stanford University. I am deeply indebted to him for his constant encouragement, his uncompromising standards of scholarship, and his friendship.

I also wish to acknowledge my gratitude to Professor Edgar Lohner of Stanford University for his enthusiastic support of this study and his stimulating criticisms; to Professor Gertrude L. Schuelke of Stanford University for her painstaking reading of the text and her astute suggestions; to Professor Robert L. Kahn, formerly of Rice University, who guided me to numerous important bibliographical sources; to Mr. James McLeod of Rice University, whose assistance in locating materials for this work spared me many hours; and to Professor Walter H. Sokel of Stanford University, who has given me much friendly encouragement and praise.

I am indebted to the Houghton Library of Harvard University and the Library of the University of Texas at Austin for their willingness to make their first editions of the *Herzensergiessungen* and *Phantasien* available to me. I am grateful to many staff members of the Fondren Library at Rice University and the Estill Library at Sam Houston State University for their generous assistance in bibliographical matters. I also wish to thank the editorial staff of The Pennsylvania State University Press for expert guidance and cooperation in the publication of this book.

Huntsville, Texas   M. H. S.
January, 1971

Contents

PART 1

INTRODUCTION

Wilhelm Heinrich Wackenroder's literary writings originated during the brief span of years between 1792 and his premature death on February 13, 1798. Including all of his extant correspondence, his travel diaries, the *Confessions from the Heart of an Art-Loving Friar* (*Herzensergiessungen eines kunstliebenden Klosterbruders*), and his contributions to the *Fantasies on Art for Friends of Art* (*Phantasien über die Kunst für Freunde der Kunst*), Wackenroder's collected works occupy little more than five hundred printed pages. But the quantity of his writing is no adequate measure of its influence and significance in the history of German and European intellectual life. Wackenroder had an impact which reached far beyond the private circle of friends for whom he intended his work. He is considered one of the principal initiators of the revival of interest in early German art. His essays on Albrecht Dürer engendered substantial attention among his *fin de siècle* readers. By praising the industriousness and diligent craftsmanship of this native German artist as well as the piety of the Dürer family, Wackenroder elevated Dürer to a position of significance in art history. His appreciation of early Italian Renaissance artists is generally regarded as having strongly influenced the Pre-Raphaelite School of painting and the "Nazarenes." The latter group of painters, among them Friedrich Overbeck and Peter Cornelius, retreated into ascetic-pietistic seclusion in an abandoned monastery in Rome, hence there is a clear affinity between Wackenroder's choice of the mask of an art-loving friar and the actual monastic retreat of the Nazarenes.

The new tone of the friar and his tender reverence for art and music also had a deep impact on such other Romantic authors as Ludwig Tieck, Friedrich and August Wilhelm Schlegel, E. T. A. Hoffmann, Achim von Arnim, and Clemens Brentano. Wackenroder's view of music as the most sublime of the arts and his desire to imitate with words the architectonic structure of symphonic music stands in a close relationship to musical Romanticism. Such

3

composers as Felix Mendelssohn, Franz von Liszt, Hector Berlioz, and Richard Wagner realized in their musical compositions ideas which are present in nuclear form in Wackenroder's essays. In addition, the preoccupation with the demonic and nihilistic side of music revealed in the essays on Joseph Berglinger directly affected Arthur Schopenhauer and Friedrich Nietzsche, as well as countless others of the nineteenth and twentieth century.

In Wackenroder's "Wondrous Oriental Tale of a Naked Saint," the anxious concern of the hermit-saint over the ceaseless revolving motion of the "Wheel of Time" serves as a metaphorical expression of the meaninglessness of life. This, together with the saving force of music, anticipates closely ideas found in Schopenhauer and Nietzsche, as well as in Thomas Mann, Hermann Hesse, T. S. Eliot, Ezra Pound, and others. Furthermore, Wackenroder's interest in the unusual, his fascination by Piero di Cosimo's grotesque *trionfo della morte* makes him a precursor of all modern intellectual movements which engage in the exploration of reality via the medium of grotesque appearances.

The impact of Wackenroder was most momentous and far-reaching in the realm of the conflict between "artist" and "world," between "art" and "actual life." For the ambivalent, desperate creative struggles of Joseph Berglinger clearly anticipate the questions of the ineffectuality and uselessness of art which have been raised repeatedly during the nineteenth and twentieth centuries. The story of Joseph Berglinger stands at an early phase in the tradition of the "novel of an artist" (*Künstlerroman*), a lengthy tradition which one can trace from Karl Philipp Moritz's *Anton Reiser* through Wackenroder, Tieck, E. T. A. Hoffmann, and Jean Paul to Hugo von Hofmannsthal, Arthur Schnitzler, Rainer Maria Rilke, Leo Tolstoy, Thomas Mann, Gottfried Benn, T. S. Eliot, indeed, to virtually all writers who have experienced the difficulty of reconciling their "art" with their "life."

Thus, generalizing in broad outlines, we can observe that Wackenroder was an initiator and a precursor of intellectual trends that have implications ranging far beyond his own modest expectations and the very limited number of pages that he wrote.

Radical, controversial, and influential when they first appeared, the *Confessions* and the *Fantasies* have continued to be the object of much scholarly attention and debate. The countless chapters in literary histories, the monographs, and the many fine articles devoted to Wackenroder provide ample evidence of the lively interest engendered by these essays on art and the process of artistic creativity. Virtually no decade has passed since 1800 without witnessing several major contributions to Wackenroder scholarship. As one would expect, most of this ferment of intellectual inquiry has centered in the German-speaking areas of Europe. However, monographs and articles have also appeared relatively frequently in France and Italy, and Wackenroder's

4

literary works have been translated into both French and Italian.[1] In the English-speaking world, however, the situation has been somewhat different. While there were sporadic references to Wackenroder in British and American magazines during the nineteenth century,[2] these occasional fleeting references did not serve to arouse any widespread awareness of the author of the *Confessions from the Heart of an Art-Loving Friar*. Although the name of Wackenroder's close friend and collaborator, Ludwig Tieck, was popularized extensively in England and America, and although *Puss-in-Boots* (*Der gestiefelte Kater*), *The Fair-Haired Eckbert* (*Der blonde Eckbert*), *Knight Bluebeard* (*Ritter Blaubart*), *The Pictures* (*Die Gemälde*), and *The Betrothal* (*Die Verlobung*) as well as various of Tieck's poems and a number of other prose works were well known and readily available in English translation by 1900,[3] the English-speaking audience was generally unaware of Tieck's productive association with Wackenroder. In the histories of German literature published in England and America during this time, brief attention was usually paid to the *Confessions*. But the tone of the discussions was frequently negative and reflected the moralizing tendency which regarded this and other products of German Romanticism as philosophically "unhealthy."[4]

In the 1930's two critics, Edwin H. Zeydel[5] and Alexander Gillies,[6] made valuable and provocative contributions to the arousing of English and American interest in the *Confessions* and the *Fantasies*. Nevertheless, despite this auspicious beginning, Wackenroder continued to gain only the attention of academic, chiefly Germanistic, circles. Not until recently has there been a

1. In French: *Fantaisies sur l'art, par un religieux ami de l'art*, trans. Jean Boyer (Paris, 1945). In Italian: *Guglielmo Enrico Wackenroder. Opere e lettere*, trans. Gina Martegiani (Lanciano, 1916). Also accessible in Japanese: *Wilhelm Heinrich Wackenroder. Geijutsu o Aisuru ichi shûdôsô no shinjô no Hireki*, trans. Eiichi Egawa (Tokyo, 1956).

2. Cf. V. Stockley, *German Literature as Known in England, 1750–1830* (London, 1929). Scott Holland Goodnight, *German Literature in American Magazines Prior to 1846* (Madison, Wisc., 1907). M. H. Haertel, *German Literature in American Magazines, 1846–1880* (Madison, Wisc., 1908).

3. Percy Matenko presents a fruitful, thorough examination of Tieck's reception in American magazines and books prior to 1900 in his study: *Ludwig Tieck and America* (Chapel Hill, 1954). Matenko also investigates the American translations of Tieck's writings and provides informative descriptions of various translations, e.g. pp. 38–47, 108, etc. See also the studies cited in n. 2 above and Bayard Quincy Morgan, *A Critical Bibliography of German Literature in English Translation, 1481–1927, with Supplement Embracing the Years 1928–1935*, 2d ed. (Stanford, 1938).

4. For documentation of this negative evaluation, cf. Haertel, pp. 356–358.

5. *Ludwig Tieck and England: A Study in the Literary Relations of Germany and England during the Early Nineteenth Century* (Princeton, 1931). Also *Ludwig Tieck, the German Romanticist* (Princeton, 1935).

6. "Wackenroder's Apprenticeship to Literature: His Teachers and Their Influence," in: *German Studies Presented to H. G. Fiedler* (Oxford, 1938), pp. 187ff. In 1948 Gillies also published an edition of the *Herzensergiessungen* together with Wackenroder's contributions to the *Phantasien* which contains an introduction in English. See the chronological list of editions of Wackenroder's literary works in the bibliography of the present study.

noticeable increase in attention to Wackenroder as part of a larger concern for the interdependence of the various forms of European Romanticism.

It is the aim of this study to present a new interpretation of Wackenroder's *Confessions* together with appropriate consideration of his contributions to the *Fantasies* and his other writings. I have attempted to be "bilingual" in the most literal sense of the term; in other words, to provide both languages when introducing quotations to document my arguments. English is used in the main text and, unless otherwise indicated, all translations are my own. The original German is presented in the footnotes.

My interpretative analysis follows an approach that is both "intrinsic" and "extrinsic."[7] In other words, my approach strives to combine historical perception with philological explication in a method which does not subordinate one to the other, but allows both to accommodate and complement each other. I seek to shed new light on the complex and multifaceted position of Wackenroder's writings in the *Geistesgeschichte* of late eighteenth- and early nineteenth-century Germany. I also examine and attempt to elucidate the overall structure of the *Confessions*, the framework provided by the mask of the *Klosterbruder*, the significance of the title, the leitmotif effect of certain terms inherited from the language of Pietism, the process of artistic creativity as revealed in the spectrum of artists' lives and, last but perhaps most far-reaching in its implications, the new problem of Joseph Berglinger.

Throughout the writing of this study, I have kept firmly in mind the fact that it is intended not only for Germanists, but also for all those English readers who have a curiosity about authors of the German Romantic period. For this reason I have not aimed at completeness in my review of the critical literature on Wackenroder. Instead, I have attempted to be selective and, whenever possible, to use the footnotes for guidelines to further study of arguments presented in broad outlines.

If this study is to be useful in the way that it is hoped, there is a secondary prerequisite, namely, the presentation of a reliable English translation of the texts under consideration. Accordingly, the second part of the book contains the first English translation of the *Herzensergiessungen eines kunstliebenden Klosterbruders* based upon the first edition, which was published in the fall of 1796 (although dated 1797) by Johann Friedrich Unger in Berlin. It also contains translations of Wackenroder's contributions to the *Phantasien über die Kunst für Freunde der Kunst*, including the essays of which the authorship has been in dispute. These translations likewise have as their textual basis the first edition (1799), published by Friedrich Perthes in Hamburg.[8]

7. René Wellek and Austin Warren, *Theory of Literature* (New York, 1949), "The Extrinsic Approach to the Study of Literature," pp. 65–135, and "The Intrinsic Study of Literature," pp. 139–282. Wolfgang Kayser, *Die Vortragsreise* (Bern, 1958), pp. 60–61.
8. F. E. Pierce has published translations into English of two essays by Wackenroder:

Appendices I and II contain critical notes to the *Confessions* and the *Fantasies* as an additional aid in the elucidation of the two texts. Here also it is not my intention to be complete in identifying proper names and terms that appear in the texts, for such factual information is readily available elsewhere. Rather, I have endeavored to present only that material which is truly relevant to my interpretation of the texts and an assistance in their clarification.

A problem of terminology arises concerning the word "romantic." That the term is not applied to German literature in the same way that it is applied to English literature (as well as other European literatures) is a fact which has long been acknowledged.[9] In addition, it is both a vague descriptive term suggesting such meanings as adventurous, picturesque, exotic, chivalrous, extravagant, and fantastic and a historical term of literary periodization. As Hans Eichner writes: "This state of affairs suggests that anyone concerned with expressing himself precisely should avoid the word altogether."[10] Yet, as Eichner and all critics would agree, it is virtually impossible to avoid use of the term in literary history. Hence the best alternative is to define one's own application of it and then attempt to stay within the boundaries of that definition. In this study I use the term "romantic" as an historical period term to refer to Wackenroder, Tieck, Novalis, Eichendorff, and those other German authors whose most significant work was published between 1796 and approximately 1830. When applied in a descriptive or normative sense, my use of the term calls into question the validity of the sharp, antinomous distinction between the "Romanticists" and the "Classicists" of German literature, a dis-

---

"Concerning two Marvellous Languages and Their Mysterious Power" from the *Confessions* and "A Marvellous Oriental Legend of a Naked Saint" from the *Fantasies*. These are contained in Pierce's anthology, *Fiction and Fantasy of German Romance. Selections from German Romantic Authors, 1790–1830* (New York and Oxford, 1937), pp. 375–383. Beyond this I was unable to find evidence of any other essays in English translation, although selected excerpts and short passages have been rendered into English in various literary histories. All of the standard bibliographies and indexes were searched for translations of Wackenroder's writings, including B. Q. Morgan, *A Critical Bibliography* (n. 3 above), *Index Translationum* (Paris, 1932–1969), *Cumulative Book Index* (New York, 1928–1969), *Whitaker's Cumulative Book List* (London, 1928–1969), *Books in Print* (New York, 1948–1969), etc.

9. To pursue various approaches to this subject, cf. Arthur O. Lovejoy, "On the Discrimination of Romanticisms," *PMLA*, XXXIX (1924), 229–253. Edwin H. Zeydel, "The Concepts 'Classic' and 'Romantic': Some Fundamental Observations," *The Germanic Review*, XIX (1944), 161–169. René Wellek, "The Concept of 'Romanticism' in Literary History," *Comparative Literature*, I (1949), 1–23, 147–172. Robert L. Kahn, "Some Recent Definitions of German Romanticism, or the Case against Dialectics," *Rice University Studies*, L (Fall, 1964), 3–19. René Wellek, "German and English Romanticism: A Confrontation," in: *Confrontations: Studies in the Intellectual and Literary Relations between Germany, England, and the United States during the Nineteenth Century* (Princeton, 1965), pp. 3–33. Hans Eichner, "The Genesis of German Romanticism," *The Queen's Quarterly*, LXXII (1965), 213–231. Arthur Henkel, "Was ist eigentlich romantisch?" in: *Festschrift für Richard Alewyn* (Cologne, 1967), pp. 292–308.

10. "The Genesis of German Romanticism," p. 3.

tinction which, although useful as a historical guideline, is frequently applied in an unjustifiably oversimplified manner.

One need only read René Wellek's essay, "Romanticism Re-Examined,"[11] in order to find abundant evidence of scholarly interest in the elements which English and German Romanticism have in common. It is hoped that the present study will contribute to the fields of English literature and comparative literature as well as Germanics by making Wackenroder's principal writings accessible to the English reader.

11. René Wellek, "Romanticism Re-Examined," written as a sequel to Wellek's earlier essay, "The Concept of 'Romanticism' in Literary History" (n. 9 above). Both essays are printed in *Concepts of Criticism* (New Haven, 1963), pp. 128–221.

1 WACKENRODER AND LITERARY SCHOLARSHIP

Literary criticism is by no means a static field of scholarship. The insights and evaluations of one generation of critics may be different from those of the next generation. One age may appreciate what the next age totally ignores. Thus, a factor of historical relativity enters into any interpretation and the critic can never free himself entirely from the prevailing *Zeitgeist*. In one way or another, this "spirit of the times" will influence both *what* he sees and *how* he expresses his insights.

The literary scholarship associated with the name of Wackenroder provides an excellent laboratory for a study of the rise and decline of critical fashions in the nineteenth and twentieth century. When speaking of "Wackenroder scholarship," one important qualification must be made. There was a complex exchange of ideas between the two close friends, Wackenroder and Tieck. Not only did Tieck eagerly encourage Wackenroder in his writing, but he also undertook to revise some of his essays and add new material of his own. In the preface to the 1799 edition of the *Fantasies*, the postscript to the novel *The Travels of Franz Sternbald* (1798), and the preface to the 1814 edition of the *Confessions*, Tieck further complicated the apparent intertwinement of the two men's minds by making certain contradictions in his allocations of the responsibility for authorship. As a result of these factors, it is virtually impossible to arrive at an indisputably clear division of the contributions of each author. Nevertheless, there is at present little doubt that the greater part of the *Confessions* and the eight essays of the *Fantasies* presented in English translation here are Wackenroder's work.[1] Hence, since this line of demarcation is being observed in my translations, it seems correct also to

1. A consideration of the previously published arguments on the question of authorship is undertaken where relevant throughout my analysis and in the critical notes to the texts.

speak of Wackenroder (and, only indirectly, Tieck) in the changing perspective of literary history.

When the little volume whose title I have translated as *Confessions from the Heart of an Art-Loving Friar* first appeared near the end of the year 1796,[2] it immediately attracted enormous attention in wide circles. The new tone of the anonymous friar, his tender and pious reverence for art and music, his perceptive portrayals of significant moments in the lives of various artists of the *Cinquecento*, and his transfer of emotions traditionally centered in the realm of religion over to the realm of art elicited strong reactions, either negative or positive, in his *fin de siècle* audience.

The publication one year later (1798) of Tieck's novel, *The Travels of Franz Sternbald* (*Franz Sternbalds Wanderungen*), which had its origin in collaborative plans and ideas of Wackenroder and Tieck, drew further attention to the two young authors. Then, in 1799, Tieck carried out the plan for a sequel to the *Confessions* and published the *Fantasies on Art for Friends of Art* as a tribute to his friend, who had died of a "nervous fever" on February 13, 1798, at the age of twenty-five. This volume contained eight hitherto unpublished essays by Wackenroder as well as twelve contributions by Tieck.

This sequel was anticipated in the preface to the *Confessions*, where the art-loving friar had said: "Heaven has ordained that I close my life in a monastery: these endeavors are, therefore, all that I am now in a position to do for art. If they are not entirely displeasing, then perhaps a second part will follow. . . ."[3] That the *Confessions* had not been "displeasing" to all of their readers is evidenced by the positive reactions of various critics. J. H. Meyer reported that the book was "well received" and "read extensively."[4] In a letter to Goethe of approximately November 20, 1799, Meyer also requested that

2. Although the year printed on the title page of the First Edition is 1797, it is a widely known fact that the *Herzensergiessungen* appeared in the fall of 1796. In a letter dated January 5, 1797, August Wilhelm Schlegel asked Böttiger for a copy of Wackenroder's chief source for artists' lives, Giorgio Vasari's *Delle Vite dé più eccellenti pittori, scultori, ed architettori* (Florence, 1550), stating therein that he needed to consult this work for a certain project that he wished to begin immediately. The project to which Schlegel was referring is generally assumed to be his review of the *Herzensergiessungen* (cf. n. 6 below). Schlegel also sent a copy of the *Herzensergiessungen* to Goethe in December of 1796.

3. *Werke und Briefe von Wilhelm Heinrich Wackenroder* (Heidelberg, 1967), p. 10. "Der Himmel hat es so gefügt, dass ich mein Leben in einem Kloster beschliesse: diese Versuche sind daher das einzige, was ich jetzt für die Kunst zu tun imstande bin. Wenn sie nicht ganz missfallen, so folgt vielleicht ein zweiter Teil. . . ." This edition, published by Lambert Schneider Verlag, was selected as the source for all references to Wackenroder's writings in the introductory chapters and the critical notes because it is the best, most readily available complete edition of Wackenroder's writings. It will be cited hereafter as W.W.

4. Johann Heinrich Meyer, *Neu-deutsche religios-patriotische Kunst* (1817), in: *Goethes Werke*, ed. im Auftrage der Grossherzogin Sophie von Sachsen (Weimar, 1887–1920), Abt. 1, XLIX, 33. "Diese Schrift (. . .) wurde in Deutschland wohl aufgenommen, viel gelesen. . . ."

Goethe "bring along" a copy of the *Klosterbruder* on his forthcoming visit, so that Büri might nourish the flame of art with it.[5]

In his charmingly phrased and highly favorable review written in 1797, A. W. Schlegel described the volume as "pleasing" (*angenehm*) and praised the tone of the language and the appropriateness of the monastic retreat. "The view of the fine arts," wrote Schlegel, "which lies at the base of this pleasing volume is not the usual one of our age. Justifiably, therefore, its anonymous author also avoided the language in vogue and selected a foreign garb, in order to find the most vital expression for his deep emotion concerning the holiness and the worth of art."[6] Schlegel also praised various specific features of the *Confessions*, including the fine manner in which Wackenroder had altered, rearranged, compressed, edited, and, at certain points, expanded with new observations the materials in his main source for the lives of Italian *Cinque-cento* artists, Vasari's *Vite*. He had thereby dramatized the artists' lives and eliminated many of Vasari's polemical and vague eulogies.[7] With these few lines of discerning critical evaluation, Schlegel, writing shortly after the *Confessions* had first appeared, drew attention to a central issue in the study of Wackenroder, namely, the specific use which he made of his source materials. Schlegel thereby pointed the way to an area of Wackenroder scholarship which, as we shall observe later in this study, has by no means been fully exhausted.

In a tirade against Merkel, the poet-dramatist Zacharias Werner wrote: "I treasure everything that he despises and I regard precisely t h o s e people whom he rudely mistreats, Tieck, the Schlegels, Wackenroder, not as Gods of this Earth or as the sole *Lumina mundi*, but as phenomena who were alone capable of again igniting the spark of German poetry, which was being extinguished under little songs of wine and satire."[8] And, two years later, Wer-

---

5. Meyer to Goethe in an undated letter of approximately Nov. 20, 1799, in: *Goethe und die Romantik. Briefe mit Erläuterungen*, 1. Theil, ed. Carl Schüddekopf and Oskar Walzel (= *Schriften der Goethe-Gesellschaft*, XIII) (Weimar, 1898), p. 325. "Bringen Sie doch geliebter Freünd den Klosterbruder mit wen in Jena jemand von unsern Bekanten dieses Werk besitzt. Büri wünscht unendlich sich entfernt von Rom wenigstens an diesem Werk zu erhohlen und der Flamme der Kunst dadurch Nahrung zu geben." On November 21, 1799, Goethe sent the "Klosterbruder" to Meyer (cf. *Tagebücher*, II, 271).

6. August Wilhelm Schlegel, *Sämmtliche Werke*, ed. E. Böcking (Leipzig, 1847), X, 363–364. "Die Ansicht der bildenden Künste, welche dieser angenehmen Schrift zum Grunde liegt, ist nicht die gewöhnliche unsers Zeitalters. Mit Recht vermied daher ihr ungenannter Verfasser auch die Sprache der Mode und wählte, um für sein inniges Gefühl von der Heiligkeit und Würde der Kunst den lebendigsten Ausdruck zu finden, ein fremdes Kostüm."

7. *Ibid.*, pp. 366–367. The source to which Schlegel refers here is Vasari's *Vite* . . . . This work is accessible in English as *Lives of Seventy of the Most Eminent Painters, Sculptors and Architects*, ed. and annotated by E. H. and E. W. Blashfield and A. A. Hopkins (New York, 1917), I–IV. This edition will be cited hereafter as Vasari, *Lives*.

8. Werner to Sander, Jan. 17, 1803, in: *Charakteristiken: Die Romantiker in Selbst-*

ner complained that not a single person in Königsberg was reading Tieck's *Genoveva*, the *Fantasies*, or the *Confessions* and that these books, which were for him unique and from which he anticipated alleviating comfort on his deathbed, were scarcely known there. He then expressed a highly emotional tribute to Wackenroder: "Great God! Why can't I scratch Wackenroder out of the Earth, in contrast to this religious colossus all the new men of art are still neophytes!"[9]

In addition to J. H. Meyer, A. W. Schlegel, and Zacharias Werner, there are numerous others who could be cited to document the positive approval the *Confessions* enjoyed. For our purposes, however, these examples must suffice. As the two passages written by Werner imply, there was also a negative side in the initial response to the *Confessions*, a side of rejection and critical disapproval. For this we must look to Weimar, where Johann Wolfgang von Goethe was well established as director of the Weimar Court Theater and generally acknowledged as the "Olympian" on the German literary scene.

Richard Benz opened his study of Goethe's relationship to Romantic art with the words: "The rediscovery of Romanticism and, especially, romantic art had to come to terms from the very outset with Goethe: not with his literature, which is exalted above all classification and conflict of principles, but with his judgment, his view of art, his art politics."[10] In the case of Wackenroder, this general statement by Benz becomes highly relevant and specifically applicable. For there is substantial reason to believe that Wackenroder was, to a large extent, a "scapegoat" for others who had irritated Goethe and that the attacks levelled against the *Klosterbruder* were political in nature. They were, in other words, not unbiased literary judgments but opinions formed as the result of external causes.

Forty-seven years old when the *Confessions* reached his hands, Goethe had left his days of storm and stress behind and was now orienting his literary and theoretical efforts around the vision of a yet-to-be-realized "higher culture." Goethe saw the poetic and archaeological prefiguration of this higher

---

zeugnissen und Äusserungen ihrer Zeitgenossen, ed. Paul Kluckhohn (Stuttgart, 1950), p. 52. ". . . ist mir Merkel die gemeinste Erscheinung am Fusse des Parnasses . . . Ich schätze alles, was er verachtet, und halte grade d i e Leute, die er unanständig misshandelt, Tieck, die Schlegels, den Wackenroder, nicht für Götter dieser Erden oder für die einzigen *Lumina mundi,* aber doch für Erscheinungen, die allein vermögend waren, den unter Wein- und Scherzliederchen erlöschenden Funken deutscher Poesie wieder anzufachen."

9. *Ibid.,* p. 54. Werner to Hitzig, Oct. 17, 1803. ". . . Grosser Gott! Warum kann ich den Wackenroder nicht aus der Erde kratzen, gegen diesen religiösen Koloss sind alle neue Kunstmenschen noch Neophyten!"

10. Richard Benz, *Goethe und die romantische Kunst* (Munich, 1940), p. 5. "Die Wiederentdeckung der Romantik und insbesondere der romantischen Kunst hat sich von Anbeginn an mit Goethe auseinandersetzen müssen: nicht mit seinem über alle Klassifizierung und Prinzipienstreitigkeit erhabenen Werk, aber mit seinem Urteil, seiner Kunstanschauung, seiner Kunstpolitik."

culture in the level of Greek civilization achieved during the age of Pericles.[11] The popularity of the *Confessions* aroused Goethe's concern and anger, for he feared the tendencies this volume would be likely to inspire. He regarded its language and content as a threat to his own vision, because he foresaw the possibility that it might precipitate a trend in painting devoted to Christian subject matter, a revival of sympathy for the Catholic Church, and a tolerance in the appreciation of art which would result in the renunciation of critical standards.

In his previously cited review, A. W. Schlegel had warned that Wackenroder's intentions with regard to Catholicism might be misinterpreted. He declared it to be historically quite understandable that the *Cinquecento* artists found their highest artistic objects in the Madonnas, Saviours, apostles, and saints of the Catholic Church. And he expressed a warning that readers of a certain type would misconstrue the actual intention of Wackenroder's ecstatic immersion in the objects of Catholic art and conclude that his love of art revealed a tendency toward conversion to Catholicism. Defending Wackenroder with his own concept of empathy (*Einfühlung*), Schlegel wrote:

> If, in accordance with the requirement that the viewer should transpose himself into the world of the poet or artist, we willingly grant to the mythological dreams of Antiquity their blissful existence, why then should we not, vis-à-vis a work of art, take a closer interest in Christian myths and customs which are otherwise foreign to our way of thinking?[12]

With perspicacious critical insight, A. W. Schlegel pointed the way to an interpretation of Wackenroder's apparent catholicizing tendency which is thoroughly justified by a close reading of the text.[13] Yet, the warning went unheeded by Goethe and those in his immediate sphere of influence. From Goethe's pen there flowed a series of scathingly critical comments and aphorisms over the next few decades, remarks which seemed on the surface intended to discredit and disparage the "art-loving friar" and his secular counterpart, Franz Sternbald.[14]

Perhaps the most famous of these commentaries are two passages which

---

11. Cf. Wilfried Malsch, *Der Geschichtliche Sinn der Kunstanschauung und der Kritik in der deutschen Klassik*, for an interesting, discerning study of this theme. Professor Malsch kindly permitted me to read his study while it was in typescript form. The book is in press.

12. *Sämmtliche Werke*, ed. E. Böcking, X, 365–366. "Wenn wir, der Forderung gemäss, dass der Betrachter sich in die Welt des Dichters oder Künstlers versetzen soll, sogar den mythologischen Träumen des Alterthums gern ihr lustiges Dasein gönnen, warum sollten wir nicht, einem Kunstwerke gegenüber, an christlichen Sagen und Gebräuchen einen näheren Antheil nehmen, die sonst unsrer Denkart fremd sind?"

13. This interpretation will be discussed in greater detail later in the present study.

14. Cf. Malsch, *Der Geschichtliche Sinn* . . . , typescript, p. 219, n. 153.

were taken up and quoted again and again by later critics of Romanticism. One appeared in a review concerning Friedrich and Johann Riepenhausen, published in the Jena *Allgemeine Literatur-Zeitung* in 1805. After citing a passage in which the Riepenhausens praised the superiority of works of art inspired by the Christian religion over those produced by the Greeks, Goethe then sharply criticized:

> To whom is the neo-Catholic sentimentality in these phrases not noticeable, the *Klosterbruder*-izing, *Sternbald*-izing excess, from which more danger confronts the fine arts than from all the intrigues that claim reality.[15]

The other key passage was written years later, when Goethe, thinking back upon the Weimar Art Exhibition of 1802, recalled: "While we exerted ourselves in every way in order to bring into practice and maintain that which has long ago been recognized as solely appropriate and advantageous for the fine arts, we heard in our halls that a new little book was present which was making a great impression; it dealt with art and claimed to establish piety as the exclusive foundation of the same. We were moved but little by this report, for how should a chain of reasoning be valid, a chain of reasoning such as this: several monks were artists, therefore all artists should be monks!"[16]

With their clear references to the *Klosterbruder*, both of these passages seem to be attacks upon Wackenroder and they were interpreted as such by readers and critics throughout the nineteenth century. However, Richard Benz points out that the angry tone of the first passage was brought on primarily by the conversion of the Riepenhausen brothers to the Catholic faith in the autumn of 1804,[17] an event which deeply irritated and disappointed Goethe. Walter Scheidig sheds new light on the second passage with his hypothesis that Goethe's memory was actually at fault when he thought back upon the year 1802, since at that time the *Confessions* were no longer new and Goethe had received a copy from A. W. Schlegel in December, 1796. Scheidig argues that the disturbing and vexatious influence which Goethe vaguely remembered in relation to the Exhibition of 1802 actually stemmed from

15. *Goethes Werke*, ed. im Auftrage der Grossherzogin Sophie von Sachsen (Weimar, 1887–1920), XLVIII, 122. "Wem ist in diesen Phrasen die neukatholische Sentimentalität nicht bemerklich, das klosterbrudrisirende, sternbaldisirende Unwesen, von welchem der bildenden Kunst mehr Gefahr bevorsteht als von allen Wirklichkeit fodernden Calibanen?"

16. *Ibid.*, XXXV, 140–141. "Indem wir nun aber uns auf jede Weise bemühten, dasjenige in Ausübung zu bringen und zu erhalten, was der bildenden Kunst als allein gemäss und vortheilhaft schon längst anerkannt worden, vernahmen wir in unsern Sälen: dass ein neues Büchlein vorhanden sei, welches vielen Eindruck mache; es bezog sich auf Kunst, und wollte die Frömmigkeit als alleiniges Fundament derselben festsetzen. Von dieser Nachricht waren wir wenig gerührt; denn wie sollte auch eine Schlussfolge gelten, eine Schlussfolge wie diese: einige Mönche waren Künstler, desshalb sollen alle Künstler Mönche sein."

17. *Goethe und die romantische Kunst*, pp. 42ff.

Schadow, who had written in 1801: "Whoever feels like a Greek, let him act accordingly." In his retrospection Goethe had inadvertently substituted Wackenroder for Schadow.[18] Wilfried Malsch carries this line of argumentation several steps further and demonstrates with precise textual examples that the *Klosterbruder* does not deserve, either historically or in terms of content, the honor of having been fashioned by Goethe into the rôle of founder of the "neo-German religious-patriotic art."[19] In his polemics Goethe very frequently has quite a different opponent in mind, for whose misguided tendencies he holds Wackenroder responsible.[20]

Whatever future scholars may uncover concerning Goethe's position vis-à-vis the *Confessions*, one fact will remain indisputable: this book was used as a target for Goethe's polemics in defense of his own ideological and artistic goals. Thus, the name of Wackenroder plays a central rôle in the arguments and counter-arguments which finally led to the sharp split of German intellectual life into a "Classical" and a "Romantic" camp.

It is important to keep in mind that the Early Romantics of Germany did not at first conceive of themselves as "romantic." Nor did they even feel any significant disparity between themselves and Goethe, whose *Wilhelm Meister* was regarded as illustrating many "modern" qualities. In 1798 Friedrich Schlegel analyzed this novel with perceptive appreciation and acknowledged its enormous impact by characterizing it as one of the three "greatest tendencies of the age." The other two were the French Revolution and Fichte's *Theory of Knowledge*.[21]

During the years between 1800 and 1820, however, there was much polemical debate stemming from both the popularizers of "Romanticism" and its stern, critical opponents. As Hans Eichner succinctly describes the situation during this period:

> The Schlegels and their friends did not normally refer to themselves as romantic. However, as they formed an easily recognizable literary fac-

18. Walther Scheidig, *Goethes Preisaufgaben für bildende Künstler, 1799–1805* (= *Schriften der Goethe-Gesellschaft*, LVII) (Weimar, 1958), 333–335. The quotation from Schadow reads in the original German: "Wer wie ein Grieche fühlt, der möge so machen."

19. *Der Geschichtliche Sinn* . . . , especially the section on the "protonazarenische" and the "nazarenische Richtung der Kunst." Cf. also n. 11 above.

20. *Ibid.*, sec. cited above. In the paragraphs under the heading: "Raffaels Beispiel einer naiven, nachgriechisch- 'antiken' Bildung in Goethes die universale Toleranz mit der regulativen Griechenvision vermittelnden Sicht," Malsch also points out that Goethe actually shares Wackenroder's admiration for Raphael and even reconciles the plea for universal tolerance with his vision of Periclean art.

21. Schlegel, *Fragmente*, in: *Athenaeum*, ed. August Wilhelm and Friedrich Schlegel (Berlin, 1798–1800), I. Photomechanical reproduction of the original journal (Stuttgart, 1960), 232. "Die Französische Revoluzion, Fichte's Wissenschaftslehre, und Goethe's Meister sind die grössten Tendenzen des Zeitalters." For Schlegel's analysis of the novel, cf. "Über Goethe's Meister," *Athenaeum*, I, 147–178.

tion, all or most of whose members frequently used this term in its striking and novel technical sense, they themselves in due course became known as romantics. At first, from about 1805, their opponents applied the expression to them as a term of abuse . . . and finally, they themselves adopted this usage.[22]

During this complex phase of increasing intellectual polarization, many of the negative statements made by Goethe were torn out of their contexts and repeated again and again as isolated "truths" by the opponents of Romanticism. This radically intensified the general progression toward an apparent polar opposition between "Classicism" and "Romanticism."

Once the polar positions had been assumed, then all common features, all shared elements of inheritance from the earlier eighteenth century, and the fundamental similarities in the ultimate vision of a "higher culture" of harmony and freedom were henceforth virtually overlooked. The stage was set for the second phase of Wackenroder scholarship, a phase during which there emerged a highly stereotyped, cliché conception that the *Confessions* were radically new, totally "romantic," and exhibited an abrupt departure from all previous aesthetic thought.

A large number of widely acknowledged scholars and literary historians, as well as many more in the underbrush of critical literature, could be cited to document the stereotyped thinking that became associated with the name of Wackenroder. Interestingly, two poets of the nineteenth century, Heinrich Heine and Joseph von Eichendorff, have also contributed to the fostering of these mistaken views.

Heine treated the Romantics with characteristic irony in his well-known satire, *The Romantic School* (*Die romantische Schule*, 1835). Of the *Confessions* he wrote:

> Through his novel *Sternbalds Wanderungen* and through the *Herzensergiessungen eines kunstliebenden Klosterbruders*, edited by him and composed by a certain Wackenroder, Mr. Ludwig Tieck has presented the naïve, crude beginnings of painting as a model also for creative artists. The devoutness and childlike quality of these works, which is revealed in their technical awkwardness, was recommended for imitation.[23]

From Heine's critical statement and from similar comments by other writers

22. "The Genesis of German Romanticism," p. 229.
23. *Heinrich Heines Sämtliche Werke*, ed. Ernst Elster (Leipzig and Vienna, 1898), V, 235. "Herr Ludwig Tieck hat durch seinen Roman 'Sternbalds Wanderungen' und durch die von ihm herausgegebenen und von einem gewissen Wackenroder geschriebenen 'Herzensergiessungen eines kunstliebenden Klosterbruders' auch den bildenden Künstlern die naiven, rohen Anfänge der Kunst als Muster dargestellt. Die Frömmigkeit und Kindlichkeit dieser Werke, die sich eben in ihrer technischen Unbeholfenheit kundgibt, wurde zur Nachahmung empfohlen."

there emerged a widespread misconception that Wackenroder praised "medieval" art to the exclusion of all other artistic forms and that he had no appreciation for technical skill and finesse in painting. Passages in which Wackenroder dwells at length upon the technical proficiency of Leonardo da Vinci and his continual attempts to increase his knowledge of the effects of light and color, the geometric proportions and relationships of objects, and such other "scientific" matters were ignored or overlooked.[24] On the other hand, passages in which he expresses his love and admiration for the "natural simplicity" of Albrecht Dürer were quoted out of context as evidence of Wackenroder's apparent preference for figures without geometric precision and harmonious grouping.[25]

In his *History of the Poetic Literature of Germany* (*Geschichte der poetischen Literatur Deutschlands*, 1857), Eichendorff looked back upon Wackenroder from the perspective of half a century and criticized the "onesidedness" with which he had established "emotion" (*Gefühl*) as the surest, most direct, indeed, the only path to the comprehension of divine matters and had thereby identified art with religion. Eichendorff then proceeded to say: "That misunderstanding consequently made fashionable, on the one hand, an artistic dilettantism, on the other hand, a dilettante catholicizing, which regarded the Church almost exclusively as a grandiose art exhibition and considered itself justified in interpreting her [the Church's] mysteries according to its own manner and mood."[26] As was the case with Goethe, so too Eichendorff seems far more concerned with the historical consequences of the *Confessions* than with the actual point of view of Wackenroder himself. Wackenroder is made almost solely responsible for the nineteenth-century revival of Catholicism. Hence, an intention is attributed to him which ranges far astray from an accurate and well balanced reading of the *Confessions* text.[27]

24. W.W., pp. 38–42.

25. *Ibid.*, pp. 61, 65–66.

26. Joseph Freiherr von Eichendorff, *Werke und Schriften*, ed. Gerhart Baumann in cooperation with Siegfried Grosse (Stuttgart, 1958), IV, 263–264. "Jenes Missverständnis hat daher, wie einerseits einen künstlerischen Dilettantismus, so auch ein dilettantisches Katholisieren in Mode gesetzt, das die Kirche fast nur als eine grandiose Kunstausstellung betrachtete und sich für berechtigt hielt, ihre Geheimnisse nach seiner Weise und Stimmung zu deuten." This criticism was written late in Eichendorff's life. It is of relevance to note that Eichendorff experienced a similar fate in the eyes of later critics and was regarded in stereotyped terms as the poet of the "forest," of "wandering," of "youth," and of the "homeland." Eichendorff clichés became entrenched in literary histories just as did those concerning Wackenroder. Only in recent years has there been a re-evaluation of Eichendorff as witnessed by the perceptive essays of Oskar Seidlin (cf. *Versuche über Eichendorff* [Göttingen, 1965]). Also important in the Eichendorff re-evaluation is *Eichendorff heute*, ed. Paul Stöcklein (Munich, 1960), which includes noteworthy studies by Richard Alewyn, Wilhelm Emrich, Hermann Kunisch, and Erich Hock.

27. The views expressed by Heine and Eichendorff regarding Wackenroder's so-called medievalism and his responsibility for a "revival of Catholicism" are repeated again and again as stereotyped ideas in the literary histories of the late nineteenth and early twentieth

Two giants of nineteenth-century criticism, Rudolf Haym and Wilhelm Dilthey, began to correct the interpretation of Wackenroder by a more accurate assessment of his position in the complex currents of thought during this epoch. In *The Romantic School* (*Die romantische Schule*), Haym stressed the crucial importance of bringing all elements of intellectual thought: poetic, philosophical, religious, and so forth into consideration in order to present an accurate portrayal of the epoch. "Since the beginning of our great epoch of literature in Germany," Haym wrote, "poetry and philosophy have always worked together and vividly intermingled. Never, however, have they permeated each other to such an extent as in the efforts of the founders of the Romantic School."[28] Haym proceeded to emphasize the importance of tracing and examining not only the literary developments from Goethe to Tieck, but also the currents of thought which led from Fichte to Schelling and from the Pietism of the Moravian Brethren to the religious doctrines of Schleiermacher.[29] With this Haym paved the way toward a more historically accurate evaluation of all the Romantics, including Wackenroder.

In the few pages devoted to the *Confessions*, Haym offered provocative thoughts which qualified and corrected several of the prevailing misconceptions. He did not misconstrue Wackenroder's attraction to Albrecht Dürer as evidence of one-sided "medievalism." Instead, he argued that both Raphael and Dürer stand equally close to Wackenroder's heart and that, polemically, his devotion to the "Middle Ages" should be interpreted as a reaction to what he disliked in his own era.[30] Although Haym did not arrive at this conclusion, he bordered upon acknowledging that Wackenroder would not have been likely to oppose the idealization of another era, such as that of Periclean Greece, as another possible prefiguration of a better age than the present one. Haym also corrected the misunderstanding of Wackenroder's "catholicizing tendency" when he wrote:

> But, notice well, his devoutness and Christianity gravitate absolutely to the side of art. Art itself becomes for him an object of devotion, his devotion is primarily devotion of art.[31]

century. Cf. in English these examples: Kuno Francke, *A History of German Literature as Determined by Social Forces* (New York, 1916), pp. 447–450 (1st ed. under the title *Social Forces in German Literature,* 1896). Calvin Thomas, *A History of German Literature* (London, 1909), pp. 307–317.

28. *Die romantische Schule. Ein Beitrag zur Geschichte des deutschen Geistes,* 1st ed. (Berlin, 1870). Photomechanical reprint (Darmstadt, 1961), p. 7. "Immer haben seit dem Beginn unsrer grossen Litteraturepoche in Deutschland Dichtung und Philosophie zusammengearbeitet und lebhaft ineinandergegriffen. Niemals jedoch haben sie sich dergestalt durchdrungen wie in den Bestrebungen der Gründer der romantischen Schule."

29. *Ibid.,* p. 8.

30. *Ibid.,* pp. 117–128; especially p. 122.

31. *Ibid.,* p. 120. "Aber wohlgemerkt, seine Frömmigkeit und Christlichkeit gravitirt durchaus nach der Seite der Kunst. Die Kunst selbst wird ihm zum Gegenstand der Andacht, seine Andacht ist wesentlich Kunstandacht."

[1]

In his outstanding Schleiermacher monograph, *Life of Schleiermacher* (*Leben Schleiermachers*), Dilthey prepared the way for an even more penetrating understanding of Wackenroder's "devotion to art" (*Kunstandacht*) by his lucid explanation of the religious experience as a "perception of the infinite through the finite" (*Anschauung des Unendlichen durch das Endliche*).[32] But the post-Haymian, post-Diltheyan generation did not pay adequate attention to the monumental contributions of these two scholars. The possibilities they opened up for an understanding of Wackenroder remained generally unexplored.

When, under the influence of Wilhelm Scherer, literary scholarship had moved toward a positivistic approach, Wackenroder proved to be a relevant subject of investigation. In 1904 Paul Koldewey published a painstaking and well documented study that has maintained its usefulness. The title, *Wackenroder and His Influence upon Tieck*,[33] is misleading, since Koldewey actually devotes only the last sixty-nine pages to that subject. The first one hundred and forty-two pages discuss with "scientific" thoroughness the use Wackenroder made of his various source materials. The technique employed is that of juxtaposing Wackenroder's text and the appropriate source, whether it be the original Italian descriptions by Vasari, Bellori, or Malvasia, or the German lines of Bohm, Mengs, Sandrart, and other less frequently used sources. Koldewey did little to interpret the parallels which he established and the significance of Wackenroder's deviations, omissions, abbreviations, and so forth. He generally contented himself with such phrases as "a typical example," "interesting parallels," "a literal repetition."[34] Yet his investigation deserves the credit for having accomplished valuable groundwork for recent interpretative studies.

In 1906–07 Ernst Dessauer contributed a fruitful two-part essay on the relationship between the *Confessions* and Vasari,[35] an essay written with a positivistic approach similar to that of Koldewey. Unlike Koldewey, however, Dessauer did not juxtapose the Italian and German texts in adjoining columns. In fact, he did not even quote passages from Vasari's *Vite*; however he made many ingenious observations regarding the points of Wackenroder's deviations. In a footnote to the first page of his study,[36] Dessauer stated that it had been written under the direction of Jakob Minor in 1903—in other words, prior to

32. *Leben Schleiermachers,* ed. H. Mulert, 2d ed. (Berlin, 1922), cf. especially pp. 340–351.

33. *Wackenroder und sein Einfluss auf Tieck. Ein Beitrag zur Quellengeschichte der Romantik* (Leipzig, 1904).

34. *Ibid.,* pp. 10, 11, 16, 26, 59, etc.

35. "Wackenroders 'Herzensergiessungen eines kunstliebenden Klosterbruders' in ihrem Verhältnis zu Vasari," in: *Studien zur vergleichenden Literaturgeschichte*, VI, 245–270, and VII, 204–235 (Berlin, 1906–1907).

36. *Ibid.,* VI, 245. Another study published during the same decade and that contains perceptive observations on Wackenroder is Helene Stöcker's *Zur Kunstanschauung des 18. Jahrhunderts. Von Winckelmann bis zu Wackenroder*, in: *Palaestra*, XXVI (Berlin, 1904).

the appearance of Koldewey's study—and had, therefore, originated totally independently of Koldewey, a statement which examination of the two studies seems to corroborate. Koldewey and Dessauer were the first critics to initiate solid, scholarly investigation of the area of "source comparison" suggested as a fruitful realm for research over one hundred years earlier by August Wilhelm Schlegel.[37]

The year 1910 witnessed publication of Friedrich von der Leyen's two-volume edition of Wackenroder's *Werke und Briefe*, an edition which deviated from the pattern of previous editions in that it separated the essays of Wackenroder from those of Tieck.[38] Tieck's contributions to the *Confessions* and the *Fantasies*, as well as his prefaces to the editions of 1799 and 1814, are printed in the first appendix to volume I (Anhang I, 197–319). In distinguishing the work of Tieck from that of Wackenroder, von der Leyen used the lines of distinction drawn by Tieck in the 1814 edition, *Phantasien über die Kunst, von einem kunstliebenden Klosterbruder*, an edition which Tieck published as a tribute to Wackenroder's memory and in which he included only what he remembered to be Wackenroder's writings.

In addition to publishing the work of the two authors in separate sections, the von der Leyen edition also printed their extant correspondence and Wackenroder's travel diary concerning the Pentecost trip with Tieck in 1793. It became the standard edition for Wackenroder research until it was superseded by the 1938 edition published by the Lambert Schneider Verlag in Heidelberg.[39]

During the 1920's there appeared a plethora of multifaceted studies on the Romantics. A great number of critics, such as Fritz Strich,[40] Ricarda Huch,[41] Paul Kluckhohn,[42] and Bonaventura Tecchi,[43] would all deserve attention in a detailed investigation of the history of Wackenroder scholarship. Each of these critics made valuable contributions, all phrased, however, within the terminological limitations of the "Classical" and "Romantic" antithesis.

The title of Strich's study, which reads in translation: *German Classicism and Romanticism, or Perfection and Endlessness: A Comparison*, already indicates the direction in which this group of scholars was headed. Through a series of brilliantly defined pairs of antonyms, Strich sought to establish once and for all the qualities which distinguished Romanticism from Classicism.

37. In Schlegel's review of the *Herzensergiessungen* cited in n. 6 above.

38. *Werke und Briefe*, ed. Friedrich von der Leyen, 2 vols. (Jena, 1910).

39. For a survey of the various editions of Wackenroder's writings and descriptive annotations of each edition, see the bibliography of the present study.

40. *Deutsche Klassik und Romantik, oder Vollendung und Unendlichkeit: Ein Vergleich* (Munich, 1922).

41. *Die Romantik*, I (Leipzig, 1922).

42. *Die deutsche Romantik* (Bielefeld and Leipzig, 1924).

43. *Wilhelm Heinrich Wackenroder* (Florence, 1927), trans. into German by Claus Riessner (Bad Homburg v. d. H., 1962).

Useful though his categories seemed to be—and they have, indeed, been used by many who sought clear, "black-and-white" definitions—they were also misleading oversimplifications. It could be argued convincingly that Strich even contradicts his own antonyms. As one of many possible examples, he defines "longing" (*Sehnsucht*) as a "romantic" quality and proceeds to state: "The essence of a classical love, as Goethe possessed it in almost antique purity, is that longing and recollection remain foreign to it. It is bound to the presence of the object."[44] Then, in the very next paragraph, he adds what seems to him a necessary qualification, namely, that Goethe did have an enduring, unquenchable "longing" for the art of sculpture. Thereupon Strich pardons this "romantic" longing in Goethe by asserting that it was directed, of course, toward the most "classical" of all arts, since Goethe "felt that sculpture alone is the art of complete and perfected realization, because it alone truly suspends the passing of time and gives shapes to space."[45] Yet, it is precisely a "longing" for an ideal of harmonious, complete, and "perfected realization" which is a recurring theme in Wackenroder's *Confessions* concerning the lives of creative artists. And, although music rather than sculpture is the medium, the "suspension of the passing of time" is the central motif of the "Wondrous Oriental Tale of a Naked Saint."

With this I do not mean to say that Strich was wrong in his definitions. But his pairs of antonyms are too general, his illustrations at times too forced. Certainly the qualities he identifies as "romantic" are not wholly applicable to the case of Wackenroder and, in the hands of later critics who lacked Strich's persuasiveness and talent for qualifying his arguments, they led to an increased rigidity of the "Classical versus Romantic" polarization.

One writer who charted quite an independent course was Josef Nadler. In *The Berlin Romanticists, 1800–1814 (Die Berliner Romantiker, 1800–1814)*, Nadler avoided altogether those terms of contrast and polarity which defined Romanticism as a counter-movement to Classicism. Instead, he looked to geographical and religious undercurrents of influence and interpreted the Berlin Romanticists as realizing not a "beginning" (*kein Anfang*), but a "new peak of an uninterrupted development" (*neue Höhe eines laufenden Vorganges*). Nadler saw the inspirational origins of Romanticism in the mystical and pietistic traditions of Silesia and Lusatia. He identified Hamann and Herder as two significant mediators between intellectual ideas of an earlier period in

---

44. *Deutsche Klassik und Romantik* . . . , p. 29. "Das Wesen der klassischen Liebe, wie Goethe sie in fast antiker Reinheit hatte, ist, dass ihr die Sehnsucht und Erinnerung fremd bleibt. Sie ist gebunden an die Gegenwart des Gegenstandes."

45. *Ibid.*, pp. 29–30. "Er fühlte eben, dass Plastik allein die Kunst der vollkommenen und vollendeten Vergegenwärtigung ist, weil sie allein in Wahrheit der fliessenden Zeit enthebt und Raum gestaltet." In his previously cited study, W. Malsch contradicts this view by arguing that Goethe gave highest credit to the "art of dancing" (*Tanzkunst*), which "realizes the highest goal of all other arts." Cf. especially chap. 1.

the eighteenth century and the Romantics.[46] Nadler correctly pointed out the historical relationship between the Berlin Romantics and undercurrents of religious emotion which can be traced from the Middle Ages through the mysticism and pietism of the seventeenth and eighteenth centuries. Concerning Wackenroder he wrote:

> Hamann's religious genius, Herder's historical impetus, Schleiermacher's intuition and emotion as a mediator to God, the best in Wackenroder was filled with all of this.[47]

On the other hand, the positive observations of Nadler's study were weakened by his erroneous, overzealous, and undocumented assertions that the feeling of chaos experienced by the Romantics originated in a chaos of racial and family relationships caused either by intermingling of the races or its opposite, inbreeding.[48]

Bonaventura Tecchi's interesting Wackenroder monograph in Italian seems to have had relatively little impact upon German scholars at the time of its publication in 1927. It did not appear in German translation until 1962.[49] Since then it has become widely known and has been cited routinely in Wackenroder bibliographies.[50]

The most recent, vigorous phase of reappraisal and re-examination of Wackenroder was initiated in 1944, when Richard Alewyn undertook to analyze two major issues: first, the grounds for attributing the idea of the *Klosterbruder* mask to Johann Friedrich Reichardt[51] and, second, the grounds for ascribing authorship of one document in the *Fantasies*, "A Letter of Joseph Berglinger" (*Ein Brief Joseph Berglingers*) to Tieck rather than to Wackenroder.[52] Concerning the latter issue, Alewyn argued convincingly that the statement in Tieck's preface to the *Fantasies*: ". . . of the Berglinger essays, the last four belong to me,"[53] should be read as a literal count from the back of

---

46. *Die Berliner Romantiker, 1800–1814: Ein Beitrag zur gemeinvölkischen Frage: Renaissance, Romantik, Restauration* (Berlin, 1921), pp. 5of.

47. *Ibid.*, p. 74. "Das religiöse Genie Hamanns, Herders geschichtlicher Trieb, Schleiermachers Anschauung und Gemüt als Vermittler zu Gott, von all dem erfüllte sich das Beste in Wackenroder."

48. *Ibid.*, pp. 55–56, 145–146, 149, 165, etc.

49. See n. 43 above.

50. An exception to this is Heinz Lippuner's study: *Wackenroder/Tieck und die bildende Kunst. Grundlegung der romantischen Aesthetik* (Zürich, 1965), which, although generally very thorough in the review of secondary sources, does not make reference to Tecchi's work.

51. "Wackenroder's Anteil," *Germanic Review*, XIX (1944), 48–58. Alewyn's findings concerning the *Klosterbruder* mask will be discussed in Chap. 2.

52. *Ibid.*, especially pp. 52–58. For the argumentation which runs counter to Alewyn's conclusions, cf. Koldewey, *Wackenroder und sein Einfluss auf Tieck*, pp. 207–210.

53. W.W., p. 136. ". . . unter Berglingers Aufsätzen gehören mir die vier letzten an."

the volume and, resultingly, should include the long poem that concludes the *Fantasies*: "The Dream. An Allegory" (*Der Traum. Eine Allegorie*). This interpretation puts "A Letter of Joseph Berglinger" in the fifth position, hence in the section ascribed to Wackenroder.

The letter, addressed to the "deeply beloved" friar, is composed in a tone of restless despair and, as Berglinger himself says, "with a highly disturbed mind and in the anxiety of an irresolute hour."[54] It raises questions of the ineffectuality and uselessness of art which clearly anticipate the conflict between "art" and "life" experienced by Tolstoy, Thomas Mann, Schnitzler, Hofmannsthal, indeed, by all those modern writers who have sought to reconcile their creativity with their social responsibility. Hence, it seemed to contradict the prevailing critical view of Wackenroder as the naïve, pious, tender, emotional advocate of a "religion of art." Following Alewyn's settlement of the authorship dispute concerning this one letter, there began a scholarly correction of the one-sided interpretation of Wackenroder's conception of art. Critics now uncovered and acknowledged the nihilistic, self-destructive, anxiety-ridden side of Wackenroder, revealed primarily in the Berglinger essays and in the "Wondrous Oriental Tale of a Naked Saint."[55]

Werner Kohlschmidt deserves special attention with regard to the reassessment of Wackenroder. Kohlschmidt first examined the antithesis between "Classicism" and "Romanticism" defined with such far-reaching effects by Fritz Strich. He noted that Strich's complete title (*Klassik und Romantik oder Vollendung und Unendlichkeit*) contains for the romantic pole the term "endlessness," a term which, in the dialectic of reality, lies very close to "nothingness," therefore, nihilism.[56] He then perspicaciously discussed Wackenroder's nihilism, a nihilism based upon an "anxiety concerning time" (*Zeitangst*), underneath which were other less consciously perceived anxieties, such as the fear of the invalidation of art as a source of meaning in life, the fear of an *Entleerung* (an "emptying") of the world, and so forth.[57]

After he had written about the "nihilistic" tendencies of Wackenroder, which foreshadowed developments of the late nineteenth and the twentieth century, Kohlschmidt took another close look at the text of the *Confessions*

---

54. Ibid., p. 229. "Ach! mein innigst geliebter, mein ehrwürdiger Pater! ich schreibe Euch diesmal mit einem hochbetrübten Gemüt, und in der Angst einer zweifelvollen Stunde . . . ."

55. Cf. Gerhard Fricke, "Bemerkungen zu Wilhelm Heinrich Wackenroders Religion der Kunst," in: *Festschrift Paul Kluckhohn und Hermann Schneider gewidmet* (Tübingen, 1948), pp. 345–371; reprinted in G. Fricke, *Studien und Interpretationen* (Frankfurt am Main, 1956).

56. "Nihilismus der Romantik," in: *Form und Innerlichkeit, Beiträge zur Geschichte und Wirkung der deutschen Klassik und Romantik* (Munich, 1955), pp. 156–176. Cf. especially p. 159 for the discussion of Strich.

57. *Ibid.*, pp. 163–168.

and came up with the conclusion that, in matters of artistic taste, Wackenroder revealed a preference for "classical" forms.[58] Thus, there emerged a new picture of Wackenroder as a "classical nihilist," or a "nihilistic classicist,"[59] or a complex composite of classical, romantic, and post-romantic, existential elements. In 1965 Kohlschmidt expressed his intention of publishing a Wackenroder monograph.[60] At the time of this writing, no monograph by Kohlschmidt has appeared. However, the confusing, provocative, often contradictory course of the Wackenroder reappraisal has provided fertile material for two excellent investigations. Heinz Lippuner's study[61] concentrates on Wackenroder and the arts of painting and sculpture, while Elmar Hertrich[62] limits the scope of his investigation to Joseph Berglinger and other materials relevant to Wackenroder's "view of music" (*Musikanschauung*). The arguments and conclusions of these two critics will be taken into consideration in the following interpretation; however, it should be noted that Hertrich's study was not published until 1969, when the present investigation had reached the final stages of preparation.[63]

There is no doubt that the writings of Wackenroder are currently undergoing a re-evaluation with far-reaching implications. They are no longer neatly stereotyped as representing the "earliest, purest, deepest and, simultaneously, most unpretentious tone of German Romanticism."[64] Instead, Wackenroder is emerging in the perspective of the 1970's as a complex literary figure with roots in the early eighteenth century and characteristics which contradict, qualify, or extend the traditional definitions of Romanticism.

It is with this complexity in mind that I now turn to my analysis of the

58. "Wackenroder und die Klassik, Versuch einer Präzisierung," in: *Unterscheidung und Bewahrung, Festschrift für H. Kunisch zum 60. Geburtstag* (Berlin, 1961), pp. 175ff; reprinted in Kohlschmidt, *Dichter, Tradition und Zeitgeist* (Bern, 1965), pp. 83–92.

59. Marianne Thalmann employs the term "nihilistischer Klassiker" in her brief remarks concerning recent Wackenroder research. Cf. *Romantik und Manierismus* (Stuttgart, 1963), p. 26.

60. Cf. "Bemerkungen zu Wackenroders und Tiecks Anteil an den *Phantasien über die Kunst*," in: *Philologia Deutsch, Festschrift zum 70. Geburtstag von Walter Henzen* (Bern, 1965), n. to p. 89.

61. For Lippuner, see n. 50 above.

62. *Joseph Berglinger, Eine Studie zu Wackenroders Musiker-Dichtung* (Berlin, 1969).

63. Two Ph.D. dissertations in English have also recently given attention to Wackenroder. These studies are: Paul Frank Proskauer, "The Phenomenon of Alienation in the Work of Karl Philipp Moritz, Wilhelm Heinrich Wackenroder and in '*Nachtwachen*' *von Bonaventura*" (Columbia University, 1966) and David Bruce Sanford, "Wackenroder and Tieck: The Aesthetic Breakdown of the *Klosterbruder* Ideal" (University of Minnesota, 1966).

64. These superlatives were applied to Wackenroder by Gerhard Fricke as recently as 1948 to begin his previously cited article: "Bemerkungen zu Wilhelm Heinrich Wackenroders Religion der Kunst." The original (p. 345) reads: "In Wackenroder erklingt der früheste, reinste, innigste und zugleich schlichteste Ton der deutschen Romantik." Fricke also gives recognition to the other side of Wackenroder's view of art, the side involving anxiety and nihilistic despair; cf. pp. 365–371.

Confessions and the *Fantasies*, not with any arrogant intention of overthrowing their classification as documents in the period of Early German Romanticism, but with the purpose of exploring their unique character and explicating specific features of central importance to an understanding of Wackenroder and his literary intentions.

2 THE MASK OF THE *KLOSTERBRUDER*

In the *Confessions* as well as in the Berglinger essays of the *Fantasies*, the fiction of a baroque friar as narrator and mediator between the life stories of the various artists and the reader is at no point interrupted. Wackenroder never speaks to the reader directly; he remains anonymous behind the mask of the "art-loving" friar.

Wackenroder's choice of this particular artistic and narrative technique can be explained from several different viewpoints, all of which shed a degree of light on the question—but none of which can claim to be "the" exclusive explanation. These viewpoints include historical-biographical, sociological, religious-philosophical, and literary-structural factors.

From the historical-biographical viewpoint, it can be observed in Wackenroder's letters to Tieck that he felt an absolute necessity of maintaining his anonymity. The fear of censure from his father, the prosperous lawyer Christoph Benjamin Wackenroder (1729–1808), who expected that his son would follow in his footsteps and pursue the practical and "enlightened" study of law, was a primary factor which prevented young Wackenroder from openly acknowledging his love of art.[1] He was abruptly thrown into a period of emotional crisis when, after he and Tieck had completed their studies at the Friedrich-Werder-Gymnasium, he was required by his father to remain in Berlin for a year and continue his studies privately—under his father's watchful eye. Meanwhile, Tieck went on to the Prussian University of Halle, where he

---

1. The investigations by E. H. Zeydel and A. Gillies cited in the Introduction above provide extensive biographical information on Wackenroder for the English reader. These studies make it possible for me to concentrate on my interpretation without repeating available facts. Cf. especially Zeydel, *Ludwig Tieck, the German Romanticist*, pp. 1–54 and 94–113. A. Gillies, "Wackenroder's Apprenticeship to Literature: His Teachers and Their Influence," pp. 187ff. *Herzensergiessungen* . . . , ed. A. Gillies, pp. ix–xliii.

[2]

matriculated as a student of theology, a study which interested him just as little as law interested Wackenroder.[2] From this crisis Wackenroder emerged privately strengthened in his inclinations toward art, although nevertheless outwardly fearful of paternal disapproval.[3]

From a broader sociological point of view, there was the fear of censure from all those elements of the late eighteenth-century Enlightenment society which represented the entrenched "Establishment": from Friedrich Gedike, for instance, the director of the Friedrich-Werder-Gymnasium, who was renowned as a strict, innovative, rationalistic educator, or from the publisher and author, Christoph Friedrich Nicolai. These were the types of authority figures in Berlin who would have caused a rather shy, introspective, and reserved young man to seek a mask behind which to hide.

Viewed from an even wider sociological perspective, Wackenroder's gravitation away from a career which he was expected to follow and into the realm of art is a part of a widespread flight away from the restrictive social situation of the eighteenth century. Precisely those young men who were expected to assume productive positions in their social environments were finding this prospect unacceptable and were fleeing "into the sphere which alone stood open for their activity: the realm of the spirit and of art."[4] With brilliant command of the historical, sociological, and cultural interrelationships and encyclopaedic thoroughness, Helmut Kreuzer, in *Die Boheme*, presents an analysis and documentation of nineteenth- and twentieth-century literary Bohemianism and establishes its roots in the eighteenth century. Kreuzer speaks of the process of "de-bourgeoisization" (*Entbürgerlichung*) of the image of the artist, a process which constituted a reaction not only against one specific social class, but against the socially well-adjusted "Non-Artist" (*Nicht-Künstler*) in general.[5] Wackenroder and Tieck were an early part of this vast, far-reaching, international phenomenon of a gradual alienation of the artist from his roots in the social structure. Kreuzer quotes Tieck as saying: ". . . since artists and educated people now stand in the most glaring contrast with the masses (. . .), anyone who wants to represent a proficient apostle of the good intellect must buy a sword for all modest considerations, for bread and clothing."[6]

2. *Ludwig Tieck, the German Romanticist*, pp. 37–38.
3. During this year of private study in Berlin, Wackenroder was permitted to study medieval German literature under the tutelage of Erduin Julius Koch (1764–1834). It is primarily through this experience that he acquired the knowledge of and appreciation for early German literature that he communicated to Tieck. Cf. their correspondence, W. W., especially pp. 275–287, 379–396, etc.
4. Cf. Eckehard Catholy, *Karl Philipp Moritz und die Ursprünge der deutschen Theaterleidenschaft* (Tübingen, 1962), p. 3. ". . . dass jene Kräfte in die Sphäre ausbrachen, die ihnen allein zur Wirksamkeit offenstand: das Reich des Geistes und der Kunst."
5. *Die Boheme, Beiträge zu ihrer Beschreibung* (Stuttgart, 1968), p. 10.
6. *Ibid.*, p. 11. ". . . da jetzt Künstler und gebildete Menschen im schneidendsten Kontraste mit der Menge stehen (. . .), muss für alle bangen Rücksichten, für Brot und

Tieck's use of the term "a proficient apostle" leads us over to another perspective on the *Klosterbruder* mask, that of its religious-philosophical implications. Behind the guise of his "art-loving friar," Wackenroder speaks openly and unrestrainedly about the early "apostles of art" (*Jünger der Kunst*), the "martyrs of art enthusiasm" (*Märtyrer des Kunstenthusiasmus*), and the "saints of art" (*Kunstheiligen*). He uses the designations of religious apostles, martyrs, and saints as terms to describe with glowing admiration both the *Cinquecento* artists and Albrecht Dürer.[7] It is, therefore, not surprising to find the contemporary figure of Joseph Berglinger identifying himself with earlier religious martyrs and exclaiming how he feels in such moments when he experiences his deepest despair:

> In such anxiety I understand how those pious, ascetic martyrs felt who, overwhelmed with sorrow at the sight of the inexpressible sufferings of the world, like despairing children subjected their bodies to the most highly selected mortifications and penances for their entire lifetimes. . . .[8]

Although Berglinger does not directly refer to himself as an "apostle" or a "martyr" of art, it is a short and easy step to this designation.

How, then, does the mask of the *Klosterbruder* play a rôle in this otherwise highly modern conception of the quasi-religious, apostolic function, and alienated martyrdom of the artist? First, the friar literally "hides" the anonymous real author and, therefore, helps to protect him from those whose censure he fears.[9] Second, the friar lives in monastic retreat and the pattern of his life seems to exemplify in every respect the orthodox life of a Catholic monastic. He distances himself from his audience at the outset by saying that his essays are "not composed in the tone of the present-day world"[10] and he claims to be living out the last days of his life without involvement in worldly affairs. Thus, there emerges an image of a South-German baroque monastic who employs the traditional metaphorical and symbolic language of the Catholic Church to

---

Kleidung ein Schwert kaufen, wer irgend einen tüchtigen Apostel des guten Geistes vorstellen will." (Cited from the Tieck edition by Kasack and Mohrhenn [Berlin, 1943], II, 195).

7. W.W., pp. 9, 23, 34, etc.

8. *Ibid*., p. 231. "In solcher Angst begreif' ich es, wie jenen frommen asketischen Märtyrern zumute war, die, von dem Anblicke der unsäglichen Leiden der Welt zerknirscht, wie verzweifelnde Kinder, ihren Körper lebenslang den ausgesuchtesten Kasteiungen und Pönitenzen preisgaben. . . ."

9. One can conclude that the mask of the *Klosterbruder* did accomplish this function to a large extent from J. H. Meyer's comment that numerous readers attributed the work to Goethe! Cf. *Neu-deutsche religios-patriotische Kunst* (1817), in: *Goethes Werke* (Weimar, 1887–1920), Abt. 1, XLIX, 33ff. "Da der Name des Verfassers auf dem Titel nicht genannt war, so wollten viele das Werk Goethen zuschreiben und folgten desto getroster den darin vorgetragenen und ihren eigenen ungefähr gleichartigen, schon vorher gehegten Meinungen."

10. W.W., p. 9. "Sie sind nicht im Ton der heutigen Welt abgefasst. . . ."

write his "confessions" of his love of art. The figure of the friar seems to all outward appearances to praise *both art and Catholicism*, and this has led many readers, including those who have favored the apparent catholicizing tendency of the essays and those who have strongly opposed it, to mislocate the gravitational center of Wackenroder's religious terminology.

If one were to undertake a thorough and systematic investigation of the vocabulary of the *Confessions* and the *Fantasies*, including such philological phenomena as the number of times that certain words reappear, the types of verbal prefixes most frequently employed, the prevailing motifs and *topoi* which recur at significant points in the portrayal of the artists' creative experiences, and so forth, one would find that the gravitational center of the art-loving friar's confessions is located highly in favor of the mystical-pietistic tradition.[11] It is important to note the fact that the emotional, individualistic outpourings of the soul-searching eighteenth-century Pietists differ radically from the confessions of the orthodox Catholic. The pietistic tradition is anchored in direct, individual, personal "communication" with God, in the analysis of experiences resulting from such communication, and in descriptive, psychological self-exploration. A philological study of word frequency and word usage in Wackenroder's writings would uncover hitherto unacknowledged affinities with other eighteenth-century writers. It would also open up new possibilities for the re-evaluation of Wackenroder's position in the intellectual currents of German literary history. Such a thorough exploration of specific words and their history (*Wortgeschichte*) lies beyond the realm of my present investigation.[12] However, a brief examination of only one word from the title of the *Confessions*, the initial word *Herzensergiessungen*, will suffice to indicate the pietistic influences upon Wackenroder's religious terminology.

Herzensergiessungen is a compound which, when divided, comprises two nouns (*Herzens/Ergiessungen*) and has the literal meaning of "Heart-Outpourings." The noun *Ergiessungen* is formed from the verb *ergiessen* ("to pour out"), which is a compound of the verb *giessen* ("to pour"). According to A. Langen, *giessen* originally carried the predominant meaning of "God (pouring) into the human soul."[13] It and its compound, *ergiessen*, car-

---

11. Cf. such studies as the following for examples of the investigation of pietistic vocabulary inherited by other eighteenth-century authors: August Langen, "Verbale Dynamik in der dichterischen Landschaftsschilderung des 18. Jahrhunderts," *Zeitschrift für deutsche Philologie*, LXX (1949), 249–318. August Langen, *Der Wortschatz des deutschen Pietismus*, 2d enlarged ed. (Tübingen, 1968). Karl Ludwig Schneider, *Klopstock und die Erneuerung der deutschen Dichtersprache im 18. Jahrhundert* (Heidelberg, 1960).

12. Where relevant and an actual contribution to an understanding of the texts, basic characteristics of pietistic language will be pointed out in my discussion and in the critical notes to the texts. I hope that some future scholar will undertake a thorough study of the pietistic influence upon Wackenroder's language.

13. *Der Wortschatz des deutschen Pietismus* (Tübingen, 1968), pp. 325–326.

[2]

ried this meaning until they gradually underwent the process of secularization and acquired new meanings, such as the "soul pouring itself into God" or into "other human souls."[14]

In addition, there is also a relationship between *giessen* (*ergiessen*) and the whole large family of "water" metaphors, including not only "pouring" but "flowing" (*fliessend*), "flooding" (*überschwemmend*), as well as many other verbal composita and a long series of related nouns: "sea," "source," "fountain," "drop," "flood," "river," "lake" (*Meer, Quelle, Brunnen, Tropfen, Flut, Fluss, Bach*). There is a major distinction between these and the "Classical" water metaphors: namely, these nouns and verbal composita all represent water in motion, while the Classical *topoi* concentrate upon water in quiet, motionless, peaceful lakes or ponds which, therefore, reflect with harmonious perfection the image of the beholder.[15] Although the Classical "mirror topos" (*Spiegeltopos*) does occur at a few points in Wackenroder's writings,[16] the metaphors involving "flowing" and "pouring out," in other words, the *Ergiessungen*, are the predominant metaphors related to water.

The second noun of the compound, *Herzens*, is the genitive form of the word *Herz* and it means, literally, "of the heart." The word "heart" has a long history in the traditions of mysticism. It occurred in the Middle Ages in compounds such as "chamber of the heart" (*Herzenskammer*), where it frequently designated a secret inner room for private conversations with God.[17] Langen does not document occurrences of the specific compound *Herzensergiessungen* prior to the period of Pietism. He hypothesizes that it is a late addition to the pietistic vocabulary, when secularizing influences were already beginning to alter the original meanings of the pietistic terms.[18]

By illuminating and clarifying the position of this one word in the tradition of pietistic language, we seek to "unmask" our *Klosterbruder* as standing quite apart from orthodox Catholic monasticism. He does not "confess" his love of art in the tone that one would expect when using the traditional Catholic ecclesiastical term for "confessions," namely, the word *Beichten*. This is quite a different tone, inherited from the emotional soul-searching of the Pietists, but transplanted into the atmosphere of a secluded, quiet monastery in order to distance the narrator from his late eighteenth-century environment.

Although the friar announces initially that he is no longer interested in the affairs of the world, we find this is also a deceptive element of his disguise. His apparent detachment from the present-day world (the world of 1796)

14. *Ibid.*, p. 326.
15. Cf. Ernst Robert Curtius, *European Literature and the Latin Middle Ages*, trans. from German by Willard R. Trask (New York and Evanston, 1953), pp. 79–105, 336.
16. These few instances are pointed out in the critical notes to the Wackenroder texts.
17. *Der Wortschatz des deutschen Pietismus*, p. 171.
18. *Ibid.*, pp. 2–19, 451–452.

does not prevent him from directing sporadic barbs against it. His own love of art, which he possessed in his early youth, has remained a strong force within him in his old age.[19] This emotion links him with the past of his youthful days; it, therefore, puts him at a critical distance from the Enlightenment society which he attacks. In his preface to the reader, the friar regrets the cold, criticizing eye with which art is judged in the present era and he rejects the writings of H. von Ramdohr, indicating that "whoever likes these may immediately put out of his hand that which I have written, for it will not please him."[20] From this point on, the essays are well sprinkled with sharp criticisms and sarcastic barbs, commentaries on the world of 1796 which have all too often been overlooked in previous studies on Wackenroder.

Since insufficient attention has been paid to this "criticism of the times" (*Zeitkritik*) which is interwoven with the friar's confessions of his love of art, it is wholly warranted that some key examples be cited here. In the essay "Raphael's Vision" (*Raffaels Erscheinung*), the friar complains that "the so-called theorists and systematizers describe to us the inspiration of the artist from hearsay,"[21] and he continues: "With how infinitely many idle words the overly clever writers of more recent times have erred concerning the subject of the ideals in the fine arts!"[22] In the essay on Francesco Francia, the friar expostulates on the value of the creations of all the *Cinquecento* artists and then proceeds to say:

> Amidst these men there occurred extraordinary things, incredible to many nowadays, because the enthusiasm which inflamed all the world during that golden age now flickers in only a few individual hearts, like a weak little lamp.[23]

After coming to the end of his chronicle of Francia's death, which resulted from a total fatigue of spirit upon seeing an original painting by Raphael and experiencing the unhappy comparison of his own artistic products with that

19. W.W., pp. 9–10.

20. *Ibid.*, p. 10. ". . . wer diese liebt, mag das, was ich geschrieben habe, nur sogleich aus der Hand legen, denn es wird ihm nicht gefallen." This polemical attack is directed against Friedrich Wilhelm Basilius von Ramdohr (1752–1822), best known for his two works: *Über Mahlerei und Bildhauerarbeit in Rom für Liebhaber des Schönen in der Kunst* (3 vols.; Leipzig, 1787) and *Charis oder Über das Schöne und die Schönheit in den nachbildenden Künsten* (2 vols.; Leipzig, 1793). Cf. n. on Ramdohr in Appendix I.

21. W.W., p. 11. "Die sogenannten Theoristen und Systematiker beschreiben uns die Begeisterung des Künstlers vom Hörensagen. . . ."

22. *Ibid.* "Mit wie unendlich vielen unnützen Worten haben sich nicht die überklugen Schriftsteller neuerer Zeiten bei der Materie von den Idealen in den bildenden Künsten versündigt!"

23. *Ibid.*, p. 18. "Es geschahen unter ihnen ungewöhnliche, und vielen jetzt unglaubliche Dinge, weil der Enthusiasmus, der itzt nur in wenigen einzelnen Herzen, wie ein schwaches Lämpchen flimmert, in jener goldenen Zeit alle Welt entflammte."

of Raphael, our art-loving friar concludes this essay with another sharply phrased barb against the intellectual, rationalistic critics of 1796:

> Those critical minds, who neither want to nor are able to believe in any extraordinary souls as in supernatural miracles and who would like very much to dissolve the entire world into prose, scoff at the tale of the old, venerable chronicler of art and say immediately that Francesco Francia died by poison.[24]

The friar's initial and concluding attacks upon the widespread disbelief in such inexplicable supernatural and psychological forces as affected Francesco Francia form a framework inside of which the story of Francia is told. This one essay is, therefore, a "microcosmic" example of the overall structure of the *Confessions*, a series of rhapsodies concerning various artists framed by the figure of a monastic who, although ostensibly unconcerned with the prevailing attitudes of the year 1796, intrudes his critical opinions into the flow of his narrations at virtually predictable intervals.[25]

Two last examples—although many more could be gathered—should serve to demonstrate the contemporary-critical attitude (*zeitkritische Einstellung*) of the friar. After vividly describing the devotion with which Albrecht Dürer sought to portray his artistic figures in the "fullness of life," he then goes on to criticize: "But the more recent artists do not seem to participate seriously in that which they portray for us; they work for aristocratic gentlemen, who do not want to be moved and ennobled by art, but dazzled and titillated to the highest degree . . . ."[26] Shortly thereafter, the friar elaborates upon his thinking with two paragraphs which surely ought to have warned all those who charged him with a "catholicizing tendency" that they were misreading (and oversimplifying) his intentions. He states with vehemence: "I must cry out woe upon our age, that it practices art merely as a frivolous plaything of the senses, while it is actually something very serious and exalted."[27] And a few lines later he proceeds to say:

24. *Ibid.*, p. 24. "Diejenigen kritischen Köpfe, welche an alle ausserordentliche Geister, als an übernatürliche Wunderwerke, nicht glauben wollen noch können, und die ganze Welt gern in Prosa auflösen möchten, spotten über die Märchen des alten ehrwürdigen Chronisten der Kunst, und erzählen dreist, Francesco Francia sei an Gift gestorben." Giorgio Vasari is the chronicler of art to whom the friar is referring here.

25. In my discussion of the process of artistic creativity, this essay will also be viewed as "microcosmically" foreshadowing the entire circle of problems of the later essays, particularly those of Joseph Berglinger.

26. W.W., p. 59. "Aber die Neueren scheinen gar nicht zu wollen, dass man ernsthaft an dem, was sie uns vorstellen, teilnehmen solle; sie arbeiten für vornehme Herren, welche von der Kunst nicht gerührt und veredelt, sondern aufs höchste geblendet und gekitzelt sein wollen . . . ."

27. *Ibid.*, p. 60. "Wehe muss ich rufen über unser Zeitalter, dass es die Kunst so bloss als ein leichtsinniges Spielwerk der Sinne übt, da sie doch wahrlich etwas sehr Ernsthaftes und Erhabenes ist."

[2]

In the writings of Martin Luther, who was very highly esteemed and defended by our Albrecht, in which, as I willingly admit, I have done some reading out of intellectual curiosity and in which much good material may be hidden, I found a remarkable passage concerning the importance of art, which now comes vividly to mind. For this man maintains somewhere very daringly and explicitly: that, after theology, music occupies the first place among all the sciences and arts of the human spirit.[28]

This latter passage sheds quite a new light on the *Klosterbruder* and is important for two reasons: first, it indicates that the friar with his supposed "catholicizing tendency" has read and appreciated the writings of the father of the Protestant Reformation; second, it anticipates the direction of the later essays, particularly those of Joseph Berglinger, by calling special attention to the high position of the art of "music" in the middle of a eulogy to the "painting"—and the simple, harmonious way of life—of Albrecht Dürer.

As our final example, we shall consider the point at which the friar initiates the narrative of the life of Joseph Berglinger. Just as in his preface "To the Reader of these Pages," the friar also makes a direct reference to his own life here. However, instead of claiming that he is no longer interested in the affairs of the present day, he reverses his position and states that he will now consider the life of a contemporary figure after all. "Again and again," he tells us, "I have turned my eyes to the past and gathered up the treasures of the art history of past centuries for my own enjoyment; but now my spirit urges me to linger at the present times for once and try my hand on the history of an artist whom I knew since his early boyhood and who was my closest friend. Alas, you unfortunately passed away from the earth so soon, my Joseph!"[29] Again there is that modest, humble tone, especially in the phrase: "try my hand on the history," a tone which is calculated to dispose the reader sympathetically toward the friar's story. But, as we shall observe at a later point, the tragedy of Joseph Berglinger is also a scathing attack upon a world

28. *Ibid.* "In den Schriften des von unserm Albrecht sehr hochgeschätzten und verteidigten Martin Luthers, worin ich, wie ich nicht ungern gestehe, einiges aus Wissbegier wohl gelesen habe, und in welchen viel Gutes verborgen sein mag, habe ich über die Wichtigkeit der Kunst eine merkwürdige Stelle gefunden, die mir jetzt lebhaft ins Gemüt kommt. Denn es behauptet dieser Mann irgendwo ganz dreist und ausdrücklich: dass nächst der Theologie, unter allen Wissenschaften und Künsten des menschlichen Geistes, die Musik den ersten Platz einnehme."

29. *Ibid.,* p. 111. "Ich habe mehrmals mein Auge rückwärts gewandt und die Schätze der Kunstgeschichte vergangener Jahrhunderte zu meinem Vergnügen eingesammelt; aber jetzt treibt mich mein Gemüt, einmal bei den gegenwärtigen Zeiten zu verweilen und mich an der Geschichte eines Künstlers zu versuchen, den ich seit seiner frühen Jugend kannte, und der mein innigster Freund war. Ach, leider bist du bald von der Erde weggegangen, mein Joseph!"

which puts the serious, dedicated artist at odds with his environment and causes him to feel dissension, isolation and abandonment.[30]

From these and the many other passages that could be cited,[31] there emerges the figure of a worldly, sophisticated friar who uses the antique rhetorical technique of claiming old age and infirmity to win the sympathy of his readers,[32] who says at the outset that he will perhaps write a second part in which he should like "to refute the evaluations of several individual works of art,"[33] who thereupon re-emphasizes that he is suffering from the infirmities of old age, including a certain distraction of mind, by expressing the modest, prayerful hope that this continuation will come into existence, "if Heaven grants me health and time to arrange the thoughts which I have jotted down regarding this and bring them into a clear exposition."[34] The friar then proceeds to sprinkle his loving and appreciative stories regarding various artists with critical barbs against the world of 1796 which show no evidence of absentmindedness, vague detachment, or unconcerned monastic retreat. The friar's "criticism of the times" is a highly involved, deeply concerned rejection of certain rationalistic forces of his age. Viewed from this perspective, it is no wonder that young Wackenroder chose the route of anonymity behind the mask of an aged friar and only reluctantly agreed to allow his friend, Tieck, to publish the *Confessions*.[35]

While the polemical position of the friar as a critic of the world of 1796 has been given only fleeting attention in Wackenroder scholarship, the two questions: "Who suggested the *Klosterbruder* mask?" and "Who actually formulated the complete title of the friar's confessions?" have been the objects of a quantity of scholarly inquiry far out of proportion to their relevance for an understanding of the *Confessions* as a literary work. However, precisely because so many critics have concerned themselves with these questions, it is essential that I also take a position in this continuing debate.

Just as with the question of authorship of several essays in the *Confessions* and the *Fantasies*, I am dealing here, too, with insufficient or contradictory testimony from the authors and their contemporaries and an overabundance of hypothetical speculation, some of which is clever and convincing.

30. For this motif or portions of it, cf. *ibid.*, pp. 115, 117, 119, 121–122, 124–127, etc.
31. Other examples of lines of criticism directed against the late eighteenth century include all of the following in *ibid.*: "die heutigen Lehrer" (p. 60); "O traurige Afterweisheit! O blinder Glaube des Zeitalters" (p. 63); "Bildersäle werden betrachtet als Jahrmärkte, wo man neue Waren im Vorübergehen beurteilt, lobt und verachtet . . ." (p. 79).
32. E. R. Curtius, *European Literature and the Latin Middle Ages*, pp. 83–85, 90.
33. W.W., p. 10. ". . . so folgt vielleicht ein zweiter Teil, in welchem ich die Beurteilungen einiger einzelnen Kunstwerke widerlegen möchte . . ."
34. *Ibid.*, ". . . wenn mir der Himmel Gesundheit und Musse verleiht, meine niedergeschriebenen Gedanken hierüber zu ordnen und in einen deutlichen Vortrag zu bringen."
35. Rudolf Köpke, *Ludwig Tieck, Erinnerungen aus dem Leben des Dichters nach dessen mündlichen und schriftlichen Mittheilungen* (Leipzig, 1885), I, 222. Cf. also Tieck's

[2]

In his Tieck biography, Köpke reports that, after Wackenroder had confided in Tieck and entrusted his writings to his friend for his perusal, Tieck then showed the material to Johann Friedrich Reichardt. Immediately approving of the essays, Reichardt agreed to publish "A Memorial to Our Venerable Ancestor Albrecht Dürer" in his journal *Deutschland*.[36] Thereupon, Köpke reports: "Reichardt also found the title under which these portrayals should be presented to the public."[37] This led to a general assumption that not only the title, but also the figure of the *Klosterbruder*, were Reichardt's inventions. It was also assumed that these inventions were quickly picked up and elaborated by Tieck, whose "penchant for play-acting" caused the idea of the mask to appeal to him.[38]

Richard Alewyn, whose opinion I share in regard to the question of Reichardt's rôle, draws attention to the fact that Tieck makes it clear on two occasions that the mask of a religious monastic was Wackenroder's own idea.[39] Alewyn refers, first, to the concluding statement of Part I of the novel *Franz Sternbalds Wanderungen*, where Tieck refers explicitly to the *Confessions* and states: ". . . he [Wackenroder] intentionally chose the mask of a religious ecclesiastic, in order to be able to express his pious emotion, his reverent love of art more freely."[40] Alewyn then points out that, in the preface to the edition of 1814, Tieck stated even more clearly that Wackenroder "while in the process of writing, began to place his words in the mouth of an ecclesiastic who was secluded from the world. . . ."[41] Alewyn therefore concludes, as do I, that the mask of the *Klosterbruder* was Wackenroder's own idea and that the

---

preface to the 1814 edition, where he mentions that Wackenroder intended his confessions only for his most intimate friends.

36. *Ibid.*, I, 221. Wackenroder's essay, "Ehrengedächtnis unsers ehrwürdigen Ahnherrn Albrecht Dürers," appeared in Reichardt's periodical, *Deutschland*, in the year 1796.

37. *Ibid.*, I, 221. "Reichardt fand auch den Titel, unter dem diese Bilder dem Publicum übergeben werden sollten." The similarity between the two titles: *Herzensergiessungen eines kunstliebenden Klosterbruders* and Jacobi's *Ergiessungen eines einsamen Denkers* was pointed out by R. Benz (*Die Deutsche Romantik* [Leipzig, 1937], p. 141), who suggests that Reichardt possibly had Jacobi's *Ergiessungen* in mind. Benz rejects Köpke's argument that Reichardt was thinking of the friar in Lessing's *Nathan der Weise*. I agree with Benz that Lessing's figure of the Crusades does not have enough in common with the "art-loving friar" to justify Köpke's contention (I, 222), unless it is the case that Reichardt was making an eclectic, uninformed comparison.

38. Cf. especially Oskar Walzel's introduction to his edition of the *Herzensergiessungen* (Leipzig, 1921), pp. 27–28. Cf. also Andreas Müller's edition in *Kunstanschauung der Frühromantik* (*Deutsche Literatur, Reihe Romantik*, III, 307). V. Santoli, *Wackenroder* (Rieti, 1929), pp. 30ff. E. H. Zeydel, *Ludwig Tieck, the German Romanticist*, p. 94. Heinrich Borcherdt, notes to his edition of the *Herzensergiessungen* (Munich, 1949), pp. 122–123, etc.

39. "Wackenroders Anteil," see n. 51 of Chap. 1 above.

40. *Ibid.*, p. 50 ". . . er wählte absichtlich die Maske eines religiösen Geistlichen, um sein frommes Gemüt, seine andächtige Liebe zur Kunst freier ausdrücken zu können."

41. *Ibid.* ". . . im Schreiben verfiel, seine Worte einem von der Welt abgeschiedenen Geistlichen in den Mund zu legen . . . ."

friar's words are an integral part of Wackenroder's writings, not an external element appended by either Tieck or Reichardt. Reichardt may, indeed, have "baptized the friar"[42] with the charmingly appropriate title of the volume, but he did not invent him.[43]

The title, which I have chosen to render into English as "Confessions from the Heart of an Art-Loving Friar,"[44] is a metaphorical prelude to the content of the essays, for it contains each of the main metaphors that reappear throughout the volume like recurring symphonic themes. The term "Confessions from the Heart" (*Herzensergiessungen*) prefigures the emotional quality which pervades all of the essays and, as I indicated earlier, connects Wackenroder with the pietistic tradition of psychological soul-searching and direct communication with the divine. The term "Art-Loving" (*kunstliebend*) presents no problem of translation and refers to the "love of art" which is, in essence, a form of devotion. The friar (*Klosterbruder*) is the principal metaphorical link between religion and art; in addition, he has a pedagogical function as the chronicler of the lives of past artists, the discoverer and transmitter of "lost" letters and other documents written by artists and friends of art,[45] and the teacher who "confesses" his own experiences of art works—while intermittently directing attacks against the "modern" tendencies of which he disapproves—in order to inspire young, beginning artists (to whom he dedicates his pages)[46] with the same love of art that he has felt throughout his lifetime.

There remains one aspect of the *Klosterbruder* mask to be explored at this time, namely, the structural function of the monastic narrator in relation

42. *Ibid.*, p. 51. "Somit ergibt sich aus Köpke nur, dass Reichardt den Klosterbruder getauft, nicht aber, dass er ihn gezeugt hat."

43. I am in agreement with E. Hertrich (*Joseph Berglinger, Eine Studie zu Wackenroders Musiker-Dichtung*, p. 12, n. 10) regarding the validity of Sievers' conclusion that much of the preface, "To the Reader of These Pages," has a tone which seems to indicate that it is Wackenroder's writing. Friedrich Schlegel was already of much the same opinion, for he wrote to August Wilhelm that Tieck did not have as large a part in the *Herzensergiessungen* as he claims, since "Tieck is not even capable of writing that type of beautiful sentimentality so simply and musically." Cf. *Charakteristiken*, ed. P. Kluckhohn, p. 114.

44. Other possible translations of the title would include: "Heart-Outpourings of an Art-Loving Monastic"; "Heartfelt Confessions of an Art-Loving Lay Brother"; "Intimate Disclosures of an Art-Loving Friar," etc. My translation was ultimately selected from the various possibilities on the grounds that it seemed to capture both the flowing tone of the original title and its metaphorical content without merely paraphrasing or transliterating the German in an awkward manner.

45. This is also a *topos* inherited from antique rhetoric and commonly known as the "discoverer *topos*." As Curtius explains, the Greeks were highly interested in the question of "Who discovered it?" The act of "discovering" was, therefore, an important occurrence according to their way of thinking. Cf. *European Literature and the Latin Middle Ages*, pp. 547–548.

46. W.W., p. 10. "Diese Blätter, die ich anfangs gar nicht für den Druck bestimmt, widme ich überhaupt nur jungen angehenden Künstlern, oder Knaben, die sich der Kunst zu widmen gedenken . . ."

[2]

to the content of the *Confessions* and the *Fantasies*. The stories he tells the reader do not relate to each other with the cohesion of an epic narrative. There is no continuous plot, no "story" that is unfolded by degrees, no clearly perceptible progression in time. The friar is "old" as he begins his confessions and not perceivably "older" at the point in the *Fantasies* where his intermittent appearances as narrator cease and the remaining contributions, which are all Tieck's work, bring the volume to a close without him.[47]

"Time" as a factor producing a chronology of events occurs only within the individual narratives concerning various artists' lives. "Time" emerges as a threatening, enchaining, ceaselessly raging force, when it traps the naked saint of the "Oriental Tale." But "time" is open, non-specific, and without chronological clarity in the overall structure of both the *Confessions* and the *Fantasies*. The art-loving friar communicates no biographical facts about himself other than that he has always felt a deep, reverent love of art and that he is now, in his old age, closing his life in the seclusion of a monastery. Beyond this he is without any individualized features and the reader must create his own mental picture of this friar, who is, essentially, hiding behind the "anonymity" of his clerical clothing—and providing, thereby, a dual anonymity for the real author.

Rather than an epic chronology of events which would make the overall flow of time perceptible, there are three distinct levels of perspective upon time.[48] First, there is the friar's perspective on the distant past and his narration of events from the age of Raphael, Leonardo da Vinci, Piero di Cosimo, Albrecht Dürer, and others; second, there is the friar's perspective on his own youth in the late baroque period, presumably when the mood and atmosphere of the seventeenth century could still be felt in a lingering after-glow, but when new influences had already begun to intrude upon the pious, harmonious relationship of the artist with the surrounding world and to create such a problem of conflict as was experienced by his youthful friend, Joseph Berglinger; third and finally, there is the perspective of the world of 1796, toward which the chronicles and the intermingled elements of "criticism of the times" are directed. The reader needs to be alert to the changes from one level of time

47. Tieck presents an apology for the lack of structural cohesion in the *Fantasies* when he states in his preface of 1799 that he and Wackenroder ". . . had decided to form an entity, so to speak, out of the individual essays" (but that) "since I have now been lacking his advice and his assistance in the working out of this, I have therefore also lacked the courage which would have inspired me in his company." Cf. W.W., p. 135. ". . . aus den einzelnen Aufsätzen gewissermassen ein Ganzes zu bilden; — aber da ich nunmehr bei der Ausarbeitung selbst seinen Rat und seinen Beistand vermisst habe, so hat mir auch der Mut gefehlt, der mich in seiner Gesellschaft beseelt haben würde."

48. The various perspectives toward "time" in Wackenroder's writings are analyzed discerningly by Dorothea Hammer in her Frankfurt dissertation, *Die Bedeutung der vergangenen Zeit im Werk Wackenroders unter Berücksichtigung der Beiträge Tiecks* (Frankfurt am Main, 1961).

perspective to another, for each of the three perspectives elicits a different epoch, a different atmosphere and mood.

As one of his structural functions, the friar-narrator directs the attention of the reader from one chronicle to another and shifts the focus of attention from epoch to epoch in time. In addition, he initiates the *Confessions* with his presence, dramatically introduces the Berglinger story, as if to say: "Pay attention now! Here comes something different!" and he then brings the *Confessions* to a close with the following lines:

> After these reminiscences about my Joseph, however, I can write nothing more.——I am concluding my book——and should only like to wish that it might be useful to one or another person for the awakening of good thoughts.[49]

To be sure, the aged friar seems to have forgotten the initial dedication of his book to "young, beginning artists" or "youths who are thinking of dedicating themselves to art," and he now concludes the volume with a far more generalized statement, namely, that he hopes it "might be useful to one or another person." Nor does he rhapsodize any longer about providing "inspiration," but rather modestly and prosaically speaks of possibly "awakening good thoughts." Without even considering the posthumous essays in the *Fantasies*, it seems as if there has been a "development" in Wackenroder's thinking, a progression from a reverent, positive faith in art to a more negative, nihilistic view. But the *Confessions* are not only the expression of a changing viewpoint toward art. They are also a literary work of art which has a structure composed of recurring metaphors and images with a symphonic-architectonic background of atmosphere and mood. Beginning, linking, guiding, and concluding this literary work is the figure of the *Klosterbruder*. He consequently forms the outer framework of what could be classified as a "narrative within a frame" (*Rahmenerzählung*).

It is common knowledge that the technique of a narrative framework or an outer structure framing an inner story (or stories) originated in the Orient and has a long, richly varied and interesting tradition which includes such famous cycles of stories as *Thousand and One Nights*, Boccaccio's *Decameron*, and Chaucer's *Canterbury Tales*. The technique of the *Rahmenerzählung* was used most successfully by many of Wackenroder's contemporaries and Late Romantic successors. A few of the numerous relevant examples are Goethe's *Unterhaltungen Deutscher Ausgewanderten* (1795) (*Conversations of German Emigrants*), Tieck's *Phantasus* (1812–1817), and, in a uniquely complex baroque intertwinement, E. T. A. Hoffmann's *Lebensansichten des*

---

49. W.W., p. 131. "Ich kann aber nach diesen Erinnerungen an meinen Joseph nichts mehr schreiben.——Ich beschliesse mein Buch——und möchte nur wünschen, dass es einem oder dem andern zur Erweckung guter Gedanken dienlich wäre."

[2]

Katers Murr nebst fragmentarischer Biographie des Kapellmeisters Johannes Kreisler in zufälligen Makulaturblättern (1820–1822).[50]

The tradition of the *Rahmenerzählung* allows the author a great deal of freedom to play with his material and create a medley of seemingly "chaotic" elements without any obvious order and coherence other than that provided by the frame. In their discussion of the literary structure of Friedrich Schlegel's *Dialogue on Poetry* (*Gespräch über die Poesie*), Ernst Behler and Roman Struc astutely clarify the Romantic observation that the "original order of things is chaotic."[51] They then further explain:

> In other words, chaotic order mirrors life and genuine Being, while systematic order is a mere shadow of life. By presenting his Romantic product in the form of a conversation, Schlegel wanted to exhibit the original order of his ideas and their so-called "chaotic symmetry."[52]

Hence, within the framework of a real conversation, one also finds such widely disparate forms of literary communication as "a lecture, a speech, a letter, and a treatise." Behler and Struc interpret the "chaotic symmetry" of Schlegel's *Dialogue* not as an accidental order, but as a highly intentional form which is the result of conscious reflection on Schlegel's part. They also make the point that this form enabled Schlegel to include in the *Dialogue on Poetry* essays which he had written at different times and for different purposes.[53]

Although the external framework provided by the *Klosterbruder* is quite different from that of Schlegel's conversational frame, the mélange of literary forms in the *Confessions* presents a parallel to Schlegel's "chaotic symmetry." It also enabled Wackenroder and Tieck to publish as a literary entity essays and rhapsodies on art which originated in unconnected contexts and at different times over a period of years.

Included among the various sub-genres represented in the *Confessions* is the popular eighteenth-century technique of the "exchange of letters" (*Briefwechsel*), which makes possible the direct communication of emotions without the narrator's intervention. First, there is the letter of the pupil to Raphael and Raphael's answer,[54] then the letter of Antonio to his friend Jacobo in Rome and Jacobo's answer,[55] finally, the letter of a young German painter in

---

50. A possible translation of Hoffmann's novel title would be: *Views Concerning Life by the Cat Murr, Along with the Fragmentary Biography of the Musical Conductor Johannes Kreisler, on Random Scraps of Paper.*

51. Fr. Schlegel, *Dialogue on Poetry and Literary Aphorisms*, trans., introduced, and annotated by Ernst Behler and Roman Struc (University Park, Pa., 1968), p. 11.

52. *Ibid.*

53. *Ibid.*, p. 12.

54. W.W., pp. 25–29, "Der Schüler und Raffael."

55. *Ibid.*, pp. 30–33. "Ein Brief des jungen Florentinischen Malers Antonio an seinen Freund Jacobo in Rom" and "Jacobos Antwort."

Rome to his friend in Nuremberg.[56] In addition, there are the "dust-covered parchments" written by Bramante, which the friar "discovered" in his monastery.[57]

The genre of lyric poetry is represented in the five stanzas of verse in "Longing for Italy," in "The Portraits of the Artists," in Joseph Berglinger's song to St. Cecilia, and the three stanzas of lament which follow shortly after the tribute to Cecilia and, most significantly, in the two descriptions of paintings (*Bildbeschreibungen*) in verse.[58] The idea of introducing the various figures portrayed in the paintings as speakers in a rhymed dialogue was highly original at this time.[59] The two paintings artistically described in this manner are not specific works of art by known artists. Instead, they are archetypes of a genre of painting which features as the key personages Mary, the Christ Child, John, and the three Wise Men from the Orient. Thus, they are thematically related to Raphael's Madonnas, Leonardo da Vinci's *Last Supper*, and other works of art with the same constellation of religious figures by Piero di Cosimo, Albrecht Dürer, Fra Giovanni Angelico da Fiesole, and an impressive list of Italian and French artists introduced and discussed in "The Chronicle of Artists."[60]

The mentioning of "The Chronicle of Artists" leads me away from the lyric poetry of the *Confessions* to another prose sub-genre of the medley of forms, the quasi-biographical chronicle of the lives of various artists. While only fleeting attention is paid to each of many artists in the above-mentioned "Chronicle," there are also far lengthier essays devoted to Raphael,[61] Francesco Francia,[62] Leonardo da Vinci,[63] Albrecht Dürer,[64] Piero di Cosimo,[65] and Michelangelo Buonarroti.[66] In several instances, these chronicles are introduced with long baroque titles reminiscent of the cultivation of elaborate

56. *Ibid.*, pp. 89–95. "Brief eines jungen deutschen Malers in Rom an seinen Freund in Nürnberg."

57. *Ibid.*, p. 13. Cf. also n. 45 above concerning the "discoverer" *topos.*

58. *Ibid.*, pp. 17, 96–98, 120–122, 47–50.

59. See the review by A. W. Schlegel cited in Chap. 1, n. 6 above. A similar technique is used in "The Portraits of the Artists," where the "Muse" and the "Youth" walk through a gallery together, commenting upon various works of art to each other in verse. Cf. *ibid.*, pp. 96–98, "Die Bildnisse der Maler."

60. *Ibid.*, pp. 99–110. "Die Malerchronik."

61. *Ibid.*, pp. 11–15. "Raffaels Erscheinung" (as well as frequent reference to Raphael in other essays).

62. *Ibid.*, pp. 18–24. "Der merkwürdige Tod des zu seiner Zeit weitberühmten alten Malers Francesco Francia, des ersten aus der Lombardischen Schule."

63. *Ibid.*, pp. 34–36. "Das Muster eines kunstreichen und dabei tiefgelehrten Malers, vorgestellt in dem Leben des Leonardo da Vinci, berühmten Stammvaters der Florentinischen Schule."

64. *Ibid.*, pp. 57–66. "Ehrengedächtnis unsers ehrwürdigen Ahnherrn Albrecht Dürers."

65. *Ibid.*, pp. 72–78. "Von den Seltsamkeiten des alten Malers Piero di Cosimo aus der Florentinischen Schule."

66. *Ibid.*, pp. 83–88. "Die Grösse des Michelangelo Buonarroti."

[2]

titles in the seventeenth century. An example is the heading for the chronicle on Leonardo da Vinci, which I translate quite literally as: "The Model of a creative and, moreover, highly learned artist, exemplified in the life of LEONARDO DA VINCI, renowned founder of the Florentine School."

This consciously baroque embellishment of titles is another aspect of the mask of the *Klosterbruder*, designed to give the reader the impression that the friar is very old and, therefore, uses the baroque style of language which he learned in his youth. But, as indicated above, the predominant vocabulary and imagery of the texts is more specifically of pietistic, pedagogical origins. The word "exemplified" in the title above gives us a hint as to the real nature of these chronicles. One is reminded of the medieval *exemplum*, which was incorporated into a sermon as a positive or a negative example of the lesson in the text.[67] Collections of *exempla* were created as sources for demonstrative proof of the power of faith in individual human lives. Frequently these *exempla* concerned the lives of saints.[68] Wackenroder's chronicles can be regarded as six *exempla* of artists' lives, all grouped loosely around the ideal figure of Raphael, who is the embodiment of the highest qualities and, hence, repeatedly characterized as the "divine" Raphael.

Wackenroder's sketches are not biographical descriptions in the sense that Vasari's *Vite* and his other source materials are. As Koldewey and Dessauer clearly pointed out,[69] there are frequent deviations, omissions, and abbreviations of the source in use. But the question remains: "To what end does Wackenroder cast aside historical accuracy and the conscientiousness of a biographer?" I suggest this answer, expressed in broad terms: namely, that Wackenroder was not interested in the "lives" of his artists. He was concerned primarily with the "process of artistic creativity" or, to use an eighteenth-century term, the "knowledge of the experience of the soul" as it created a work of art.[70] In modern terms, he was an early student of the "psychology of the artist." For this reason, he was not concerned with presenting well-balanced, factually accurate biographical sketches. Instead, he sifted through the factual material available to him and selected one event or psychological moment, generally a period of crisis in the artist's creative life. He then ex-

67. E. R. Curtius defines the *exemplum* (*paradeigma*) as a technical term of antique rhetoric which was used from the time of Aristotle onwards and which also occurred in the form of the "exemplary figure," i.e. "the incarnation of a quality." Cf. *European Literature and the Latin Middle Ages*, pp. 59–60.

68. The parallel between Wackenroder's descriptions of artists' lives and medieval legends of saints' lives was first observed by Heinrich Wölfflin. Cf. "Die Herzensergiessungen eines kunstliebenden Klosterbruders," in: *Studien zur Literaturgeschichte: Michael Bernays gewidmet* (Hamburg, 1893), pp. 61–73.

69. See Chap. 1 above.

70. The term *Erfahrungsseelenkunde* ("knowledge of the experience of the soul") became popularized through the journal edited and, to a large extent, written by Karl Philipp Moritz, "ΤΝΩΘΙ ΣΑΥΤΟΝ oder Magazin zur Erfahrungsseelenkunde als ein Lesebuch für Gelehrte und Ungelehrte," 10 vols. (Berlin, 1783–1793).

amined and elaborated upon this crisis as a new and interesting element in his
ever-widening collection of *exempla* concerning the creative process.

In addition to the exchanges of letters, the lyric poetry, the poetic descriptions of paintings, and the chronicles, there are two other sub-genres of prose
which complete the mélange of forms in the *Confessions*. Werner Kohlschmidt
speaks of the three "quasi-theoretical pieces"[71] in reference to the following essays: "A Few Words concerning Universality, Tolerance and Human Love in
Art,"[72] "Concerning two wonderful Languages and their mysterious Power,"[73]
and "How and in what Manner one actually must regard and use the Works
of the great Artists of Earth for the Well-Being of his Soul."[74] The word
"quasi" is as appropriate here as it was when applied to the adjective "biographical" above. Wackenroder is not a theoretician concerning art. The theoretical explorations among his writings are founded not on his "reason" (*Ver-
nunft*), but on his "feeling" (*Gefühl*) concerning art and, as we shall observe
in the last sub-genre of the *Confessions*, this emotional substratum can and
does experience volatile change. It is inaccurate, therefore, to speak of Wackenroder's "philosophy of art," at least not as the term applies to Humboldt, Schiller, Schelling, Hegel, and others. The remaining sub-genre of the *Confessions*
approaches the style of the "short story" and, therefore, if the essential qualifi-
cations are made, it can be classified under the German term *Novelle*. This sub-
genre is represented by the final sections of the *Confessions*, containing Parts I
and II of the life of Joseph Berglinger, the lengthiest sustained narrative in the
entire book.[75]

In summary, we can distinguish six different literary forms, including
prose and verse, using the techniques of reminiscence, discovery, correspondence by letter, dialogue, and rhapsodic eulogy, incorporated within the framework provided by a "baroque" friar and involving three distinct levels of time
perspective. If we also consider Wackenroder's contributions to the *Fantasies*,
we acquire a fairy-tale as an additional sub-genre with all of its traditional ac-
coutrements.[76] How, then, can one approach this complex mosaic of elements
only loosely connected by the friar in order to determine its intention, its content, and its position in the *Geistesgeschichte* of the epoch?

71. "Der junge Tieck und Wackenroder," in: *Die deutsche Romantik*, ed. H. Steffen
(Göttingen, 1967), pp. 30–44, especially p. 35. ". . . drei quasi-theoretischen Stücke."
72. W.W., pp. 51–56. "Einige Worte über Allgemeinheit, Toleranz und Menschenliebe
in der Kunst."
73. *Ibid.*, pp. 67–71. "Von zwei wunderbaren Sprachen und deren geheimnisvoller
Kraft."
74. *Ibid.*, pp. 79–82. "Wie und auf welche Weise man die Werke der grossen Künstler
der Erde eigentlich betrachten und zum Wohle seiner Seele gebrauchen müsse."
75. *Ibid.*, pp. 111–131. "Das merkwürdige musikalische Leben des Tonkünstlers Joseph
Berglinger. In zwei Haputstücken."
76. *Ibid.*, pp. 197–202. "Ein wunderbares morgenländisches Märchen von einem
nackten Heiligen."

One way is to use the text as a quarry for the excavation of ideas which can be labeled "classical," "romantic," "alienated," "nihilistic," and so forth.[77] Another way is to seek influences and track down elements in various essays inherited by Wackenroder from Herder, Hamann, Reichardt, Karl Philipp Moritz, et al. Or one can take a third route and seek the influence which Wackenroder exercised upon the Pre-Raphaelite School of painting, upon E. T. A. Hoffmann, or even upon R. M. Rilke and Stefan George. But each of these approaches, if applied to the exclusion of the others, will necessarily yield one-sided results. However valid the insights that are gained may be, they will not help the reader to comprehend the *Confessions* as a literary entity. I shall follow an approach which, first, seeks a unifying element in this literary mosaic and, second, examines the thematic and structural development of that element as it recurs in the text and acquires a gradually widening range of implications.

77. See the survey of Wackenroder scholarship in Chap. 1 above.

3   THE PROCESS AND THE PROBLEM OF ARTISTIC CREATIVITY

When one seeks a "unifying idea" for Wackenroder's work or, to speak more poetically, a "heart" for the *Herzensergiessungen,* one does not find it in the figure of the friar. His rôle, important though it is, has a limited scope. Nor does one find that Wackenroder's widely discussed "religion of art" provides a sustained unifying concept for all of the essays.[1] The dominant underlying idea reflected again and again in various thematic constellations is the "process of artistic creativity." Wackenroder is attracted to the Italian *Cinquecento* artists and to Albrecht Dürer not so much because he is interested in their artistic products; these are only of secondary importance to him. Above all he seeks to explore the process of "how the artist creates" his art work. In the tradition of pietistic soul-searching, yet still in the pre-psychoanalytic era, Wackenroder "analyzes" the action of the artist's brain during moments of creativity and what I shall term "periods of creative crisis." As discussed above, the gravitational center of Wackenroder's language lies in the pietistic tradition, but the terminology is not applied to the religious individual *qua* religious individual. It has been transferred over to the creative artist. Where Wackenroder speaks of "inspiration" entering into the artist's "soul," today's neurosurgeon or psychiatrist would speak of "impulses" from the "brain" which result in creative behavior. This comparison is not intended to be trite; rather, its intention is to

---

1. Even Gerhard Fricke, a strong proponent of a literal interpretation of Wackenroder's formulations concerning the "direct divine assistance" required for artistic creativity, acknowledges that the "religion of art" as exemplified by Raphael, Leonardo da Vinci, Dürer, etc. . . . becomes "art without religion" in the Berglinger biography. Cf. "Bemerkungen zu Wilhelm Heinrich Wackenroders Religion der Kunst," especially pp. 362–366.

place Wackenroder's investigations in their historical perspective as a part of the widespread pre-psychoanalytic phase of research into such mental phenomena as hypnosis, somnambulism, mental telepathy, and so forth. That Wackenroder's interest was centered so intently upon the processes of artistic creativity could be explained with the most probable degree of accuracy by his own life story. Certainly critics have regularly drawn the autobiographical parallel between Berglinger and Wackenroder.[2] However, this parallel lies outside the boundaries of the present interpretation. My question is: *How* does Wackenroder explore the process of "artistic creativity" and, if by recurrent themes, what are these themes?

Throughout the span of years during which Wackenroder lived and on into the nineteenth century, the act of artistic creativity was a topic of extensive investigation. The terms employed, the degree of complexity described, the style of presentation, and the philosophical depth of the analyses varied greatly from one author to another. But again and again the formula reappeared which described the creative act as the coming together of two opposing drives or forces.

In his pioneering study of Wilhelm von Humboldt's poetic theory, Kurt Müller-Vollmer sheds new light on Humboldt's terminology and clarifies his definition of these two opposing forces as "activity of the self" (*Selbsttätigkeit*) and "receptivity" (*Empfänglichkeit*).[3] Müller-Vollmer then points out the resemblance between Humboldt's dualism and Schiller's "form drive" (*Formtrieb*) versus "content drive" (*Stofftrieb*).[4]

Karl Philipp Moritz's two opposing terms, "power of creativity" (*Bildungskraft*) and "capacity of feeling" (*Empfindungsvermögen*)[5] identify and define another problem area of the creative process, namely, the distinction between the truly creative artist and the individual who is capable of artistic appreciation, but who cannot "create." Moritz defines the higher creative gift as a product of the *Bildungskraft*. The *Empfindungsvermögen* is a secondary quality, left to those who do not have the inspiration to create and, thus, to experience the highest pleasure of bringing forth great works of art. Moreover, Moritz further explains:

The more complete the *Empfindungsvermögen* for a certain genre of the beautiful is, it is all the more in danger of deceiving itself, of taking itself

2. Cf. D. B. Sanford, "Wackenroder and Tieck: The Aesthetic Breakdown of the *Klosterbruder* Ideal," especially pp. 85–117. See also P. R. Proskauer, "The Phenomenon of Alienation in the Work of Karl Philipp Moritz, Wilhelm Heinrich Wackenroder . . . ," pp. 172–207.

3. *Poesie und Einbildungskraft: Zur Dichtungstheorie Wilhelm von Humboldts* (Stuttgart, 1967), p. 21.

4. *Ibid.*

5. Cf. "Über die bildende Nachahmung des Schönen," in: Karl Philipp Moritz, *Schriften zur Ästhetik und Poetik*, ed. Hans Joachim Schrimpf (Tübingen, 1962), pp. 63–93.

to be *Bildungskraft*, and in this manner, through a thousand unsuccessful attempts, destroying its peace with itself.[6]

Hans Joachim Schrimpf was the first critic to discuss the influence of Moritz's theoretical concepts upon Wackenroder, particularly upon his characterization of Joseph Berglinger.[7] The personal contact between Wackenroder and Moritz in Berlin had previously been well researched in the studies by A. Gillies and is documented further by Schrimpf.[8] Since the year 1964 the principles of Moritzian *Bildungskraft* versus *Empfindungsvermögen* have been applied to the figure of Berglinger with excellent argumentation on only one occasion known to this author: by Elmar Hertrich in his study of Joseph Berglinger published in 1969. Hertrich quotes the friar's desperate question: "Shall I say that he [Berglinger] was perhaps created more to enjoy art than to practice it?"[9] Thereupon he draws a parallel between this dualism in the Berglinger biography and the "opposition between the power of feeling and the power of creating" (*Gegensatz von Empfindungs- und Schaffenskraft*) which is at the root of the creative problems and the "half-artistry" of Anton Reiser.[10]

In the light of our previous observations regarding the concern for the psychic processes of creativity during this era, it should not be a surprise that the novel of a young man struggling to achieve status as a full-fledged artist, Karl Philipp Moritz's novel, *Anton Reiser*, carries the subtitle "A psychological Novel" (*Ein psychologischer Roman*). This is the first occurrence of the word "psychological" in the title of a German novel. Nor should it be a great surprise that Moritz also wrote a theoretical essay concerning the "hearing" of music and, in this instance, again used the word "psychological" in his title, "The Effects of the External Senses in Psychological Perspective: Concerning Musical Hearing."[11] Thus, it is a disappointment that P. R. Proskauer, who, in his Columbia dissertation (1966) concentrates on the timely, hitherto un-

6. *Ibid.*, p. 79. "Je vollkommner das Empfindungsvermögen für eine gewisse Gattung des Schönen ist, um desto mehr ist es in Gefahr sich zu täuschen, sich selbst für Bildungskraft zu nehmen, und auf die Weise durch tausend misslungne Versuche, seinen Frieden mit sich selbst zu stören." In other passages Moritz occasionally uses the term *Tatkraft* interchangeably with the term *Bildungskraft*.

7. "W. H. Wackenroder und K. Ph. Moritz: Ein Beitrag zur frühromantischen Selbstkritik," *Zeitschrift für deutsche Philologie*, LXXXIII (1964), 385–411. It should be pointed out, however, that Schrimpf's essay was by no means the first study to link Moritz with the German Romantics as a group. As early as 1928, E. H. Zeydel had outlined characteristics which Moritz had in common with the Romantics. Cf. "The Relation of K. Ph. Moritz's *Anton Reiser* to Romanticism," *The Germanic Review*, III (1928), 295–327.

8. For Gillies, cf. n. 6 of the Introduction above. Schrimpf, "W. H. Wackenroder und K. Ph. Moritz . . . ," especially pp. 386–387.

9. *Joseph Berglinger, Eine Studie zu Wackenroders Musiker-Dichtung*, p. 151. "Soll ich sagen, dass er [sc. Berglinger] vielleicht mehr dazu geschaffen war, Kunst zu g e n i e s s e n   a l s   a u s z u ü b e n?"

10. *Ibid.*

11. "Die Wirkungen der äussern Sinne in psychologischer Rücksicht: Über das musikalische Gehör," in: Moritz, *Schriften zur Ästhetik und Poetik*, pp. 129–135.

[3]

explored "phenomenon of alienation" as it reoccurs in Moritz, Wackenroder, and *Bonaventura's 'Nachtwachen,'* fails to take into consideration any of Moritz's theoretical writings and their relevance in the evolution of Wackenroder's thinking.[12]

During the initial stages of the present study, I believed that it would be possible to interpret the essays on Joseph Berglinger as they have been generally understood and interpreted up to the present time. I thought that they could be considered quite apart from the essays on the artists of the past and that they contained "modern," "nihilistic" elements which indicated a break in Wackenroder's thinking and a new, devastatingly negative view of art as "a seductive, forbidden fruit."[13] But it became increasingly clear that there is no abrupt psychic, thematic, or structural discontinuity between the earlier essays and the Berglinger sequence. The change is far more subtle than has hitherto been realized. It is a gradual widening of the thematic background, with the same themes recurring in new constellations to provide an architectonically structured continuity.

Underlying Wackenroder's discussion of each artist is his dominant concern for the process of artistic creativity, a process which is regarded in dualistic terms. In discussing the terminology of Humboldt and Moritz, two distinct sets of terms were observed, Humboldt's opposing forces of "activity of the self" (*Selbsttätigkeit*) and "receptivity" (*Empfänglichkeit*), which came together in the creative act, and Moritz's terms of "power of creativity" (*Bildungskraft*) and "capacity of feeling" (*Empfindungsvermögen*), which distinguish the creative artist from the non-creative appreciating dilettante. Without pursuing the question of direct influences and personal contacts in Berlin, I shall seek now to provide demonstrative evidence that both of these dualisms were of important concern to Wackenroder—not just in the Berglinger essays, but from the essay "Raphael's Vision" all the way through to "A Letter of Joseph Berglinger."

The first artist whom Wackenroder considers is Raphael and, immediately, in the midst of a barrage of polemical attack upon the errors of the "overly clever writers of more recent times,"[14] the kernel of the creative act is defined as "divine inspiration."[15] But this is not divine inspiration in any orthodox

12. "The Phenomenon of Alienation in the Work of Karl Philipp Moritz, Wilhelm Heinrich Wackenroder and in 'Nachtwachen' von Bonaventura." This dissertation title promises more than Proskauer delivers. Although well written in a flowing style, the topic is overly ambitious for a study of 270 typed pages. Proskauer traces the "problem of the alienated artist" (p. 2) through all of the following works: *Anton Reiser; Andreas Hartknopf: Eine Allegorie; Andreas Hartknopfs Predigerjahre;* and *Die neue Cecilia* all by K. Ph. Moritz; Wackenroder's *Herzensergießungen* and *Phantasien;* and the *'Nachtwachen' von Bonaventura.* This is obviously an immense undertaking which, although quite perceptive with regard to Moritz's novels, is too eclectic in its gathering up of passages to *prove* the common trait of alienation in all seven works.

13. W.W., p. 230. "Die Kunst ist eine verführerische, verbotene Frucht; . . ."

14. *Ibid.*, p. 11. ". . . die überklugen Schriftsteller neuerer Zeiten . . ."

15. *Ibid.*, p. 12. ". . . göttliche Eingebung . . ."

sense; it is the mysterious assistance of a supernatural force which is beyond the rational explanations that mankind can devise. It can be and is described, therefore, with a variety of adjective-noun combinations such as "divine omnipotence," "the direct assistance of God," "the divine spark," "a heavenly genius," or noun-noun combinations such as "the grace of heaven," "the genius of art," and so forth.[16] These terms are the point of departure for an understanding of Wackenroder's view of artistic creativity, which is incorporated into and embodied most perfectly and harmoniously in the figure of the "divine" Raphael.

The anecdote that Wackenroder selects to narrate first concerns Raphael's struggles to create a picture of the Madonna that would meet his ideal of heavenly perfection. The only factual element in this anecdote is the quotation from a letter of Raphael to Baldassare Castiglione, in which Raphael says:

> Since one sees so few beautiful womanly personages, I hold myself to a certain mental image, which enters into my soul.[17]

The rest of the anecdote, including its supposed source on "sheets by the hand of Bramante" which the friar claims to have "discovered" in his monastery,[18] is Wackenroder's own invention. Even the application of Raphael's words to one of his Madonnas is a deviation from the truth, since Raphael is known to have made this statement in connection with his painting of the sea-goddess of Greek antiquity, Galatea.

Much attention has been given by scholars to this substitution of the Christian Madonna for the pagan Galatea. Ladislao Mittner acclaimed, for instance, that this was the first step toward the Romantic replacement of the "antiquated heathen mythology" with a new, or renewed, Christian medieval mythology.[19] Yet, it seems far more probable that this substitution occurred quite accidentally on the part of Wackenroder and that he had in mind the Madonna at Pommersfelden, which he had believed to be the work of Raphael.[20] Certainly there is no evidence of opposition to the classical Greek ideal of beauty in Wackenroder's description of the Pommersfelden Madonna:

16. *Ibid.*, pp. 15, 19, 21, 32, 35, etc.
17. Raphael's original Italian line reads: "Essendo carestia di belle donne, io mi servo di certa idea che me viene al mente." Koldewey (*Wackenroder und sein Einfluss auf Tieck*, p. 5) argues convincingly that Wackenroder used the following work as his source for Raphael's letter to Castiglione: Giorgio Pietro Bellori, *Descrizione delle imagini dipinti da Rafaëllo, . . .* (Rome, 1695), p. 100.
18. See Chap. 2, n. 45, above.
19. "Galatea: Die Romantisierung der italienischen Renaissancekunst und -dichtung in der deutschen Frühromantik," *Deutsche Vierteljahrsschrift*, XXVII (1953), 555–581. On p. 556: ". . . den ersten, entscheidenden Schritt (. . .), die veraltete heidnische Mythologie durch eine neue oder erneuerte christliche zu ersetzen . . ."
20. Cf. *Katalog der Alten Pinakothek München. Amtliche Ausgabe 1957* (Munich, 1957), p. 25, W.A.F. 153, *Bildnis einer Frau*. See also H. Lippuner, *Wackenroder/Tieck und die bildende Kunst*, Chap. 1, n. 10. Lippuner explains that the painting was ascribed to Raphael until 1880, then to Leonardo da Vinci and, after the mid-nineteenth century, to Antonio Solario.

Mary is seated at the left, in an erect position, in the most blessed peacefulness. In her countenance the celestial, universal form of Greek ideal beauty is united most successfully with the most eloquent, attractive individuality.[21]

The echoes of Winckelmann's "noble simplicity and quiet greatness" (*edle Einfalt und stille Grösse*) are unmistakable here. The emphasis placed upon "the most blessed peacefulness" of the Madonna portrait indicates Wackenroder's preference for the harmonious, well-balanced work of art which is "perfected in itself" (*in sich selbst vollendet*).[22] There are a number of other passages which also reflect a "classical" taste in works of art.[23] In addition, the pietistic concept of "quietness" (*Stille*) or total peacefulness of the soul is present as a value to be found in the perfect work of art. With all this in mind, there is little doubt that the substitution of the Madonna for Galatea is not the major step toward the creation of a new Christian medieval mythology that Ladislao Mittner considers it to be. Wackenroder's taste in matters of art still conforms in many respects with Winckelmann's ideal of beauty—and the Madonna portrait that he admires combines in her countenance "the celestial, universal form of Greek ideal beauty" with the modern element of "individuality."

The crucial factor in this essay is not the issue of the Madonna, but the struggle of Raphael to "create" his work of art. The creative activity of the artist or, to apply Humboldt's term, his *Selbsttätigkeit*, is conveyed by such lines as: "Day and night his mind had constantly worked on her picture in abstraction; but he had not been able to perfect it at all to his satisfaction; it had always seemed to him as if his fantasy were working in the dark."[24] The struggle continues and Raphael's soul becomes more and more excited, until suddenly the unfinished picture hanging upon his wall becomes illuminated one night and he envisions a "perfect and truly living image" of his Madonna. Having also the quality of receptivity (*Empfänglichkeit*), Raphael is able to absorb the impression of this vision so completely that it remains "firmly stamped in his mind and his senses for eternity."[25] Thereafter he is capable of portraying the

21. W.W., p. 569. This passage, in the travel diary "Reise ins Bayreuthische und Bambergische" reads: "Maria sitzt links, in gerader Stellung, in der seligsten Ruhe. In ihrem Antlitz ist die überirdische, allgemeine Form griechischer Idealschönheit, mit sprechendster, anziehender Individualität aufs glücklichste vereinigt . . ."

22. Cf. "Versuch einer Vereinigung aller schönen Künste und Wissenschaften unter dem Begriff des in sich selbst Vollendeten," in: Moritz, *Schriften zur Ästhetik und Poetik*, pp. 3–9.

23. For discussions of other similar passages, cf. H. Lippuner, *Wackenroder/Tieck und die bildende Kunst*; also D. B. Sanford, "Wackenroder and Tieck; the Aesthetic Breakdown of the *Klosterbruder* Ideal."

24. W.W., p. 14. "In Gedanken habe sein Gemüt beständig an ihrem Bilde, Tag und Nacht, gearbeitet; allein er habe es sich gar nicht zu seiner Befriedigung vollenden können; es sei ihm immer gewesen, als wenn seine Phantasie im Finstern arbeitete."

25. *Ibid.*, p. 15. ". . . die Erscheinung sei seinem Gemüt und seinen Sinnen auf ewig fest eingeprägt geblieben . . ."

Madonna repeatedly just as she had appeared to him in this vision. The source of the inspiration is, as has been pointed out above, "divine" and, thus, it places the truly creative artist in a special relationship with God. As the recipient of "divine inspiration," the artist is an extraordinary human being who stands apart from ordinary men and serves as a holy receptacle of the "divine spark" and, through the medium of his created artistic product, as a mediator between the ordinary mortal and the "divinity." It is this special relationship with the source of "divine inspiration" that makes the artist different from other men and gives him a function which had hitherto been ascribed only to the realm of religion.

The chronicle of Francesco Francia provides a clear statement of the second theoretical dualism underlying the *Confessions* and the *Fantasies*. Like Raphael, Francia was also a zealous and industrious artist, who, "with his untiring diligence and his constantly striving spirit,"[26] had reached a high level of acclaim and had become the progenitor of a school of painting in Bologna. He is described by Wackenroder as the "founder and, simultaneously, the first prince of this newly established sovereignty,"[27] namely, that of Renaissance art in Lombardy. Francia enjoys great prestige and eminence; he also has the respect and admiration of Raphael, who has demonstrated this in letters to Francia. Due to his great success, Francia believes at the outset that there is a "heavenly genius"[28] dwelling within him. He feels that the only other contemporary artist who could possibly be considered his competitor is Raphael. Although the latter had seen some of Francia's paintings, Francia had never been fortunate enough to see a work created by Raphael.

Quite unexpectedly a letter arrives from Raphael asking that Francia receive an altar painting of Saint Cecilia which he had just completed. The request is made that Francia repair any damage, improve, or correct the painting in whatever way that he deems necessary, and arrange that it be appropriately set in its place at the Church of Saint John (San Giovanni-in-Monte) in Bologna. It is at this point in the chronicle that Wackenroder begins to deviate in a major way from his source in Vasari's *Vite*. He shifts the emphasis over to the psychological factors and intentionally depicts a build-up of emotional tension which leads to a "creative crisis," a crisis that results in Francesco Francia's death. The technique used by Wackenroder to intensify the emotional aspect is that of lengthening the time intervals between the major events, so that excitement and psychological stress are increased.

26. *Ibid.*, p. 19. ". . . durch seinen unermüdeten Fleiss und seinen immer hinaufstrebenden Geist . . ."
27. *Ibid.*, p. 20. ". . . und in der Lombardei war gerade er der Stifter, und gleichsam der erste Fürst dieser neugegründeten Herrschaft."
28. *Ibid.*, p. 21. ". . . sein lebhafter Geist (. . .) an einen himmlischen Genius in seinem Inneren zu glauben anfing."

[3]

First, the letter from Raphael asking for Francia's assistance arrives long before the painting itself reaches him. Thus, Francia and his pupils await the arrival of Raphael's work most impatiently. Second, when it finally arrives, the pupils place it in a favorable light in Francia's studio and, upon their master's return from an excursion, they rush up to him and tell him with great joy of the painting's arrival. Thereupon Francia rushes in, beside himself. He is "thunderstruck" at the sight of Raphael's work and his "soul is pierced through." He feels as if he were falling to his knees before a "higher being" in total contrition of heart. Francia immediately experiences deep repentance for his arrogant presumption that his works of art could rival those of Raphael. From that moment on, his life moves steadily downward, his emotions are in "constant turmoil," and he suffers from "fatigue of the spirit." Wackenroder reports that his pupils found him lying dead in bed not long thereafter. Then the concluding paragraphs contain an important idea, namely, that Francia became "truly great" because he felt himself to be so insignificant in comparison with Raphael. Thereby he earned the halo which is his due as a true "martyr of art enthusiasm."[29]

The long wait for Raphael's painting and the highly emotional language describing Francia's response to it are Wackenroder's own stylistic devices, which intentionally dramatize the contrast between the "divinely inspired" Raphael and Francesco Francia. The chronicle in Vasari's *Vite* which served as Wackenroder's source reads quite differently. There the letter and the painting arrive simultaneously at a time when Francia is at home. Since he has had no advance notice of its arrival, he has not experienced any period of anxious expectation. The tone of Vasari's description is far more matter-of-fact. There is no crowd of eager pupils standing around and awaiting the reaction of their master. And, although the cause of death is described as "grief" stemming from his own foolish presumption, there is no mention of any "martyrdom" due to enthusiasm for art. The psychological causes of Francia's sudden death are not dramatized as they are by Wackenroder. In the final paragraph of his account, Vasari even calls them into question when he writes:

> There are, nevertheless, many who declare his death to have been so sudden as to give rise to the belief, which was confirmed by various appearances, that it was caused by poison or apoplexy, rather than anything else.[30]

Wackenroder's deviations from Vasari's account allow us to establish certain hypotheses concerning his own theoretical attitude toward art. First, it can be observed that the works of art themselves are not of central importance. The paintings by Francia are only the medium through which he developed his

29. Cf. *ibid*., pp. 21–24, for the words and passages cited above.
30. Vasari, *Lives,* II, 315. (For the first reference to this English translation, see Chap. 1, n. 7, above.)

illusion that he was a rival of Raphael. Raphael's portrait of St. Cecilia, the patron saint of music, is significant not in and of itself, but because of the enormous emotional impact it had upon Francia. And the entire chronicle is the artistic expression of a dualistic contrast between Raphael, in whom the drive to create and the receptivity to divine inspiration are harmoniously united, and Francesco Francia, who feels the same creative urge but suffers, in the end, from a lack of the "divine spark." Thus, he is called a "martyr of art enthusiasm," an interesting designation which combines an element of quasi-religious suffering with an element of Moritz's art theory. The passage cited earlier in which Moritz states that "the more complete the *Empfindungsvermögen* . . . , the more in danger it is of deceiving itself, or taking itself to be *Bildungskraft* . . ." has relevance when applied to the chronicle of Francia, who is, indeed, deceived concerning his own "heavenly genius." As an artist who dies in a paroxysmal reaction to his own feelings of inadequacy and uselessness, Francesco Francia is a spiritual predecessor of Joseph Berglinger. Even the fact that the painting which triggers Francia's negative response is Raphael's "St. Cecilia" foreshadows Berglinger's poem in honor of St. Cecilia[31] and the entire problem of the musical art.

In summary, the two earliest chronicles in the *Confessions*, "Raphael's Vision" and "The remarkable death of the old artist, Francesco Francia . . . ," establish several themes which recur like the musical themes of a symphony, not in any clearly established sequence of developmental stages, but in an ever-widening, organically growing intensification. The same themes are reflected repeatedly in new contexts and with new atmospheric backgrounds. Certain metaphorical images are also repeated in association with these themes. As Murray H. Abrams states in *The Mirror and the Lamp*:

> In Germany, such writers as Tieck, Wackenroder, and E. T. A. Hoffmann (following the lead of Herder) praised symphonic music as the art of arts, just because it is indefinite, innocent of reference to the external world, and richly, because impressively suggestive.[32]

And Abrams continues shortly thereafter: "In another aspect, literature was made to emulate music by substituting a symphonic form—a melody of ideas and images, a thematic organization, a harmony of moods—for the structural principles of plot, argument, or exposition."[33] It is this musical, thematic organization to which I shall now turn my attention.

31. W.W., pp. 120–121.
32. *The Mirror and the Lamp: Romantic Theory and the Critical Tradition* (New York, 1953), p. 94.
33. *Ibid.*

[3]

4 THE "THEMATIC" STRUCTURE OF THE *CONFESSIONS*

Raphael represents for Wackenroder the highest level of true artistry, which combines technical skill and active striving with receptivity to "divine inspiration." Each other artist is measured and examined against the model of Raphael, whether this comparison is openly stated or tacitly implied. As has been discussed above, Wackenroder invented and dramatically elaborated the story of the "image" which entered into Raphael's "soul." His only factual basis for this nocturnal vision was a sentence from a letter written by Raphael to Castiglione in a totally different context. But the outcome of this vision is a highly positive one for Raphael. Once he has seen the vision of his "Madonna," he is henceforth capable of re-creating her again and again with quiet, harmonious confidence. While some artists experience feelings of virtually irresolvable conflict, Raphael is a model of infinite harmony and composure. He is at peace with himself and the world.

The theme of harmonious creativity established in the essay of "Raphael's Vision" is continued with a slight differentiation of emphasis in the chronicle on Leonardo da Vinci. Particularly stressed in this essay is the idea that true artistic creativity cannot result from "divine inspiration" alone. This divine spark must be united with the active knowledge and skilled craftsmanship of the artist himself. The goddess Minerva, who includes among her attributes such qualities as intelligence, inventiveness, and practical skill in the arts, is said to be the willing and desirable companion of the "genius of art." Wackenroder describes Leonardo as "the model in a truly scholarly and thorough study of art and as the symbol of an untiring and, at the same time, gifted diligence."[1]

1. W.W., p. 34. ". . . das Muster in einem wahrhaft gelehrten und gründlichen

He closes his second paragraph in praise of Leonardo with the thematically recurring idea of the beautifully reflected harmony of the true artist, when he states that "in such a large and open soul, even if it is directed toward one principal endeavor, nevertheless, the entire multifariously compounded picture of human knowledge is reflected in beautiful and perfect harmony."[2]

Wackenroder departs, at this point, from his consideration of the creative process as it functions in Leonardo and falls into a biographical style, narrating historical facts from Leonardo's life. He speaks highly of Leonardo's father, who perceptively recognized the dexterity and wit in his son's nature and wisely knew that he should be allowed to develop according to his own free will. "Leonardo's father acted in that way," Wackenroder writes, "by leaving the boy to the inclination which was by nature innate within him and placing him in the apprenticeship of the very renowned and deserving man, Andrea Verocchio in Florence."[3] Thus, we observe a sharp contrast between the understanding action of Leonardo's father and the rigid behavior of Joseph Berglinger's father, who despised all the arts and "from the beginning had regarded with displeasure the fact that his Joseph had become so very fond of music."[4] As Joseph's inclinations grew even stronger, his father made "a persistent and serious attempt to convert him from the ruinous inclination"[5] over to his own field of medicine. Implied in the praise of Leonardo's father is also Wackenroder's underlying anxious criticism of his own father, who was attempting to guide his son away from art into his profession of law.

After this brief, but significant, digression into the realm of factual biography, Wackenroder returns to his discussion of the "creative personality" of Leonardo or the "psychology" of the artistic mind. He speaks of the "lively and animated spirit" required for creativity, "for, through gradual painstaking effort a finished work is finally to be brought forth for the pleasure of all the senses; and sad, withdrawn temperaments have no inclination, no desire, no courage and no constancy to be creative."[6] These passages and numerous others

---

Studium der Kunst, und als das Bild eines unermüdlichen, und dabei geistreichen Fleisses . . ."

2. *Ibid.*, p. 35. ". . . in einer grossen und offenen Seele, wenn sie auch auf ein Hauptbestreben gerichtet ist, doch das ganze, vielfach zusammengesetzte Bild menschlicher Wissenschaft sich in schöner und vollkommener Harmonie abspiegelt."

3. *Ibid.*, p. 35. "So tat Leonardos Vater, indem er den Knaben seiner ihm von Natur eingepflanzten Neigung überliess, und ihn der Lehre des sehr berühmten und verdienten Mannes, Andrea Verocchio zu Florenz, übergab."

4. *Ibid.*, p. 117. "Schon von jeher hatte er es mit Missvergnügen gesehen, dass sein Joseph sich so sehr an die Musik gehängt hatte."

5. *Ibid.* ". . . machte er einen anhaltenden und ernstlichen Versuch, ihn von dem verderblichen Hange (. . .) zur Medizin (. . .) zu bekehren."

6. *Ibid.*, p. 36. ". . . denn es soll ja durch allmähliche mühsame Arbeit endlich ein vollkommenes Werk, zum Wohlgefallen aller Sinne, hervorgebracht werden, und traurige und in sich verschlossene Gemüter haben keinen Hang, keine Lust, keinen Mut und keine Stetigkeit hervorzubringen."

on the remaining pages of the chronicle emphasize repeatedly Leonardo's zeal, his industrious observation of all forms of natural life, his constant efforts to widen the range of his painting and make himself universal. Thus, in contra-distinction to Raphael, the emphasis of the Leonardo chronicle lies on the side of "activity of the artist," rather than on the side of "receptivity" to divine inspiration.

The spectrum is widened and the complexity of Wackenroder's thinking elucidated when one adds to Raphael and Leonardo da Vinci the figures of Michelangelo Buonarotti and Albrecht Dürer. Concerning Michelangelo, Ernst Dessauer observes that Wackenroder excludes all biographical information and disregards all chronological sequence, thus vastly contracting and abbreviating the material in his source, Vasari's *Vite*.[7] Once again we find the explanation for this extensive deviation from the source in the fact that it was not Michel-angelo's "life" which interested Wackenroder, but the kernel of his creativity. Wackenroder even seems to treat Vasari with a trace of sarcasm here, for he comments on how Vasari "rejoices deeply" that he and Michelangelo "shared the same little area of earth" as their mutual homeland. He also notes that Va-sari, throughout his lengthy description of the life of Michelangelo, "frequent-ly acts very happily proud that he enjoyed his most intimate friendship."[8] And, thereupon, Wackenroder assumes his own independent position with the statement:

> However, we do not want to content ourselves merely with marveling about this great man but, instead, we want to penetrate into his inner spirit and press close to the unique character of his works.[9]

He then makes a direct comparison between Raphael and Michelangelo, in which he dramatically calls Raphael the artist of the New Testament and Michelangelo the artist of the Old Testament. He explains this dissimilarity on the basis of the individual creative temperaments of the two artists and, there-by, gives clear expression to the already implicit idea that there are not only different degrees of inspired, harmonious, artistic creativity, but also different sources of "divine inspiration." "For," as Wackenroder writes, "the silent, di-vine spirit of Christ—I dare to express the bold thought—rests upon the former —upon the latter the spirit of the inspired prophets, of Moses and the other

7. "Wackenroders *Herzensergiessungen* (. . .) in ihrem Verhältnis zu Vasari," Part IV, p. 217.
8. W.W., p. 85. ". . . tut oft recht gutmütig=stolz darauf, dass er seiner vertrautesten Freundschaft genossen."
9. *Ibid.* "Doch wir wollen uns nicht an dem blossen Anstaunen dieses grossen Mannes begnügen, sondern vielmehr in seinen inneren Geist hineingehen, uns in den eigentüm-lichen Charakter seiner Werke hineinschmiegen." It should be noted that, despite the latter part of this line, Wackenroder does *not* discuss any of Michelangelo's paintings. He concerns himself solely with the "creative process" as manifested in Michelangelo in contrast with Raphael and as imitated by later artists.

poets of the East."[10] Without belaboring the point, it is clear that Wackenroder conceives of the "divine" element in the creative process as potentially emanating from various sources, including Old as well as New Testament prophets and Oriental poets and visionaries. Far from revealing an overt "catholicizing tendency," this view encompasses a wide range of possible sources of the "divine spark" in art. It is, therefore, a tolerant, relatively secularized position which acknowledges that there is a "secret" (*Geheimnis*) of a spiritual nature involved in the genuine creative act, but that this mysterious divine force can make its presence felt in many different ways and through many different media.

The idea of tolerance comes into the foreground even more vividly when Wackenroder turns his attention away from Rome, Bologna, and Florence to Albrecht Dürer in the German city of Nuremberg. His first chronicle on Dürer actually precedes the Michelangelo essay in the sequence of the *Confessions*. The second Dürer chronicle was published posthumously as the initial essay of the *Fantasies*; therefore it technically lies outside the boundaries of the present discussion, although it develops the same theme. The first chronicle, "A Memorial to our venerable ancestor Albrecht Dürer," begins with a rhapsodic tribute to the city of Nuremberg and mentions not only Dürer, but also Hans Sachs, Adam Kraft, and Wilibaldus Pirkheimer, all of whom lived in Nuremberg during the vibrant and exciting age of Renaissance in German art. The tone of Wackenroder's fond expression of love for Nuremberg's "quaint streets" and "antiquated houses and churches" closely resembles the tone used by Karl Philipp Moritz in his descriptions of Rome.[11] The parallel becomes even more provocative as a comparison when Wackenroder mentions Rome and Germany in one sentence:

> You, who see boundaries everywhere where there are none! Are not Rome and Germany situated on one earth? Has the heavenly Father not made pathways from North to South and from West to East across the globe? Is a human life too brief? Are the Alps insurmountable?—Then, more than one love must also be able to live in the breast of man.[12]

This eloquent plea for universal tolerance and for appreciation of more than

10. *Ibid.*, p. 86. ". . . denn auf jenem—ich wage den kühnen Gedanken auszusprechen —ruhet der stille göttliche Geist Christi,—auf diesem, der Geist der inspirierten Propheten, des Moses und der übrigen Dichter des Morgenlandes."

11. Cf. *Die neue Cecilia*, photomechanical reprint of the first edition of 1794 (Stuttgart, 1962), especially pp. 23, 33–35.

12. W.W., p. 58. ". . . ihr, die ihr überall Grenzen sehet, wo keine sind! Liegt Rom und Deutschland nicht auf einer Erde? Hat der himmlische Vater nicht Wege von Norden nach Süden, wie von Westen nach Osten über den Erdkreis geführt? Ist ein Menschenleben zu kurz? Sind die Alpen unübersteiglich,—Nun so muss auch mehr als eine Liebe in der Brust des Menschen wohnen können."

one artistic form, a viewpoint which Moritz, Wackenroder, and others of the late eighteenth century inherited primarily from Herder,[13] concludes the introduction of the figure of Albrecht Dürer. From this point on in the Dürer chronicle of the *Confessions*, Wackenroder's underlying concern for the creative process again receives attention and the friar-narrator makes his narrative seem more immediately and intensely important by employing the form of a conversation, as if he were speaking directly to this native German artist of Nuremberg's past. In his one-sided dialogue—"one-sided" because Dürer does not respond—the art-loving friar says: "I imagine that I see you, how you stand meditating before the picture you have begun—how the conception that you want to make visible hovers very animatedly before your soul (. . .), and you then accurately and painstakingly convey to the panel the beings allied with your lively imagination."[14]

Once again we can observe a recurrence of the two elements of the creative process first introduced in the essay which opened the *Confessions*, "Raphael's Vision." These two elements are the eager, painstaking effort on the part of the artist and the "conception" which "hovers very animatedly" before his soul. But, here again, there is a shift of emphasis which differentiates Dürer from Raphael, for there is no mention made of "divine assistance," but only the vague postulate of a "conception" which is defined no further. In addition, Dürer's "provincialism" receives attention, and Wackenroder acknowledges that Dürer's "blood was not Italian blood" and that "he was not born for the perfection and the lofty grandeur of a Raphael."[15] Nevertheless, he achieved admirable artistic results in the quiet simplicity of sixteenth-century Nuremberg. Hence, the friar's nocturnal vision of Raphael and Dürer standing hand in hand, gazing at their paintings hanging side by side in a magnificent gallery, symbolizes the equivalent accomplishment of each of the two artists in relationship to their separate artistic environments. Raphael achieved the highest level of true artistry, but Albrecht Dürer also deserves our loving recognition for his excellent accomplishments amidst surroundings which were far less sophisticated in matters of art. At the close of the Dürer chronicle, Wackenroder expresses one of the passages that has been quoted frequently as evidence of his supposed advocacy of medievalism:

13. Cf. Johann Gottfried von Herder, "Ideen zur Geschichte und Kritik der Poesie und bildenden Künste," in: *Sämmtliche Werke: Zur schönen Literatur und Kunst* (Stuttgart and Tübingen, 1829), XV, 63–294.

14. W.W., p. 59. "Mich dünkt, ich sehe euch, wie ihr nachdenkend vor eurem angefangenen Bilde stehet,—wie die Vorstellung, die ihr sichtbar machen wollt, ganz lebendig eurer Seele vorschwebt (. . .), und wie ihr dann, mit inniger Teilnahme und freundlichem Ernst, die eurer lebendigen Einbildung befreundeten Wesen, auf die Tafel treu und langsam auftraget."

15. *Ibid.*, p. 63. ". . . sein Blut war klein italienisches Blut. Er war für das Idealische und die erhabene Hoheit eines Raffaels nicht geboren."

True art sprouts forth not only under Italian sky, under majestic domes and Corinthian columns—but also under pointed arches, intricately ornamented buildings, and Gothic towers.[16]

W. D. Robson-Scott, whose opinion I share with regard to Wackenroder's aesthetic position concerning the Middle Ages, argues that this contrast, when examined in its complete context, "in fact, is a geographical one—a contrast between Italian and German art, not, as is usually claimed, between classical art and the art of the Middle Ages."[17] All that Wackenroder is actually saying is that Dürer, as well as Raphael, is an artist who is worthy of attention and esteem.

We have examined Wackenroder's chronicles concerning four genuine, gifted, harmoniously balanced artists: Raphael, Leonardo da Vinci, Michelangelo Buonarotti, and Albrecht Dürer. We have observed differentiations in specific points of emphasis, but an underlying concern for the process of artistic creativity which serves as a unifying theme. In contrast, we have observed that the finished works of art, the "products" of the creative process, are given only fleeting, superficial attention. The zeal, the enthusiasm, the diligence, the craftsmanship of the artist—plus that elusive, inexplicable factor of "inspiration"—are the elements which come together in the moment of creativity. The atmosphere surrounding each of these genuine artists also deserves our attentive examination. Preceding Raphael's vision there is a period of darkness, a metaphorical inability to conceptualize the Madonna. Then, on one dark night, Raphael is awakened by a bright light on the wall opposite his bed and, from this point on, the imagery shifts to a piling up of metaphors concerning light. A gentle "beam of light" illuminates Raphael's picture of the Madonna. He arises as if newly born on the "next morning." And he is described metaphorically as the "shining sun" among all the artists.

The epoch of Italian Renaissance art is described as that "golden age" when art enthusiasm "inflamed all the world."[18] The versatility of Leonardo receives special attention with another "flame" metaphor, for Wackenroder lauds this quality in Leonardo and says of such an artist that "when he, moreover, is not merely devoted to one single art but unites several within himself, perceives their hidden relationship, and feels in his inner self the divine flame which flickers in all of them, then this man is certainly elevated above other human beings in an amazing way . . . ."[19]

16. *Ibid.*, p. 66. "Nicht bloss unter italienischem Himmel, unter majestätischen Kuppeln und korinthischen Säulen;—auch unter Spitzgewölben, kraus verzierten Gebäuden und gotischen Türmen wächst wahre Kunst hervor."

17. "Wackenroder and the Middle Ages," *Modern Language Review*, L (1955), 160.

18. W.W., p. 18. ". . . weil der Enthusiasmus (. . .) in jener goldenen Zeit alle Welt entflammte."

19. *Ibid.*, p. 41. "Und wenn er überdies nicht bloss einer einzigen Kunst ergeben ist, sondern mehrere in sich vereinigt, ihre geheime Verwandtschaft fühlt, und die göttliche

Similar metaphorical terms involving "flame," "fire," "light," and related adjectives, adverbs, and nouns recur at many points where artistic inspiration and creativity are revealed. In the opening paragraph of the Michelangelo chronicle, Wackenroder speaks from behind his mask of the "art-loving friar" and discusses his "favorite object" (*Lieblingsgegenstand*) in the realm of art, the painters of Italy's past. He tells us that it is this realm "to which my mind often turns spontaneously, like the sunflower to the sun."[20] At another point the landscapes of Italy are described as those "beautiful, bright regions"[21] where art thrives.

In surprisingly similar language Wackenroder enthusiastically apostrophizes the city of Nuremberg during the era of Albrecht Dürer. "Blessed be to me your golden age, Nuremberg!" he writes, "the only age when Germany could boast of having its own native art."[22] He employs the word "sunflower" again to describe the scene at Dürer's gravesite, where his grave is located amidst numerous other gravestones, "between which tall sunflowers spring up in multitudes, which make the cemetery into a lovely garden."[23] And he speaks of Nuremberg's churches, "where, through colorfully painted windows, the sunlight splendidly illuminates all the objects of art and paintings of the past age!"[24] A metaphor of light is once again employed in the passage where Wackenroder first gives expression to his concept of tolerance in artistic matters.[25] "Beauty in art," he writes, "is not something so poor and scanty that one human life could exhaust it; (. . .) rather, its light splits up into thousands of beams, the reflections of which are cast back into our enchanted eyes in various ways by the great artists whom heaven has placed upon earth."[26] The closer one looks, the more one discovers that Wackenroder's descriptions of truly creative artists and their art works revolve around changing combinations of a very limited number of metaphors, all of which are variations of a single basic metaphor of the artist as the "shining reflection" of the "divine" element in-

---

Flamme, die in allen weht, in seinem Inneren empfindet, so ist dieser Mann von der Hand des Himmels gewiss auf eine wunderbare Weise vor andern Menschen hervorgehoben . . . ."

20. *Ibid.*, p. 83. ". . . zu welchem mein Geist sich oft unwillkürlich, wie die Sonnenblume zur Sonne, hinwendet."

21. *Ibid.*, p. 16. ". . . die schönen, hellen Gegenden . . ."

22. *Ibid.*, p. 66. "Gesegnet sei mir deine goldene Zeit, Nürnberg! die einzige Zeit, da Deutschland eine eigene vaterländische Kunst zu haben sich rühmen konnte."

23. *Ibid.*, p. 58. ". . . zwischen denen sich hohe Sonnenblumen in Menge erheben, welche den Gottesacker zu einem lieblichen Garten machen."

24. *Ibid.*, p. 57. ". . . wo der Tag durch buntbemalte Fenster all das Bildwerk und die Malereien der alten Zeit wunderbar beleuchtet!"

25. See n. 13 of the present chapter regarding the origin of Wackenroder's concept of tolerance.

26. W.W., p. 20. "Denn allerdings ist die Schönheit in der Kunst nicht etwas so Armes und Dürftiges, dass Eines Menschen Leben sie erschöpfen könnte; (. . .) ihr Licht zerspaltet sich vielmehr in tausend Strahlen, deren Widerschein auf mannigfache Weise von den grossen Künstlern, die der Himmel auf die Welt gesetzt hat, in unser entzücktes Auge zurückgeworfen wird."

volved in artistic creativity. Whether the words be "sun," "sunlight," "sunflower," "daylight," "lightbeam," the adjectives "bright," "shining," "brilliant," "golden," or the "fire" vocabulary: "flame," "spark," "inflamed," and so forth, they recur consistently as a metaphorical background to the theme of artistic and creative inspiration. They are employed in describing each of the artists along the spectrum extending from Raphael to Leonardo, Michelangelo, Dürer, and those artists who are only briefly introduced in "The Chronicle of Artists."

In sharp contradistinction to the metaphorical language involving light in all of its variations, there is an opposing set of metaphors related to "night," "darkness," "inability to see," and similar concepts such as "storms," "stormclouds," "illness," and "death." All of these words form a metaphorical background to those periods we described earlier as "periods of creative crisis." In other words, they are associated with artists who *are not*, at that time, truly creative and who are in disharmony with their surroundings.

As an example, the imitators of Michelangelo are described in the chronicle concerning that artist as "pitiable followers" who "wander about blindly!"[27] As a second example, Francesco Francia, upon realizing the presumptuousness which led him to regard himself as Raphael's rival, falls into a disharmonious turmoil of emotions which leads directly to his death. And, contrasted strikingly with the "divine" Raphael, Piero di Cosimo is an artist whose spirit is constantly in restless activity and who never achieves the serenity and harmony which characterize the mind of Raphael. Of Cosimo it is said that "Nature had filled his soul with a continuously seething fantasy and had covered his mind with heavy and dark storm clouds, so that his spirit was constantly in restless toil and moved about amidst extravagant pictures, without ever being reflected in simple and serene beauty."[28] Much of the imagery surrounding the figure of Cosimo is imagery of heavy storm clouds, wild, dark, seemingly ominous landscapes, night, and death.

Concerning the theme of death, Wackenroder enters into extensive detail in his depiction of the gruesome *trionfo della morte*, which Cosimo secretly arranges and stages on the very night when all of Florence is rejoicing at carnival time. Suddenly, in the eery light of early dawn, a black, terrifying wagon approaches, drawn by four black buffalo and marked with the bones of the dead and with white crosses. "A huge victor-figure of death,"[29] armed with the dreadful scythe, struts about on the wagon and all around him there are coffins. Wackenroder's description continues with the vivid portrayal of how these coffins slowly open up and white skeletons with half a body climb out, sit on their

27. *Ibid.*, p. 87. "Die jämmerlichen Nachbeter (. . .), irren blind herum . . ."
28. *Ibid.*, pp. 72–73. "Die Natur hatte sein Inneres mit einer immer gärenden Phantasie erfüllt, und seinen Geist mit schweren und düstern Gewitterwolken bezogen, so dass sein Gemüt immer in unruhiger Arbeit war, und unter ausschweifenden Bildern umhertrieb, ohne jemals sich in einfacher und heiterer Schönheit zu spiegeln."
29. *Ibid.*, p. 75. ". . . eine mächtig grosse Siegergestalt des Todes . . ."

[4]

coffins, and fill the air with ominous, blood-curdling songs about the horrors of death, whereupon they then chant a psalm of David with "hollowly trembling voices."

Werner Kohlschmidt[30] compares Wackenroder's lengthy elaboration of the motif of this weird and ominous carnival wagon with the much shorter version of the same in either the second or an even later edition of Vasari's *Vite*. Kohlschmidt points out that the first edition of the *Vite* does not yet contain this motif, therefore it could not have served as Wackenroder's source. He then draws attention to the fact that Vasari initiates his chronicle of Piero di Cosimo with a tribute in praise of this Tuscan artist, whereupon Vasari explains the wild excesses of Piero's fantasy and his tendency toward disharmonious absentmindedness as the direct result of the "intensity" with which he worked. Kohlschmidt accurately points out that Wackenroder omits Vasari's positive evaluation of Piero and elaborates upon the weird, wild, fantastic features of Piero's creative spirit. Following Kohlschmidt's interpretation further, one finds that he uses these deviations from Vasari to argue that Wackenroder levels a "negative characterization"[31] against Piero. Because Piero does not reflect the harmony, clarity, and beauty of a "classical" artist, he is, therefore, judged negatively for his wild fantasy and his untamed, weird spirit. He does not reflect the "classical direction of taste" (*klassische Geschmacksrichtung*) which Kohlschmidt argues to be the basic aesthetic position of Wackenroder.

However, there are several unsolved difficulties in Kohlschmidt's interpretation. First, it does not take into account the paragraph immediately following the description of Piero's grotesque carnival wagon:

> It is very remarkable that this unanticipated procession of the dead, despite the terror that it spread at the beginning, was nevertheless regarded by all of Florence with the greatest pleasure. Painful and unpleasant sensations reach into the soul with force, cling to it firmly, and compel it, as it were, to participation and to enjoyment; and if they also assail and excite the fantasy with a certain poetic verve, then they can keep one's emotions in sublime and inspired tension.[32]

It is apparent from these lines that Wackenroder perceives a sort of "positive"

30. "Wackenroder und die Klassik," first printed in *Unterscheidung und Bewahrung, Festschrift für H. Kunisch zum 60. Geburtstag* (Berlin, 1961). Cited from the reprint in *Dichter, Tradition und Zeitgeist: Gesammelte Studien zur Literaturgeschichte* (Bern, 1965), pp. 83–92.

31. *Ibid.,* p. 89.

32. W.W., p. 76. "Es ist sehr merkwürdig, dass dieser unerwartete Totenaufzug, soviel Schrecken er auch anfangs verbreitete, doch von ganz Florenz mit dem grössten Wohlgefallen betrachtet ward. Schmerzliche und widrige Empfindungen greifen mit Macht durch die Seele, halten sie fest und zwingen sie gleichsam zur Teilnahme und zum Behagen; und wenn sie überdies mit einem gewissen poetischen Schwunge die Phantasie anfallen und aufregen, so können sie das Gemüt in einer hohen und begeisterten Spannung erhalten."

emotional value in the effect of Piero's grotesque procession upon the assembled witnesses. Second, he speaks of a "marvelous secret power" which seems to enable such "excellent souls" as Piero to "capture the minds even of the common masses by means of the strange and extraordinary things that they do."[33]

This characterization does not seem, in my opinion, to represent a totally negative rejection of Piero. On the contrary, it seems more accurate to regard the Piero di Cosimo chronicle as another example of Wackenroder's deeply rooted concern for the "psychological" aspects of the creative process as they manifest themselves in the artist's behavior as well as in his creations. Vasari's quick, rational "explanation" of Piero's extreme fantasies as the result of "intensity of work" is not an adequate explanation for Wackenroder, therefore, he omits it. Instead, he explores the conflict in Piero's restless, dark fantasy, a conflict which, in his old age, could cause him to "quarrel with his shadow or go into a rage over a fly."[34] Again we can observe the background of metaphorical language involving "darkness," "storm clouds," "shadows," and "mental disharmony." The final paragraphs which sum up the chronicle about Piero are particularly important in relation to the "thematic structure" of the *Confessions*. For they clearly indicate how Wackenroder mirrors one artist in the reflection of another, how he contrasts the various artists whom he has selected for close examination, and how he implicitly uses the set of distinctions defined by Karl Philipp Moritz to separate the "true artist" with actual *Bildungskraft* from the "half-artist" who has a high degree of *Empfindungsvermögen* and often mistakes himself for a truly creative artist. Wackenroder begins his summation with the words: "Let him think what he wish, nevertheless, I cannot believe that this Piero di Cosimo was truly a genuine artist."[35] He then draws a direct comparison between Piero and Leonardo da Vinci, but concludes that even though both were driven about by lively imaginations, their resemblance is only superficial, for Piero was driven "into dark, cloudy regions of the sky,"[36] while Leonardo was driven "into the midst of all substantial Nature,"[37] in other words, into a harmonious absorption and beautiful re-creation of the elements of Nature.

If one were to describe in a few sentences the "thematic" structure of the *Confessions*, one could perhaps best approach this medley of seemingly disparate elements through the atmospheric background provided by the metaphorical language of "light" and "darkness," "day" and "night," "harmony" and

33. *Ibid.* ". . . durch die fremden und ausserordentlichen Dinge, welche sie tun, die Köpfe, auch des gemeinen grossen Haufens, einzunehmen."
34. *Ibid.*, p. 77. "Er konnte sich mit dem Schatten zanken und über eine Fliege in Zorn geraten."
35. *Ibid.*, p. 78. "Dem sei nun wie ihm wolle, so kann ich nicht glauben, dass dieser Piero di Cosimo ein wahrhaft-echter Künstlergeist gewesen sei."
36. *Ibid.* ". . . in finstere Wolkenregionen der Luft."
37. *Ibid.* ". . . unter die ganze wirkliche Natur."

[4]

"disharmony," "life" and "death." For it is this language of dualisms that provides the medium through which Wackenroder explores selected episodes of the creative process in a wide spectrum of artists. The "shining" example at the most "divinely inspired" end of the spectrum is the figure of Raphael, who earns Wackenroder's highest evaluation. Yet, each of the others along the spectrum is a source of new insight into the creative process. Each has his own unique qualities of spirit and, as the reader progresses from artist to artist, each seems to locate himself closer to one or the other side of the spectrum. Assuming positions close to Raphael are the other "harmonious" and truly creative artists, who include Michelangelo, Albrecht Dürer, and Leonardo da Vinci. Assuming positions at the other end of the spectrum are the more problematic, disharmonious "martyrs" of art and—to use a fully secularized term—the "victims" of art. These would include Francesco Francia, the pupil Antonio, Piero di Cosimo, and, as the polar opposite of Raphael, the figure of Joseph Berglinger, to whom we shall turn our attention in the next chapter.

To label Wackenroder a "classical" writer fails to take into account the complexity of his eighteenth-century inheritance. Even the more cautiously phrased argument that he has a "classical direction of taste"[38] loses its persuasiveness when inconsistencies are discovered upon close examination. Hence, I would tend to agree with Hans Eichner, who points out the futility of "attempts at deciding whether the poet X or the novelist Y is more classical or more romantic, whereas, in fact, he is neither . . ."[39] Wackenroder is complex in his thinking and ambivalent in his outlook on art; hence, he cannot be easily categorized and neatly labeled within the conventional periods of German literary history. He is traditionally regarded as one of the Early Romantics, yet he anticipates trends and currents of thought which emerged in full force at a much later date. His "newness," his "revolutionary" quality lies in the fact that he seeks out the psychological kernel of the creative process and the psychological factors involved in the response of the individual to works of art. He thereby transfers the emotions which had been traditionally centered in the realm of organized religion over to the realm of art. The creation and the experience of art works becomes a unique, highly individual, emotion-centered experience. This experience is frequently "indescribable" and it involves a "secret" for which the inherited language of the soul-searching Pietists proves to be the most appropriate available terminology. The word "available" is used consciously here, since it must be kept in mind that this is the epoch during which modern psychology was born. It is the pre-psychoanalytic phase of interest in the human mind and its processes. Hence, the psychological terminology with which the modern reader is well acquainted did not yet exist and, since the re-

38. Cf. D. B. Sanford, "Wackenroder and Tieck: The Aesthetic Breakdown of the *Klosterbruder* Ideal."
39. "The Genesis of German Romanticism," p. 214.

sponse Wackenroder himself felt in regarding works of art resembled a deeply religious emotion of prayerful reverence, it is understandable that he would generalize this emotion of reverence and maintain that it is the way in which *all* should regard the works of the great artists of earth. Demands are herewith placed upon the appreciator of art works which supersede all previous expectations. In the essay "How and in what Manner one actually must regard and use the Works of the Great Artists of Earth . . . ," Wackenroder makes his position clear when he writes: "I compare the enjoyment of the more noble works of art to the prayer."[40] He then describes the truly appreciative and receptive mind with the same imagery of "light" he used to elucidate the creative process in Raphael. "That one," writes Wackenroder, "is, however, a favorite of heaven who waits with humble longing for the chosen hours when the gentle, heavenly beam comes down to him voluntarily, splits open the shell of earthly insignificance with which the mortal spirit is generally covered, and releases and displays his more noble inner self; then he kneels down, turns his open heart toward the brilliance of heaven in silent rapture, and saturates it with the ethereal light; . . ."[41] The one who regards works of art must do so with the same spiritual involvement and receptivity as the creative artist himself. With quiet, humble attentiveness and in a solitude that elevates the heart, he must await those favorable hours when he is enabled by divine inspiration to immerse himself in the work of art. He must lay aside all of his own concerns, including whatever distractive or disturbing influences surround him, and "enter into" the work, experiencing the deepest intention of the artist. In thus approaching the work of art, he will be "touched" and "moved," perhaps even brought to tears by the impact it has upon his emotions. Wackenroder's descriptions of such moments of highly involved "appreciation" are filled with the vocabulary of the pietistic tradition. The emotions are felt "inwardly" (*inniglich*) and they are frequently associated with weeping. The word "tears" (*Tränen*) recurs again and again in the *Confessions*.[42] August Langen brings out the fact that the idea of "inwardness" and the word "inward(ly)" (*innig*) must be considered as additional important elements in Wackenroder's favorite vocabulary.[43]

There is a clear thematic parallel between the truly creative artist and the truly appreciative observer of art works, for they both combine the two ele-

40. W.W., p. 79. "Ich vergleiche den Genuss der edleren Kunstwerke dem Gebet."
41. *Ibid.*, p. 80. "Der aber ist ein Liebling des Himmels, welcher mit demütiger Sehnsucht auf die auserwählten Stunden harrt, da der milde himmlische Strahl freiwillig zu ihm herabfährt, die Hülle irdischer Unbedeutenheit, mit welcher gemeiniglich der sterbliche Geist überzogen ist, spaltet, und sein edleres Innere auflöst und auseinanderlegt; dann knieet er nieder, wendet die offene Brust in stiller Entzückung gegen den Himmelsglanz, und sättiget sie mit dem ätherischen Licht; . . ."
42. *Ibid.*, pp. 13, 14, 22, 30, 31, 47, 70, 91, 93, etc.
43. *Der Wortschatz des deutschen Pietismus*, p. 160.

[4]

ments of activity and receptivity. In the former instance, this combination results in the creation of an artistic product; in the latter case, it precipitates a response which opens the heart and enriches the soul. Thus, both the artist and the one who truly appreciates art enter into a realm of experience which resembles religion in the impact it has upon them. As Wackenroder writes: "He whose finer nerves are once active and receptive to the secret charm which lies hidden in art is often deeply moved in his soul where another passes by indifferently."[44]

The specific requirement upon the one who is regarding and appreciating art works is *not* that he judge them, compare them, and estimate the degree of their technical perfection; rather, he should seek to "feel his way into" the world of the artist and fully recognize what the artist's intentions were—as perceived within the particular historical context of that artist's life. The "biographies" of past artists are important to Wackenroder solely for the information that they provide concerning the creative process and the creative intentions of the artist. As Klaus Weimar explains in his interesting study of the premises and the origin of Romanticism, Wackenroder is the first among the Romantic authors to call for a "historical" approach to the appreciation of art.[45] However, at the very outset of German Romanticism, Wackenroder already points beyond Romanticism. For, as far as can be established concerning the sensitive young soul hiding behind the mask of the *Klosterbruder*, he does not believe that the "historical" conditions which made the art of Raphael, Leonardo da Vinci, Michelangelo, and Dürer possible can be resurrected or reestablished in a new future. Contrary to so many authors of this epoch, among them Goethe, Schiller, the Schlegels, Novalis, Hölderlin, and so forth, Wackenroder does not see in the harmonious accomplishments of the past—whether they be those of Periclean Greece, Renaissance Italy, or sixteenth-century Nuremberg—a prefiguration of a new, great era of harmonious perfection in art and life. At the point where he departs from the lives of past artists and tells the quasi-autobiographical story of Joseph Berglinger, a whole new set of problems is introduced. The atmospheric, stylistic change is not abrupt. Such figures as Francesco Francia, the pupil Antonio, and Piero di Cosimo are thematically related to Berglinger and have paved the way for an understanding of his "desire" to be truly creative and his awareness of his limitations. But they have not raised the question of a conflict between the artist and the surrounding world, for, in the times during which they lived, no conflict of this nature existed.

44. W.W., p. 82. "Wessen feinere Nerven einmal beweglich, und für den geheimen Reiz, der in der Kunst verborgen liegt, empfänglich sind, dessen Seele wird oft da, wo ein anderer gleichgültig vorübergeht, innig gerührt."

45. Cf. *Versuch über Voraussetzung und Entstehung der Romantik* (Tübingen, 1968), pp. 56ff. (Wackenroder was following the "historical" approach to art initiated primarily by Herder; cf. especially "Auch eine Philosophie der Geschichte zur Bildung der Menschheit," 1774, in: *Sämmtliche Werke*, ed. Bernhard Suphan, V (Berlin, 1891), 477–586.

5   THE MUSICAL WORLD OF JOSEPH BERGLINGER: CREATIVE ECSTASY AND NIHILISTIC DESPAIR

"Art is a seductive, forbidden fruit; whoever has once tasted its innermost, sweetest juice is irretrievably lost to the active, lively world."[1] With this startlingly revolutionary statement, Wackenroder sets up the problem of the conflict between "art" and "life," a conflict that has obsessed all writers who have experienced difficulty in achieving a harmonious balance between their artistic creativity and their responsibility to the "active" world. Although the inspiring harmony of symphonic music is the force which motivates Joseph Berglinger, the tenor of his life in the world of ordinary, daily routine and responsibility is one of disharmony and guilt.

As in previous chronicles, the friar once again begins his narrative with biographical facts concerning his friend Berglinger. He speaks of the impoverished financial circumstances of Joseph's family, of the fact that his mother had died while bringing him into life, and of the five sisters who also relied upon the work of their father for support. The stage is set for Joseph's feelings of guilt when the friar characterizes Joseph's father as becoming increasingly despondent over the wretchedness of his poverty and his old age. As a medical doctor, his greatest joy had always been in helping, giving counsel, and alms; hence, his inability to do so caused him much unhappiness.

The initial part of the Berglinger biography tells of Joseph's first experi-

---

1. W.W., p. 230. "Die Kunst ist eine verführerische, verbotene Frucht; wer einmal ihren innersten, süssesten Saft geschmeckt hat, der ist unwiederbringlich verloren für die tätige, lebendige Welt."

ence away from his family situation. "No one," says the friar, "could fit into this family less than Joseph, who was always existing in a realm of beautiful fantasy and divine dreams."[2] His trip to the episcopal residence city and his experience of symphonic music while visiting there are described in complex and, to an eighteenth-century rationalistic audience, unorthodox terms. It is stated, for example, that at times the symphonic sounds "caused a wonderful mixture of gaiety and sadness in his heart, so that he was on the verge of both smiling and weeping."[3] This tension of mixed emotions causes Joseph to experience a high degree of alert, attentive receptivity to symphonic music. But there is no "classical" balance in his reactions, for Berglinger is not a moderate and harmonious individual. On the contrary, he is tossed from one emotional extreme to the other—from great joy to deep grief—from creative ecstasy to nihilistic despair.

The subjectivism of Joseph Berglinger's emotions lies in the same tradition as that of Goethe's early novel, *The Sufferings of Young Werther* (*Die Leiden des jungen Werther*). This "Storm-and-Stress" novel of 1774 had by no means ceased to exercise widespread influence during the years of Wackenroder's boyhood. The previously discussed pietistic concept of "inwardness" (*Innerlichkeit*) has its direct applicability here as well, for it is in those quiet moments of self-involvement and self-insulation from all distractive external factors that Berglinger experiences the effects of music most deeply. As Elmar Hertrich correctly points out: "The inwardness that is characteristic of Berglinger and which seems to be the only appropriate milieu for him is a quality that he has in common with heroes of 'sentimental' novels."[4] Hertrich proceeds to draw the parallel between Werther and Berglinger in stressing the fact that both of them experience a total breakdown caused by their inability to fit themselves adequately into a firmly founded relationship to reality, above all, to social reality.[5]

With his characteristic ease and finesse, Lawrence Ryan illuminates an important distinction between the manner in which ecstatic emotions are ex-

2. *Ibid.*, p. 113. "In diese Familie konnte niemand weniger passen als Joseph, der immer in schöner Einbildung und himmlischen Träumen lebte."

3. *Ibid.*, p. 116. "Ein andermal wieder wirkten die Töne eine wunderbare Mischung von Fröhlichkeit und Traurigkeit in seinem Herzen, so dass Lächeln und Weinen ihm gleich nahe war; . . ."

4. *Joseph Berglinger, Eine Studie zu Wackenroders Musiker-Dichtung*, p. 75. "Die Innerlichkeit, die Berglinger auszeichnet und die als der ihm einzig gemässe Lebensraum erscheint, hat er mit Helden empfindsamer Romane gemein."

5. *Ibid.* Proskauer also makes this point in "The Phenomenon of Alienation in the Work of Karl Philipp Moritz . . ." (pp. 3–4) and adds to the list of alienated artists who were precursors of Berglinger not only Werther, but also Goethe's Torquato Tasso and the key figures of all three novels by Moritz: *Anton Reiser, Andreas Hartknopf,* and *Die neue Cecilia.* Despite the weaknesses of this study (see Chap. 3, n. 12 above), Proskauer corrects the general misconception that Berglinger is the first character in German literature to represent an artist who is estranged from his surrounding world.

perienced by Werther and by Hölderlin's Hyperion. He regards the kernel difference as lying in the fact that in Werther's subjectivity "the 'divine' world is reduced, as it were to the 'small world,' to a world which is continuously based upon the feeling individual."[6] Ryan also clarifies this distinction by explaining that this "inner sanctuary" of emotion is, indeed, quite different from Hyperion's ecstatic yearning to merge himself with all of Nature and become "one with all that lives."[7] The same distinction holds true for Wackenroder. Like Goethe's Werther, Wackenroder's Joseph Berglinger does not at any point leave the realm of the small and narrowly restricted world of his own immediate subjective experiences. The often quoted lines of Hyperion:

> To be one with all that lives, in blessed self-forgetfulness to return to the totality of Nature, that is the summit of thoughts and joys, that is the holy mountain peak, the location of eternal peace, . . .[8]

express a yearning for transcendence of self in the experience of union with the universe. In contrast to this, Joseph's basic nature is one of self-involvement and subjectivity. He is concerned with the sensations which enter in upon his own "self"—not with the overcoming of separateness through the ecstatic union with "all that lives." This is demonstrated by such a passage as: ". . . he [Joseph] valued his own inner soul above all else and kept it concealed and hidden from others."[9] Further evidence of Joseph's subjective self-involvement is provided by the effect of music upon him, as for example, in the following descriptive lines: ". . . the music penetrated his nerves with gentle tremors and, as it changed, it caused various pictures to rise up before him."[10] Joseph's response to music is a private and personal response. "At many a point in the music," writes the friar, "a particular beam of light seemed to fall into his soul."[11] Thus, we observe the same metaphorical imagery of light used earlier to signal moments of inspiration in artists of the past. In addition, although the use of pietistic, religious terminology recedes to a certain extent in the Berglinger essays, nevertheless the emotional soul-searching with its pietistic un-

6. *Hölderlins "Hyperion," Exzentrische Bahn und Dichterberuf* (Stuttgart, 1965), p. 71. "Hierin liegt der Kern der Wertherschen Subjektivität: die 'göttliche' Welt wird gleichsam zur 'kleinen Welt' reduziert, zu einer Welt, die durchgehend auf das empfindende Ich bezogen wird."

7. *Ibid.*

8. Friedrich Hölderlin, *Sämtliche Werke* (Grosse Stuttgarter Ausgabe), ed. Friedrich Beissner (Stuttgart, 1944–1968), III, 9. "Eines zu seyn mit Allem, was lebt, in seeliger Selbstvergessenheit wiederzukehren in's All der Natur, das ist Gipfel der Gedanken und Freuden, das ist die heilige Bergeshöhe, der Ort der ewigen Ruhe, . . ."

9. W.W., p. 113. ". . . sein Inneres schätzte er über alles und hielt es vor andern heimlich und verborgen."

10. *Ibid.*, p. 114. ". . . die Musik durchdrang seine Nerven mit leisen Schauern und liess, so wie sie wechselte, mannigfache Bilder vor ihm aufsteigen."

11. *Ibid.*, p. 115. ". . . bei manchen Stellen der Musik endlich schien ein besonderer Lichtstrahl in seine Seele zu fallen . . ."

dercurrent links Berglinger closely to other key figures of earlier eighteenth-century "sentimental" novels.[12]

The second section of the Berglinger biography is a structural counterpart to the first section. After having returned home from the episcopal residence city and suffered for more than a year in the restrictive, depressing circumstances of his family circle, Joseph had finally taken flight back to this "magnificent" city. We encounter him there in the position of orchestra conductor, however he is now close to the point of despair. He is no longer the youthful boy who joyfully immerses himself in the sensations which music arouses within him. Instead, he is now being called upon to "create" music and, moreover, to do so within the framework of a social world which he has grown to resent. "How much more ideally I lived at that time," he writes in a letter to the friar, "when in unconstrained youth and quiet solitude I still merely enjoyed art; than now, since I practice it amidst the most blinding splendor of the world, surrounded by nothing but silk clothes, stars, and crosses, nothing but cultivated and refined people!"[13] There is resentment in these unhappy words; there is disgust and despair; there is also disillusionment. The artist, Joseph Berglinger, who had abandoned his aging father and his five sisters for the sake of his love of art, has found that even so radical a "flight" from his social responsibilities has not disentangled him from the realities and superficialities of the world. Nor has art proven to be the deeply moving, soul-shaking force he at first expected it to be. In this second part of Joseph's biography in the *Confessions*, there is already a strong trace of the nihilistic thinking which is to re-appear in the later Berglinger essays of the *Fantasies*. Joseph begins to question the whole purpose of art. He even employs the word "nothing" (*nichts*) when he questions: "What is it, truly and in actuality, if it is Nothing for all people and only Something for me alone?"[14] And, thereupon, he speaks of art most pejoratively when he questions whether one should devote one's life to this "art, which has no other role in real, earthly life than card-playing or every other pastime."[15]

The "creative crisis" in Joseph's life is precipitated on an evening when, just after receiving a worthy and moving tribute from his audience for the

---

12. In *Joseph Berglinger: Eine Studie zu Wackenroders Musiker-Dichtung* (pp. 76–77), Hertrich stresses in particular J. M. Miller's *Siegwart. Eine Klostergeschichte,* where Threse's response to the reading of Klopstock's odes closely resembles the effect of music upon Berglinger.

13. W.W., p. 127. "Wie weit idealischer lebte ich damals, da ich in unbefangener Jugend und stiller Einsamkeit die Kunst noch bloss genoss; als itzt, da ich sie im blendendsten Glanze der Welt und von lauter seidenen Kleidern, lauter Sternen und Kreuzen, lauter kultivierten und geschmackvollen Menschen umgeben, ausübe!"

14. *Ibid.,* p. 128. "Was ist sie denn wirklich und in der Tat, wenn sie für alle Menschen nichts ist und für mich allein nur etwas?"

15. *Ibid.* ". . . Kunst, die im wirklichen irdischen Leben keine andre Rolle spielt als Kartenspiel oder jeder andre Zeitvertreib?"

conducting of a musical piece he himself had composed, he meets his youngest sister in the street, most wretchedly clothed, who had come to give him the news that their father was dying. Hereupon he is abruptly confronted with the "conflict" between devotion to art and social responsibility—a conflict that has haunted the subconscious levels of his mind since early boyhood. He rushes home to witness the miserable condition of his father and see him die wretchedly.

Thereafter, the paroxysm of creative energy which enables Joseph to fulfill his obligation of composing new Passional music for the approaching Easter celebration is another study of the psychology of creativity. Again the leitmotif of tears (*Tränen*) recurs, and we find that "hot streams of tears poured forth from him whenever he was about to sit down to the work; . . ."[16] Suddenly, he pulls himself together and, "in a marvelous state of enthusiasm, but with continuous, violent swings of emotion"[17] composes a musical masterpiece of the highest order.

The intense emotional impact of this experience and the exertion and excitement of conducting the oratorio on Easter Sunday leave Berglinger in a psychological state which parallels that of Francesco Francia near his death. Just as Francia suffers from "fatigue of the spirit" after absorbing the impact of Raphael's painting of St. Cecilia, so does Berglinger also experience extreme fatigue and enervation. Both artists live on for a short while in a state of gradual deterioration of their nervous systems, whereupon they both die.

As I stated earlier, a close examination of the *Confessions* as a literary entity reveals that there is no abrupt psychic, thematic, or structural discontinuity between the earlier essays and the Berglinger sequence. Rather, there is a gradual widening of the thematic background through the examination of first one, then another artist along the spectrum from the harmonious and "divine" Raphael to the disharmonious and conflicted Joseph Berglinger. The underlying concern which unifies the entire "medley" of varied literary elements is Wackenroder's concern for the "process of artistic creativity." Whether Joseph Berglinger possesses the true "power of creativity" (*Bildungskraft*) or only the "capacity of feeling" (*Empfindungsvermögen*) remains an ambivalent matter. For, on the one hand, Berglinger does truly create musical masterpieces, particularly the Easter oratorio, which is implied to have eternal worth. On the other hand, the upheavals of emotional energy and the negative questioning of the value of art associated with his creativity raise the issue which the friar expresses when he asks:

16. *Ibid.*, p. 130. "Helle Ströme von Tränen brachen ihm aber hervor, sooft er sich zur Arbeit niedersetzen wollte; . . ."

17. *Ibid.* ". . . und schrieb in einer wunderbaren Begeisterung, aber immer unter heftigen Gemütsbewegungen, eine Passionsmusik nieder . . ."

Shall I say that he was perhaps created more to enjoy art than to practice it?—Are those perhaps fashioned more fortunately, in whom art works silently and secretly like a veiled spirit and does not disturb them in their activities upon earth? And must the constantly enthused one perhaps also boldly and strongly interweave his lofty fantasies into this earthly life as a firm woof, if he wants to be a true artist?[18]

The art-loving friar concludes his *Confessions* with these profound and probing questions. He briefly refers back to Raphael, to Guido Reni, and to Albrecht Dürer. These quick references serve as structural links between the beginning, the middle, and the end of the *Confessions*. However, the phrasing of these concluding references deserves the closest attention. Raphael, hitherto repeatedly described as "divine" and "inspired," is said to have produced "in all innocence and naïveté the most highly spiritual works."[19] "Innocence"—"naïveté"—precisely the same adjectives that have been applied so frequently to Wackenroder by nineteenth- and twentieth-century critics. Yet here, behind his *Klosterbruder* mask, Wackenroder applies *them* to Raphael!

Guido Reni was not the subject of any discussion earlier in the *Confessions*, yet here, at the close, he is brought in to demonstrate an interesting balance of psychological forces, for his life and his art were totally at odds, yet he nevertheless experienced no devastating inner conflict. How is it possible to comprehend "a Guido Reni, who led such a wild gambler's life, [yet] created the gentlest and holiest pictures."[20] Even the aura of harmonious peacefulness surrounding Albrecht Dürer is shattered here at the close of the *Confessions*, when we are told that this "unpretentious Nuremberg citizen prepared very tender works of art with assiduous, mechanical diligence in the very same room in which his ill-tempered wife quarreled with him daily; ..."[21] With these three examples it becomes quite clear that the question of "how it is possible to be truly creative" is the underlying thematic concern of the *Confessions*. Wackenroder's posthumously published essays in the *Fantasies* expand and continue the exploration of this question, but they also leave it

18. *Ibid.*, p. 131. "Soll ich sagen, dass er vielleicht mehr dazu geschaffen war, Kunst zu geniessen als auszuüben?—Sind diejenigen vielleicht glücklicher gebildet, in denen die Kunst still und heimlich wie ein verhüllter Genius arbeitet und sie in ihrem Handeln auf Erden nicht stört? Und muss der Immerbegeisterte seine hohen Phantasien doch auch vielleicht als einen festen Einschlag kühn und stark in dieses irdische Leben einweben, wenn er ein echter Künstler sein will?"

19. *Ibid.* "Ein Raffael brachte in aller Unschuld und Unbefangenheit die allergeistreichsten Werke hervor . . ."

20. *Ibid.* ". . . ein Guido Reni, der ein so wildes Spielerleben führte, schuf die sanftesten und heiligsten Bilder; . . ."

21. *Ibid.* ". . . Albrecht Dürer, ein schlichter nürnbergischer Bürgersmann, verfertigte in eben der Zelle, worin sein böses Weib täglich mit ihm zankte, mit emsigem mechanischem Fleisse gar seelenvolle Kunstwerke; . . ."

open and unanswered. For this reason it is entirely possible to argue that Wackenroder's writings represent a late contribution to the literature of "sentimentalism" (*Empfindsamkeit*), that they contain the soul-searching terminology of the Pietists, the emotionalism of Werther and the "Storm-and-Stress" period, the ideal of harmonious, integrated beauty of the Classicists, and—in addition to all of this inheritance—the despairing, modern, nihilistic thought that the integration of the artist into the social structure is, for complex and incomprehensible reasons, no longer possible. It is true that Wackenroder's youthful and sensitive mind absorbed impulses and influences from virtually all of the directions which converged on Berlin during the late eighteenth century. However, to single out any one of these intellectual currents of thought and give it priority over the others is to misread—and oversimplify—Wackenroder's intentions.

Wackenroder uses selected events and periods of crisis in the lives of artists of the past as his medium for exploring the process of creativity. But the creative moment is not merely a fortunate juxtaposition of activity on the artist's part and receptivity to inspiration. It is a moment of intuitive insight into a higher spiritual reality. The artistic product is, therefore, man's "chiffre" for that intuited reality. Words are incapable of conveying the metaphysical intuition which art can communicate. The work of art is a hieroglyphic for this exalted, divine reality. As such it is a "language" that speaks to man's emotions in a symbolic manner—as a copy of God's creation which is Nature. Oskar Walzel[22] perceptively analyzes Wackenroder's concept of creativity as resting ultimately on a divinely inspired emotional experience. In contrast to the philosopher-philologist Johann Georg Hamann, Wackenroder does not seek to explain and interpret rationally the moment of artistic intuition via the emotions. Rather, he searches primarily to experience it himself. In the process of his striving, he temporarily establishes a balance between his desire to be creative and the conflicting, dichotomous demands of his actual life. But the balance is a precarious one, and the tragic ambivalence of Joseph Berglinger is a seemingly accurate portrait of Wackenroder's own emotional struggles.

Thus, Wackenroder's search for the "kernel" of the creative process is simultaneously a search for a higher metaphysical reality. This reality cannot be defined in orthodox religious terms, for art is here assuming the function traditionally attributed to orthodox religion. From the *Confessions* and the *Fantasies* it is only a short step to the fully formulated concept of the artist as an extraordinary human being, as a mediator (*Mittler*) between the infinite and the finite—between the divine and the ordinary mortal—and all of its historical ramifications.

22. Cf. "Die Sprache der Kunst," in: *Vom Geistesleben Alter und Neuer Zeit* (Leipzig, 1922), pp. 262–315.

[5]

6 NOTE ON THE PRESENT TRANSLATION AND THE LANGUAGE OF THE *CONFESSIONS* AND *FANTASIES*

The following translations attempt to reproduce the *Confessions* and Wackenroder's contributions to the *Fantasies* according to the principal characteristics of their style and tone. As stated in the Introduction, the first editions of these two works were used as the textual basis for the translations.

Because of the inaccessibility of these first editions to the general reader, I elected to use the latest complete edition of Wackenroder's writings: *W. H. Wackenroder: Werke und Briefe* (Heidelberg: Lambert Schneider Verlag, 1967) as the source for all references to the texts in my introductory interpretation and in the critical notes. This procedure seemed most appropriate, since the Lambert Schneider edition is currently readily accessible. The Schneider edition does not attempt to reproduce the words which are s p a c e d o u t for emphasis and the interesting title layouts of the first editions, hence there are occasional deviations where the Schneider edition is cited in a footnote without the spacing that I have indicated in the English texts.

The reader will quickly observe that these translations are not "modern English" versions of the original eighteenth-century texts. My intention was not to "modernize" Wackenroder's style. Rather, I have attempted to render the effusive, emotion-laden language of the *Confessions* and the *Fantasies* into an equivalent level of English. Such an approach necessarily involves the retention of a tone that may seem unfamiliar and antiquated. But it consequently provides a more faithful reproduction of the characteristics that are unique in Wackenroder. Wilhelm von Humboldt prefaced his translation of Aeschylos' *Agamemnon* with a discerning introduction which explains his philosophy toward the problems of translation. "Translation (. . .)," writes Humboldt, "is one of the most necessary efforts in literature, partly in order to introduce forms of art and humanity to those who do not know the language, through which every nation always gains substantially, partly however—and primarily—in order to expand the significance and the capacity for expression of one's own language."[1] It is in this spirit that I have undertaken to expand the limits of the English language into a realm of expression which is not always the standard form of modern English. In the preface to the *Confessions*, the art-loving friar says to his readers that the essays "are not composed in the tone of the present-day world."[2] The same statement would be equally appropriate as an explanation of my English translations to twentieth-century readers.

I have chosen to set up the title of each essay as it was printed in the first editions and to s p a c e o u t those words which Wackenroder spaced out, since this was the contemporary technique for drawing special attention to key passages. In modern English italicized words would be the closest equivalent to the spaced-out words.

It seems advisable to mention that I have intentionally abided by the original punctuation to the extent that this was at all feasible. I have, therefore, included most of the colons, semicolons, and exclamation points which are distinguishing features of Wackenroder's flowing, emotional style. In addition, I have retained all of the long dashes, whether they occurred inside sentences, between sentences, preceding, or following paragraphs. These dashes clearly do not conform to modern usage. However, for Wackenroder they served as a reinforcement of the other punctuation and they therefore have a definite syntactical purpose.

In some instances it proved impossible to reproduce the complex sentence structure of the original text; therefore it was necessary to break a lengthy German sentence into shorter English sentences. Otherwise Wackenroder's flowing, lively, highly embellished style is re-created in order to give the English reader a text which approximates the original as closely as possible.

The verbal prefixes constituted a special problem in these translations, for there is frequently no way of rendering the many composite verb forms used by Wackenroder into clear and comprehensible English without rearranging the order of the various sentence elements. This was done whenever it was required and great effort was employed to select the most appropriate

---

1. *Wilhelm von Humboldts Gesammelte Werke*, ed. von der Königlich Preussischen Akademie der Wissenschaften (Berlin, 1905–1920), VIII, 130. "Das Uebersetzen . . . ist vielmehr eine der nothwendigsten Arbeiten in einer Literatur, theils um den nicht Sprachkundigen ihnen sonst ganz unbekannt bleibende Formen der Kunst und der Menschheit, wodurch jede Nation immer bedeutend gewinnt, zuzuführen, theils aber und vorzüglich, zur Erweiterung der Bedeutsamkeit und der Ausdrucksfähigkeit der eignen Sprache."

2. W.W., p. 9. "Sie sind nicht im Ton der heutigen Welt abgefasst, . . ."

English verbal prefix for the German compound. The nouns presented only minor difficulties, since the inherited German pietistic terms generally have English equivalents. When there is a problem of terminology between Wackenroder's German and the English text, the critical notes provide explanatory information.

PART 2

INDEX

IV Albrecht Dürer: Assumption and Coronation of the Virgin (1509). *Reproduction permission granted by the Historisches Museum, Frankfurt am Main.*

III Raphael: Self-Portrait (circa 1506). *Reproduction permission granted by the Palazzo Pitti, Florence, through the office of the Soprintendenza alle Gallerie, Gabinetto Fotografico, Piazzale degli Uffizi.*

WILHELM HEINRICH WACKENRODER
AND LUDWIG TIECK

Confessions from the heart
of an
Art-Loving Friar

Berlin

Published by Johann Friedrich Unger

1797

To the Reader of these Pages

The following essays have come into existence little by little in the solitude of a monastic life, from which I only occasionally think back dimly to the distant world. In my youth I loved art inordinately and this love, like a faithful friend, has accompanied me up to my present age: without realizing it, but acting out of an inner compulsion, I wrote down my reminiscences, which you, beloved reader, must view with an indulgent eye. They are not composed in the tone of the present-day world because this tone is not within my power and because, if I am to speak entirely honestly, I also am unable to like it.

In my youth I was involved in the world and in many worldly affairs. My strongest inclination was toward art and I wished to dedicate to it my life and all my limited talents. According to the judgment of several friends I was not without skill in sketching and my copies, as well as my own creations, were not totally unpleasing. But I continuously thought about the great, blessed saints of art with quiet, holy awe; it seemed strange, indeed, almost absurd to me that I should be guiding the charcoal or the paintbrush in my hand whenever the name of Raphael or Michelangelo came into my mind. I may, indeed, admit that I occasionally had to weep out of an indescribable melancholy fervor, when I pictured to myself most vividly their products and their lives: I could never manage —— indeed, such a thought would have seemed impious to me, —— to separate the Good from the so-called Bad in my chosen favorites and, in the end, to place them all in a row in order to observe them with a cold, criticizing eye, as young artists and so-called friends of art tend to do nowadays. Therefore, I am willing to admit openly that I have read only very little in the works of H. von R a m d o h r[1] with pleasure; and whoever likes these may immediately put out of his hand that which I have written, for it will not please him. I dedicate these pages, which I initially did not intend for the press at all, only to young, beginning artists or to boys who intend to dedicate themselves to art and who still carry in a quiet, uninflated heart holy respect for the time which has passed by. Perhaps they will be even more touched by my otherwise insignificant words, inspired to a still deeper respect; for they read with the same love with which I have written.

Heaven has ordained that I close my life in a monastery: these endeavors are, therefore, all that I am now in a position to do for art. If they are not entirely displeasing, then perhaps a second part will follow, in which I should like to refute the evaluations of several individual works of art, if Heaven grants me health and time to arrange the thoughts which I have jotted down regarding this and bring them into a clear exposition. ——

RAPHAEL'S VISION[2]

From time immemorial the inspirations of poets and artists have been a great cause for and object of contention in the world. Ordinary men cannot comprehend what the circumstances of these are and they form very false and preposterous notions about them. For this reason, just as many absurdities have been methodically and unmethodically debated and chattered about, w i t h i n and o u t s i d e o f systems, concerning the inner revelations of artistic geniuses as concerning the mysteries of our holy religion. The so-called theorists and systematizers describe to us the inspiration of the artist from hearsay. They are perfectly satisfied with themselves when, with their vain and profane philosophisms, they have compiled paraphrasing words for something concerning which they know neither the spirit, that cannot be grasped in words, nor the significance. They speak about the artist's inspiration as if it were an object that they had before their eyes; they interpret it and tell a great deal about it; and they fittingly ought to blush in uttering the holy word, for they do not know w h a t they are expressing with it.

With how infinitely many idle words the overly clever writers of more recent times have erred concerning the subject of the i d e a l s in the fine arts! They grant that the painter and sculptor must arrive at his ideals by way of a more extraordinary path than the path of ordinary nature and experience; they admit that this occurs in a m y s t e r i o u s way; and yet, they delude themselves and their students into believing that they know the way; —— for it seems as if they would be ashamed if anything were to lie concealed and hidden in the soul of man, concerning which they could give inquisitive young people no information.

Others are, in actuality, unbelieving and deluded jeerers, who totally deny with mockery the divine element in art enthusiasm[3] and are absolutely unwilling to admit any special distinction or consecration of certain unusual and exalted intellects, because they themselves feel all too distant from them. Meanwhile, these people stand totally apart from my course and I do not speak with them.

However, I wish to instruct the sophists whom I have pointed out. They are injuring the young minds of their pupils by teaching them such boldly and rashly dogmatic opinions about divine matters as if they were human matters and, thereby, inculcating in them the illusion that it is within their power to grasp impudently what the greatest masters of art, —— I may say it openly, —— have achieved only through divine inspiration.

So many anecdotes have been noted down and told again and again, so many significant slogans of artists preserved and continually repeated; and how has it been possible that people listened to them merely with such superficial admiration, so that no one came to suspect in these expressive signs the most holy aspect of art toward which they were pointing and to acknowledge here also, as in the rest of nature, the trace of the finger of God?

I, for my part, have preserved this belief within myself all along; but my dim belief has now become enlightened to the brightest conviction. I am happy that heaven has elected me to extend its glory through penetrating proof of its unperceived miracles; I have succeeded in building a new altar to the honor of God. ——

R a p h a e l, who is the shining sun among all painters, left behind for us in a letter to the Count of Castiglione[4] the following words, which are worth more to me than gold and which I have never been able to read without a mysterious, deep feeling of respect and admiration. He says therein:

"Since one sees so few beautiful womanly personages,
I hold myself to a certain mental image,
which enters into my soul."

To my inner delight, a bright light was quite unexpectedly kindled within me recently concerning these meaningful words.

I searched through the wealth of old manuscripts in our monastery and, amidst many a useless, dust-covered parchment, found several sheets by the hand of Bramante.[5] How they arrived at this place is not known. On one sheet the following was written, which, without further digression, I wish to set down here in German:

For my own pleasure and in order to preserve it for myself exactly, I want to record here a marvelous occurrence which the beloved Raphael, my friend, confided to me under the seal of silence. Recently, when I let him know most sincerely my admiration of his so exquisitely painted Madonnas and Holy Families and pressured him with a great many requests to tell me from where in the world he had derived the incomparable beauty, the touching gestures, and the unequalled expression in his pictures of the Holy Virgin; then, after he had resisted me for awhile with the youthful modesty and reticence peculiar to him, he finally became very moved, fell upon my neck in tears, and disclosed his secret to me. He told me how, from his early childhood on, he had always carried within himself a certain holy feeling for the Mother of God, so that occasionally he had become extremely melancholy even upon hearing her name uttered openly. Later on, when his faculties were directed toward painting, it had always been his highest desire to paint the Virgin Mary in all her heavenly perfection; but he had not had the confidence to do it. Day and night his mind had constantly worked on her picture in abstraction; but he had not been able to perfect it at all to his satisfaction; it had always seemed to him as if his fantasy were working in the dark. And yet, occasionally the picture had fallen into his soul like a heavenly beam of light, so that he had seen the figure before himself with vivid features, just as he wished it to be; and yet, that had always been only a moment and he had not been able to retain the conception in his mind. Thus, his soul had been tossed about in constant agitation; he had always caught sight of the features only sporadically and his dim presentiment had never been on the point of dissolving into a clear image. Finally, he had no longer been able to restrain himself and, with trembling hand, he had begun a portrait of the Holy Virgin; and during the work his soul had become more and more excited. Once, during the night, when he had prayed to the Virgin in a dream, as had often happened to him before, he had suddenly started out of his sleep, violently disturbed. In the dark night his eye was attracted by a bright light on the wall opposite his bed and, when he had looked closely, he had perceived that his picture of the Madonna, still uncompleted, had been hung upon the wall, illuminated by the gentlest light, and had become a perfect and truly living image. The divinity in this picture had so overpowered him that he had broken out into hot tears. It had looked at him with its eyes in an indescribably touching manner and, at each moment, had seemed as if it wanted to move; and it had seemed to him as if it also really were moving. The most wonderful aspect of all was that he felt as if this picture were precisely the one which he had always sought, although he had only had a dim and confused conception of it. How he had fallen asleep again, he absolutely did not know. The next morning he had arisen as if newly born; the vision had remained firmly stamped in his mind and his senses for eternity. And, thereupon, he had succeeded in portraying the Mother of God each time just as she had appeared to his soul, and he himself had always felt a certain reverence in the presence of his paintings. —— My friend, my dear Raphael, told me this and this miracle has seemed to me so important and remarkable that I have written it down for myself, for my own pleasure. ——

Such is the content of the invaluable sheet which fell into my hands. Will people now clearly envision what the divine Raphael means by the remarkable words, when he says:

I hold myself to a certain mental image, which enters into my soul.

Will they, instructed by this obvious miracle of divine omnipotence, understand that his guileless soul expressed a very deep and great truth in these simple words? Will they not now at last realize that all the profane babbling about the artist's inspiration is veritable sin, —— and be convinced that it is actually a matter of nothing else but the direct assistance of God?

But I shall add nothing more, in order to leave each person to his own thoughts concerning this so important object of serious consideration.

Longing for Italy[6]

Through a strange coincidence the following little page has been preserved until now among my possessions. I composed it in my early youth, when I was unable to find peace because of my desire to see for once at last I t a l y, the famed land of art.

By day and in the night my soul thinks only of the beautiful, bright regions which appear before me in all my dreams and call me. Will my desire, my longing always be in vain? So many a one travels there and returns and then does not know where he has been and what he has seen, for no one loves so deeply the land with its native art.

Why does it lie so far away from me that my feet cannot reach it in a journey of several days? so that I then might kneel down before the immortal works of the great artists and confess to them all my admiration and love? that their spirits might hear it and welcome me as the most faithful disciple? ——

If, by chance, the map is opened up by my friends, I always feel compelled to look at it with emotion; in my mind I wander through cities, country towns and villages, —— alas! and feel only too quickly that everything is merely imagination.

I desire for myself no glittering earthly happiness; but is it not even to be granted unto me to live once, O holy art, totally for you?

> Shall I simply pine away,
>   And languish in myself with love?
> Will Fate send no help my way,
> But watch my longing every day
>   With displeasure from above?

> Am I, then, fully forlorn,
>   Abandoned to the exiled men?
> O blessed he, who alone was born
> That he may the arts adorn,
>   And dedicate heart and life to them.

> Alas, my joy still lies so distant,
>   Will not yet come near to me!
> Surely I'd despair this instant, ——
> Were the stars not turning, turning, ——
>   Finally, finally it will be!

> Then no hesitations,
> After long meditations,
>   After deep calm,
> Through forests and bowers,
> Through fields full of flowers
>   To that homeland!

> Then will fly toward me,
> With blessings reward me
>   Genii, bewreathed,
>   With lightbeams sheathed!
> They will lead the weary one
> To joys and sweet rest,
>   To a peaceful fresh start,
>   To the homeland of art!

The remarkable death of the old artist
FRANCESCO FRANCIA,
the first of the Lombard School,
widely renowned in his day⁷

Just as the epoch of renaissance of the sciences and scholarship brought forth the most many-sided, as human beings most remarkable, most intellectually powerful men, so too the period in which the art of painting emerged like a phoenix from its long quiet ashes was characterized by the most eminent and most noble men of art. It is to be regarded as the true h e r o i c a g e of art and one is tempted to sigh (like Ossian) because the power and greatness of this heroic period has now disappeared from the earth. Many rose up at numerous places and elevated themselves entirely by means of their own power: their lives and their creations had weight and were worth the effort of being preserved for posterity in detailed chronicles, such as we possess from the pens of those who admired art at that time; and their minds were as venerable as are their bearded heads today, which we regard with reverence in the valuable collections of their portraits. Amidst these men there occurred extraordinary things, incredible to many nowadays, because the enthusiasm which inflamed all the world during that golden age now flickers in only a few individual hearts, like a weak little lamp. The degenerate descendants doubt or laugh at so many a story preserved from these times as if it were a fairy tale, because the divine spark has totally deserted their souls.

One of the most remarkable stories of this type, which I have never been able to read without astonishment and which my heart was never tempted to doubt, is the story of the death of the early artist F r a n c e s c o F r a n c i a, who was the ancestor and progenitor of the school which arose in Bologna and in Lombardy.

This Francesco was born of humble craftspeople, but, with his untiring diligence and his constantly striving spirit, he had soared to the highest peak of fame. In his youth he first worked with a goldsmith and created such artistic objects in gold and silver that they moved to astonishment everyone who saw them. For a long time he also engraved the stamps for all commemorative coins and all the princes and dukes of Lombardy considered it an honor to be portrayed on their coins by his stylus. For that was still the age when all the aristocrats of the land and all fellow-citizens were able to make the native artist proud by their continuous, loudly resounding applause. Infinitely many princely personages came through Bologna and did not fail to have their portraits sketched by Francesco and, afterwards, cut and imprinted in metal.

But Francesco's perpetually active, fiery mind strove toward a new field of endeavor. The more his ardent ambition was satisfied, the more impatient he became to open up for himself an entirely new, yet untravelled road to fame. When he was already forty years old, he entered the lists of a new art; with indomitable patience he practiced the use of the paintbrush and directed all his attention to the study of composition on a large scale and the effect of colors. And it was most extraordinary, how quickly he succeeded in producing works which aroused all of Bologna to admiration. Indeed, he became a superior artist; for, even if he had numerous rivals and although the divine R a p h a e l was even working in Rome at the time, nevertheless his works could always justly be considered among the most distinguished. For, to be sure, beauty in art is not something so poor and scanty that o n e human life could exhaust it; and its glory is not a lottery prize which falls to one chosen man alone: rather, its light splits up into thousands of beams, the reflections of which are cast back into our enchanted eyes in various ways by the great artists whom heaven has placed upon earth.

Francesco lived amidst the very first generation of eminent Italian artists, who were enjoying all the greater and more widespread respect because they were establishing an entirely new, brilliant empire on the ruins of barbarism: and in Lombardy the founder and, simultaneously, the first prince of this newly established sovereignity was none other than he. His skillful hand completed an innumerable quantity of magnificent paintings, which spread not only all through Lombardy (in which no city wanted to have said of it that it did not own at least o n e sample of his work), but also into the other regions of Italy and loudly proclaimed his fame to all eyes who were so fortunate to see them. The Italian princes and dukes were eager to possess his pictures; and eulogies streamed in to him from all directions. Travellers transplanted his name to all the places which they reached and the flattering echo of their words resounded in his ear. Bolognese who visited Rome praised their native artist to Raphael and he, who had also seen and admired several products of Francesco's brush, demonstrated in letters to him his respect and admiration with the easy congeniality characteristic of him. The writers of that time could not resist interweaving praises to him in all their works; they direct the eyes of posterity to him and they report with an air of great importance that he is worshipped like a God. One of them is even bold enough to write that, at the sight of his Madonnas, Raphael had abandoned the dullness which had clung to him from the School of Perugia and had acquired a grander style.

What other effect could these repeated successes have had on the mind of our Francesco than that his lively spirit soared up to the most noble artistic pride and he began to believe in a heavenly genius within himself? Where does one find this exalted pride now? One hunts for it in vain among the artists of our times, who are, indeed, v a i n a b o u t t h e m s e l v e s, but not p r o u d o f t h e i r a r t.

Of all the artists who were his contemporaries, R a p h a e l was the only one whom he possibly allowed to be considered as his competitor. He had, however, never been fortunate enough to see a picture from his hand, for he had never in his life gone far from Bologna. However, after hearing numerous descriptions he had mentally formulated for himself a firm picture of Raphael's style and, particularly because of the latter's modest and very obliging tone towards him in his letters, he had convinced himself that he was Raphael's equal in most of his artistic products and even his superior in many. Not until his elderly years was it granted to him to see a picture by Raphael with his own eyes.

Quite unexpectedly he received a letter from Raphael, in which he communicated to him that he had just completed an altar painting of Saint Cecilia,[8] which was intended for the Church of Saint John in Bologna; moreover, Raphael wrote that he would send the work to him, as his friend, and requested that he do him the favor of having it appropriately set in its place and, if it had been damaged anywhere during the trip or if he himself should perceive any oversight in the picture or any mistake, that he improve it and correct it as a friend. This letter, in which a R a p h a e l humbly put the paintbrush into his hands, caused him to be beside himself with joy and he could scarcely await the arrival of the picture. He did not know what was in store for him!

One day, when he arrived home from an excursion, his pupils rushed up to him and told him with great joy that Raphael's painting had arrived in his absence and that they had already placed it in the most favorable light in his studio. Francesco rushed in, beside himself. ——

But how shall I describe for the world of today the emotions which the extraordinary man felt tear his heart at the sight of this picture. He felt as one must feel who, full of delight, is about to embrace his brother who has been separated from him since childhood and, instead, suddenly sees an angel of light before his eyes. His soul was pierced through; he felt as if he were falling to his knees before a higher being in total contrition of heart.

Thunderstruck, he stood there and his pupils crowded around the old man and held him up, asked him what had come over him, and did not know what they should think.

He had recovered somewhat and stared continuously at the picture, divine above all else. How he suddenly had fallen from his elevation! How sorely he had to repent the sin of having all too arrogantly elevated himself to the stars and having presumptuously placed himself above him, the inimitable Raphael.

He beat his gray head and wept bitter, smarting tears that he had consumed his life in conceited, ambitious toil and, in the process, had only made himself increasingly foolish and that he now, close to death, had to look back with open eyes upon his entire life as upon a wretched, uncompleted bit of bungling. Along with the elevated countenance of Saint Cecilia, he also lifted his eyes, showed heaven his wounded, penitent heart, and prayed humbly for forgiveness.

He felt so weak that his pupils had to take him to bed. While leaving the room, he caught sight of several of his own paintings, particularly his dying Cecilia, which was still hanging there, and he almost passed away in pain.

From that time on, his emotions were in constant turmoil and there was almost always a certain absentmindedness about him. The infirmities of age and fatigue of the spirit, which had been engaged for so long in ever more strenuous exertion in the creation of so many thousands of figures, supervened to shake the house of his soul from its very foundation. All of the infinitely manifold forms, which had always originated in his artistic mind and had gone over into reality in colors and lines on the canvas, now darted through his soul with distorted features and were the tormentors which frightened him in his fevers. Before his pupils were prepared for it, they found him in his bed lying dead. ——

Thus, this man became for the first time truly g r e a t because he felt himself to be so insignificant in comparison with the divine Raphael. The guardian spirit of art also long ago canonized him in the eyes of the consecrated ones and encircled his head with the halo which is his due as a true martyr of art enthusiasm. ——

The above story of the death of Francesco Francia was transmitted to us by old V a s a r i, in whom the spirit of the first fathers of art still prevailed.

Those critical minds, who neither want to nor are able to believe in any extraordinary souls as in supernatural miracles and who would like very much to dissolve the entire world into prose, scoff at the tale of the old venerable chronicler of art and say immediately that Francesco Francia died by poison.

The Pupil and Raphael

At that time, when the admiring world still saw R a p h a e l living in its midst, —— whose name does not easily pass over my lips without my involuntarily calling him the Divine One, —— at that time, —— O, how gladly I would renounce all the cleverness and wisdom of later centuries in order to have been in that one! —— there was living in a little town of the Florentine region a young man whom we shall call A n t o n i o, who was training himself in the art of painting. From childhood on, he had a very zealous drive toward painting and, as a young boy, he industriously copied all of the pictures of saints which fell into his hands. However, along with all the constancy of his zeal and his truly indefatigable desire to produce something superior, he simultaneously possessed a certain imbecility and narrow-mindedness, in the presence of which the blossom of art always has a stifled and frail development and can never shoot up freely and healthily toward heaven: an unfortunate constellation of spiritual qualities, which has already put many a half-artist into the world.

Antonio had already trained himself in the style of various masters of his age and had succeeded well enough so that he himself took great pleasure in the similarity of his imitations and he kept a very precise account of his gradual progress. At last he saw several drawings and paintings by Raphael; he had already heard his name spoken frequently with high praise, and he prepared himself for the moment when he would work from the products of this highly esteemed man. However, when he totally failed to achieve successful copies and did not know what the matter was, he impatiently set down the paint-brush, considered what he wanted to do, and finally wrote the following words:

> "To the most excellent of all painters,
> Raphael of Urbino."[9]

Forgive me, that I do not know how I should address Thee, for Thou art an incomprehensible and extraordinary man; and I am, more-over, not at all practiced in guiding a pen. I have pondered for a long time whether it is appropriate that I write to Thee, without ever having seen Thee in person. But since one hears everywhere of Thy genial and friendly disposition, I finally have dared to do it.

Yet I do not want to rob Thee of Thy valuable time with many words, for I can imagine how industrious Thou must be; rather, I want to open my heart to Thee immediately and very urgently make my request of Thee.

I am a young beginner in the splendid art of painting, which I love above all else and which delights my whole heart, so that if I (of course), exclude Thee and other famous masters of these times, I can scarcely believe that anyone else could bear such a profound love and such an incessant craving for art. I exert myself as much as possible constantly to advance a little closer to the goal which I see before me in the distance. I am not idle any day, indeed, I would almost like to say any hour; and I notice that each day I make some progress, however little it may be. I have already trained myself in the style of many of today's renowned men; however, since I began to imitate T h y works, it has seemed to me as if I knew nothing at all and ought to start from the beginning once again. I have already brought into being on panels so many a head in which nothing false or inappropriate could be found, neither in the contours nor in the highlights and shadows; but when I transfer to my panel line for line the heads of Thy Madonnas and the Christ-child, with such exactitude that my eyes would like to burst, —— and when I then view the entire thing and compare it with the original, I am shocked to see that my copy is worlds apart from it and an entirely different countenance. And yet, when one looks at Thy heads for the first time, they seem almost easier than others; for they have such a natural appearance and it is as if one immediately recognized in them the people whom they are supposed to represent and as if one had already seen them in real life. Moreover, I do not find in Thy work such difficult and extraordinary foreshortenings of the limbs, with which other contemporary masters tend to demonstrate the perfection of their art and to torment us poor pupils.

Therefore, as much as I have pondered over it, nevertheless I absolutely do not know how to explain the particular quality which Thy works have about them and I cannot ascertain actually why it is that one cannot imitate Thee accurately and can never entirely approach Thee. O, give me Thy assistance in this, —— I urgently and imploringly ask Thee for it; and tell me (for Thou certainly knowest it best) what I must do in order to become only in some measure like Thee. O, how deeply I shall impress it upon my memory! how zealously I shall follow it! —— It has, —— forgive me, —— at times occurred to me that Thou must possess some secret in Thy work, concerning which no other person has been able to form an idea. I should like all too willingly to watch Thee at work for only half a day; but Thou perhaps admitteth no one. Or, if I were a great lord, I would offer Thee thousands and thousands of gold pieces for Thy secret.

Alas, be tolerant with me, that I presume to chatter to Thee so much. Thou art an extraordinary man, who doubtless must look down upon all other people with disdain.

No doubt Thou worketh day and night in order to accomplish such magnificent things; and, during Thy youth, Thou hast certainly progressed as far in one day as I do not in a year. But, henceforth, I also want to exert myself as much as I am possibly able to do so.

Others, who see more clearly than I, also praise the expression in Thy pictures above all else and maintain that no one knows as well as Thou how to depict the mental disposition, as it were, of individuals in such a way that, from their bearing and gestures, one could, so to speak, guess their thoughts. However, these are matters of which I as yet understand little.

But I must at last cease inconveniencing Thee. O, what a refreshing solace it would be for me, if Thou imparteth Thy advice, even in just a few words

to Thy
Honoring Thee above all else
Antonio.

Thus read Antonio's letter to Raphael; —— and the latter smilingly wrote him the following answer:

My good Antonio,

It is fine that you have such great love of art and train yourself so industriously; you have pleased me very much with this. But, that which you want to know from me, I unfortunately cannot tell you; not because it is a secret that I would not want to disclose, —— for, from the bottom of my heart I would gladly communicate it to you and to everyone, —— but because I myself do not know it.

I can see that you don't believe this of me; and yet, it is so. Just as little as one can account for the source of his rough or pleasing voice, so little am I able to tell you why, under my hand, pictures assume such a character and no other.

The world seeks much that is exceptional in my pictures; and when one makes me aware of this or that good aspect in them, then I myself sometimes have to regard my work smilingly, that it has succeeded so well. However, it is carried out as if in a pleasant dream and, during the work, I have always thought more about the object itself than about how I wanted to portray it.

If you cannot wholly comprehend and imitate that which you find special in my works, then I advise you, dear Antonio, to select instead one or another of the justly famous masters of current times as your model; for, each has something worthy of imitation and I have educated myself profitably from them and still nourish my eye on their numerous qualities of excellence. However, that I now have precisely this and no other style of painting, as everyone tends to have his own, that seems to have been rooted in my nature all along; I did not acquire it through bitter effort, and something such as this cannot be deliberately studied. Continue, nevertheless, to practice art with love and may you fare well.

––––––––––

A Letter
of the
young Florentine painter
A N T O N I O
to his friend Jacobo in Rome

––––––––––

Beloved Brother!

Do not be surprised that I have not written to you for such a long time, because all sorts of pursuits have occupied my time incredibly. However, I now want to write to you more frequently, for I wish to communicate my thoughts and feelings to you as my dearest friend. You know my complaints that, in the past, I always felt as if I were an entirely unworthy, pitiful pupil of the noble art of painting; but now my soul has received a marvelous, incomprehensible life, so that I breathe more freely and boldly and no longer stand there, humbly blushing, before the pictures of the great masters.

And how shall I portray for you now in what way and through what means this has happened? The human being is very impoverished, dear Jacobo; for even if he carries a truly precious treasure in his breast, he must hide it like a miser and can tell or show nothing of it to his friend. Tears, sighs, a clasp of the hand are then all the language that we have. So it is with me now, and for this reason I should like to have you before me, in order to take your dear hand and place it upon my beating heart. —— I do not know whether other people have, in the past, felt as I do, —— whether it has already been granted unto others to find through love such a beautiful path to the worship of art. For, if one word is to express my feelings, then it must be love, which is now governing my heart and my mind.

I feel as if a curtain had been drawn away from my life and I now were seeing for the first time what people always call the nature and the beauty of the world. All mountains, all clouds, the sky and its sunset are now different and have come down closer to me. With love and inexpressible desire, I would like to embrace Raphael, who is now dwelling among the angels because he was too good and too exalted for us and this earth: hot tears of enthusiasm, of the most genuine reverence come into my earthly eye and make my senses divinely intoxicated, when I now stand before his works and impress them deeply upon my mind and heart. I can truly say that I am now feeling for the first time what distinguishes art from all other activities and occupations of mortal men: I have become purer and holier and, for this reason, I have at last been admitted to the holy altars. How I now worship the Mother of God and the exalted apostles in those inspiring pictures, which I formerly desired only to copy, stroke by stroke, with a cold heart and a semi-skilled paintbrush: —— now tears well up in my eyes, my hand trembles, I am moved in the depths of my heart, so that I convey the colors to the panel almost (I should like to say) without consciousness, and, nevertheless, the work turns out so well that I am satisfied with it afterwards. O, if only Raphael were still living, so that I could see him, speak to him, tell him my feelings! He must have been familiar with them, for I discover them, I discover my entire heart again in his works: all of his Madonnas resemble my beloved Amelia.

I also hit upon grand and truly daring inventions on my own now: I have already begun several things and, in many an hour, when I rise from a meal or have just carried on an insignificant conversation, I am myself astonished at my foolhardy undertaking. But, inwardly, my guiding spirit then urges me on again, so that, in spite of all this, I do not lose courage.

How dissimilar the tightly closed bud is to the gorgeous lily, which looks toward the sun like a large silver star on its dark stem: so dissimilar am I to myself in my previous condition. I want to do a great deal yet, and with untiring vigor.

When I am sleeping, the name Amelia is stretched out above me like a golden, protecting tent. I wake up often, because I hear this name spoken in a sweet tone, as if one of the Raphaelian infant angels were calling me teasingly and caressingly. Then, little by little, rippling sounds close the breach again and most charming dreams come down upon my eyes with gentle wings. ——

Alas, Jacobo, believe me, I am now for the first time truly your friend, but do not jeer at

your

happy Antonio.

Jacobo's Answer

Your dear letter, my most beloved Antonio, gave rise to a joyful feeling in me. I do not need to wish you happiness, for you are now truly happy; and far be it for me to jeer at you, for then I would not deserve the grace of heaven, which has chosen me as an instrument of its glorification, as an artist.

I understand very well your urge to work and your constantly lively inventiveness. I praise, indeed, I envy you; but you will not be offended with me, if I add a few words over and above this: for, because I have had so many a year, so many an experience ahead of you, I may thereby perhaps have a right to speak.

What you write to me about art does not please me so absolutely. Many a one has already walked your pathway, but I do not believe that the great artist must stop there where you are now standing. To be sure, love opens our eyes concerning ourselves and the world; the soul becomes quieter and more devout, and thousands of smoldering emotions break out into bright flames from all the corners of the heart: at that time one learns to understand religion and the miracle of heaven; one's mind becomes more humble and more full of pride; and art, in particular, speaks to us in the depths of our hearts with all its harmonies. However, at this point the artist all too easily faces the danger of seeking h i m s e l f in every work of art; all his emotions are poured out in o n e direction, and he thereby sacrifices his many-sided talent to a single emotion. Guard against this, dear Antonio, because otherwise you can be led to the narrowest and, in the end, the most insignificant style. The artist must come across every beautiful work already potential within himself, but not seek himself laboriously therein; it must be second in esteem only to religion; it must be a religious love, or a beloved religion, if I may express myself thusly: —— earthly love may, indeed, follow after this. Then a magnificent, refreshing wind will blow all emotions, all beautiful flowers into this conquered land, which is covered by the aurora of dawn and penetrated by divine desire.

Do not misinterpret my words, my deeply beloved Antonio: my devotion to art speaks from me in this way and, thus, you will interpret everything for the best. —— Farewell.

The Model
of a
creative and, moreover, highly learned artist,
exemplified in the life
of
LEONARDO DA VINCI,
renowned founder of the Florentine School

The age of the revival of the art of painting in Italy brought forth men to whom the world of today fittingly ought to look up as to hallowed saints. One would like to say of them that t h e y first subdued and, simultaneously, charmed wild Nature with their powers of sorcery, —— or rather that t h e y were the first to kindle the spark of art from the confusion of the universe. Each of these was resplendent with his own noteworthy perfections and, for many of them, altars have been erected in the temple of art.

From amidst these men I have, for the time being, chosen the famed founder of the Florentine School who can never be lauded enough, L e o n a r d o d a V i n c i, in order to present him to whomever it may interest, as the model in a truly scholarly and thorough study of art and as the symbol of an untiring and, at the same time, gifted diligence. May the apostles of art who are eager to teach learn from him that it is not sufficient merely to take an oath to a flag, to drill one's hand in the nimble control of the paintbrush and, armed with superficial and fleeting pseudo-enthusiasm, take the field against serious, well-founded scholarship. Such an example will teach them that the genius of art does not pair itself unwillingly with earnest Minerva and that a large and open soul, even if it is only directed toward one principal endeavor, nevertheless reflects the entire multifariously compounded picture of human knowledge in beautiful and perfect harmony. ——

The man about whom we are speaking was born in the little town of Vinci, which is situated down in the Arno Valley, not far from the magnificent city of Florence. As tends to occur with such select mentalities, the dexterity and the wit that he had inherited as a part of his nature revealed itself in his early youth and came forth in the variegated figures which his childish hand created in play. This is like the first bubbling of a gay little spring, which later becomes a mighty and admired river. Whoever is acquainted with it does not restrain the waters in their course, for otherwise they would break out through walls and dikes; rather, he leaves them their free will. Leonardo's father acted in that way by leaving the boy to the inclination which was by nature innate within him and placing him in the apprenticeship of the very renowned and deserving man, A n d r e a V e r o c c h i o in Florence.

But, alas! who among us still knows and who uses these names, which shone like sparkling stars in the sky in those days? They have faded away and nothing more is heard about them, —— people do not even know whether they ever existed.

And this Andrea Verocchio was not at all commonplace. He was devoted to the holy trefoil of all the fine arts: painting, sculpture, and architecture, —— for at that time it was not unusual that the mind of o n e human being had space enough for such a threefold love and capability. In addition to this, he was also well versed in mathematical perceptions and an ardent friend of music. It may well be that this model, which impressed itself at an early age upon Leonardo's tender soul, influenced him greatly; none the less, the seeds must have been there in the depths of his soul. But who is able to detect all the fine threads between causes and effects in the history of the development of a person's mind, when the individual himself is not even always aware of this interconnection during the course of his actions.

A lively and animated spirit is required for the learning of every fine art, even if it is to depict serious or sad things; for, through gradual painstaking effort a finished work is finally to be brought forth for the pleasure of all the senses; and sad, withdrawn temperaments have no inclination, no desire, no courage and no constancy to be creative. The youth Leonardo possessed this kind of lively spirit; and he trained himself with fervor not only in drawing and in the laying on of colors, but also in sculpturing, and, for relaxation, he played the violin and sang pretty songs. Thus, wherever his many-sided mind turned, it was always accompanied by the Muses and the Graces, floating in their atmosphere as their darling; it never touched the soil of daily life, not even in the hours of relaxation. Of all his pursuits, however, painting was closest to his heart; and to the embarrassment of his teacher, he advanced therein so far that, after a short while, he surpassed him. Proof that art cannot actually be learned and taught but that its current gushes forth unrestrainedly from the artist's own soul, if it only is led and directed along a short distance.

His imagination was so fruitful and rich in all sorts of significant and expressive figures that during his youth, when all his talents pressed forth within him forcibly, his spirit displayed itself not in the usual insipid imitations, but in extraordinary, rich, indeed, almost eccentric and strange images. Once he painted our first forefathers in paradise in this manner. He enriched and embellished the picture with all possible types of wonderful and strangely shaped animals and with an infinite, painstaking variety of plants and trees, so that one had to marvel at the multiplicity and could not turn his eyes away from the picture. Even more wonderful was the Medusa's head which he once painted upon a wooden shield for a peasant: he composed it from the limbs of all imaginable ugly crawling things and frightening monsters, so that one would not care to see anything more terrible. Later on, the experience of years regulated this wild, exuberant wealth in his spirit.

But I want to hasten to the main point and attempt to give a description of the all-encompassing zeal of this man.

In the art of painting he strove for higher and higher perfections with untiring eagerness and not in   o n e,   but in   a l l   styles; and he combined with the study of the secrets of the paintbrush the most industrious o b s e r v a t i o n,   which, as his guardian angel, led him through all the scenes of ordinary life and enabled him to gather the most beautiful fruits for his favorite field on all his pathways, where others did not suspect them. Thus, he himself was the greatest example for the teachings which he imparts in his excellent work on paintings, namely, that an artist ought to make himself   u n i v e r s a l.   He must not depict all things with one single habitual motion of the hand but must portray each according to its unique characteristics; —— and, then, that one should not rely upon one master but himself freely explore Nature in all its forms, since one otherwise would deserve to be called a grandchild, but not a son, of Nature.

From this particular writing, the only one of his scholarly works which has reached the eyes of the world and which one justly could call the golden book of Leonardo, it becomes apparent to us how seriously he always combined the precepts and rules of art with the practice of the same. He had the constitution of the human body so well under his command in all conceivable forms and positions, up to the smallest detail, as if he himself had created it; and he always proceeded directly to the precise meaning and the physical as well as spiritual significance which was supposed to be in each figure. For, as he himself makes clear in his book, every work of art must rightly speak a double language, one of the body and one of the soul. At several points in his book he gives instruction concerning how one ought to paint a battle, a storm at sea, a large gathering; and there his imagination is so active and effective that it quickly brings together the clearest and most expressive traits verbally in a remarkable entity.

Leonardo knew that the spirit of art is a flame of a very different nature from the enthusiasm of the poet. It does not have the intention of bringing forth something entirely from its own mind; the artistic spirit ought rather to roam about assiduously outside of itself and seek out all the forms of creation with agile dexterity and preserve their shapes and imprints in the storehouse of the mind; so that the artist, when he puts his hand to work, may find

already within himself a world of all things. Leonardo snatched up and contributed to his treasure every little part of the human body which pleased him in anyone passing by, every transitory charming position and expression. Unusual faces with strange hair and beards pleased him immensely; on their account he sometimes followed such people for a long while in order to fix them firmly in his mind, since he then painted them at home as naturally as if they had actually sat for him. Moreover, when two people were talking with each other totally naturally and left to their own inclination, without thinking that they had a spectator, or when a violent argument broke out or he otherwise came across human emotions and agitations in their full existence and their total force, then he never hesitated to take note of the outlines and the arrangement of the parts to the whole. Although it may seem ridiculous to many, he also often spent long periods of time totally lost in himself, gazing at old ruins upon which time had played with all sorts of strange figures and colors or at vivid stones with strange designs. During this fixed contemplation, there suddenly occurred to him many a fine idea about landscapes or battle throngs or strange settings and faces. For this reason he even sets down in his book the rule that one should assiduously contemplate such things for pleasure, because the mind would be incited to discoveries by such entangled things. ——
One can see how the extraordinary intellect of Leonardo, equalled by no one after him, knew how to draw gold out of all things, even the smallest and the least esteemed.

In the s c i e n c e of his art there was perhaps never a painter more experienced and more learned than he. The knowledge of the inner parts of the human body and of the entire mechanism of wheels and levers in this machine, —— the knowledge of light and of colors and how they affect each other and how one unites with the other, —— the theory of the relationships according to which things seem smaller and fainter at a distance; —— all these disciplines, which actually belong to the true original foundation of art, he had penetrated into their deepest abysses.

As has already been mentioned, however, he was not merely a great painter but also a good sculptor as well as an eminent architect. He was experienced in all branches of the mathematical sciences, a profound connoisseur of music, a pleasing singer and violinist, and a clever poet. In short, if he had lived during mythical times, then he would inevitably have been considered to be a son of Apollo.[10] Indeed, he took pleasure in distinguishing himself in all sorts of skills, even when they were entirely apart from his course. Thus, he was so well practiced in riding and in the managing of horses as well as in the handling of the sword that an uninformed person would have thought he had devoted his entire life to this alone. He was so familiar with marvelous mechanical objects of art and with the secret powers of nature's forms that one time, on a festive occasion, he constructed from wood the figure of a lion which moved by itself; and another time he had made out of a certain thin material little birds which floated freely up into the air by themselves. His mind had an inborn impulse to devise something new continuously, which kept him in constant activity and exertion. But all his talents were enhanced by noble and captivating manners, like precious stones by a golden setting. And, in order that the extraordinary man might seem outstanding and excellent even to the most vulgar and most stupid eyes, generous Nature had endowed him with splendid physical strength and, in addition to all this, finally with a very admirable education and a face that one had to love and respect.

The investigating mentality of the serious sciences seems so dissimilar to the creative spirit of art that, upon the first impression, one almost would like to imagine two separate genres of beings for both. And, in actuality, only a few mortals are so constructed that they could sacrifice to this twofold genius. But, whoever finds within his own soul the native land of all of the perceptions of forces, which as a rule m a n y divide between themselves, and whose mind calculates truths through conclusions of reason and, with the same zeal and good fortune, brings forth in visible representations creations of his inner sensuality through the toil of his hand: —— such a one must elicit astonishment and admiration from the entire world. And when he, moreover, is not merely devoted to one single art but unites several within himself, perceives their hidden relationship, and feels in his inner self the divine flame which flickers in all of them, then this man is certainly elevated above other human beings in an amazing way and many will not even be able to come close to him with their thoughts.

The court of the Milanese duke, Lodovico Sforza, was the principal theater where Leonardo da Vinci, as the highest administrator of the Academy, displayed his numerous skills. Here he proved himself with excellent paintings and artistic works; here he disseminated his good taste in the architecture of buildings; he was regularly employed in the ranks of the musicians as a violinist; with profound insight he directed the difficult construction of a water canal over mountains and valleys, —— and, thus, he represented solely in his own person almost an entire academy of all human perceptions and skills. Before he took charge of the construction of the canal, he went to Valverola, the country-seat of one of his distinguished friends and, with the encouragement of the pastoral Muse, applied himself with great diligence to the mathematical aspects of architecture. Later he spent several years on this quiet country estate and devoted himself with a philosophical spirit to mathematical studies and to all other studies in any way appertaining to a fundamental theory of the fine arts. He became totally immersed in serious speculations. In his external appearance as well, he conveyed the impression of contemplative wisdom, for he had allowed his hair and beard to grow so long that he had the exterior of a hermit; —— and some also want to see in his untiring diligence

the motivating reason why he remained unwed throughout his lifetime. ——
During his sojourn in rustic solitude, he also compiled in detailed volumes the
results of his study, refined and clarified by his intellect and sprinkled with
his own very penetrating thoughts and observations. These works, composed
in his own cherished handwriting, are still located today in the magnificent
Ambrosian book collection in Milan.

But alas! like so many another very old manuscript covered with venerable dust in the rare book collections of the great, this also is an untouched
relic which the uncomprehending sons of our age p a s s b y with, at
best, an empty display of reverence. The manuscript is still awaiting that one
person who shall awaken the spirit of the old painter, which is sleeping be-
witchedly therein, and release it from its long-endured bondage.

My pen is not capable of analyzing all the beauties and admirable qualities in the many paintings of our Leonardo. His most famous picture is
doubtless the depiction of the Last Supper in the refectory of the Dominicans
in Milan. People admire in this the soulful expression in the faces of Christ's
disciples, how each seems to be asking the Lord: Lord! am I the one? The
old chroniclers of art say that Leonardo had hesitated for a while after he had
finished the other figures and had pondered and debated with himself or (to
speak perhaps more exactly), waited for happy inspirations as to how he
should most perfectly express the traitorous face of Judas and the exalted
countenance of Jesus; whereupon the prior of the monastery had given revealing proof of his own lack of understanding by chastising him like a day-
laborer about his hesitation.

I must make mention of one other painting of Leonardo because of a
noteworthy circumstance. I refer to the portrait of Lisa del Giocondo (the
wife of Francesco), upon which he worked for four years without stifling the
spirit and the life of the total entity by the most careful and minute working
out of every little hair. Now, whenever the noble lady sat for him, he always
called hither several people who had to entertain her with pleasant and lively
instrumental music, accompanied by the human voice. A very clever idea, for
which I have always admired Leonardo. He knew only too well that a dull
and vacant earnestness usually tends to appear on the faces of people who are
sitting for portraits and that, when it is set down in permanent features in the
painting, such an expression takes on an unpleasing or even ominous appearance. On the other hand, he knew the effect of gay music, how it is reflected in the facial expressions, how it relaxes all the features and sets them
into charming, alert activity. Thus, he transferred the eloquent charms of
this countenance onto the panel a s i f t h e y w e r e a l i v e
and, in the practice of the one art, he knew how to make use of the other as
assistant so successfully that the latter cast its reflection upon the former.

One can imagine how many skilled artists emanated from Leonardo's school and how distinguished and universally respected he was during his lifetime. Once, when he had done only the first sketch for a large altar-painting in a monastery outside of Florence, the fame of this sketch became so great that for two days crowds of people from the city made pilgrimages to that place and one would have thought that a festival or a procession were being celebrated.

After Duke Lodovico Sforza of Milan had suffered complete defeat during Italy's age of strife, and the Academy in Milan had become totally dispersed, Leonardo da Vinci had settled down in Florence again. In his later years he was called from Florence to F r a n c e by King Francis I.[11]

The monarch esteemed him above all else and received the elderly seventy-five-year-old man with particular friendliness and respect. However, it was not his lot to live a long while in his new country. The hardships of the journey and the difference in the national character and customs must have brought on the illness which he contracted not long after his arrival. The king visited him regularly during his illness and showed signs of being very concerned about him. One day, when he came to him once again, stepped up to his bed, and the old man wanted to sit up in bed in order to thank the king for his kindness, he was suddenly overcome by weakness, —— the king supported him with his arms, —— but the breath went out of him, —— and the s p i r i t which had produced so many great things, that still exist today in all their perfection, was blown away with a single breath, like a leaf from the earth. ——

If the radiance of royal crowns is the light which particularly furthers the flourishing of the arts, then one can regard the scene which stands at the close of Leonardo's life to a certain extent as an apotheosis of the artist; in the eyes of the world, at least, it must have seemed a worthy reward for all the deeds of the great man that he pass away in the arms of a k i n g. —— ——

Now, people will perhaps ask me: Whether I intended to nominate this Leonardo da Vinci, praised so highly here, as the most excellent and the foremost of all painters and to urge all students that they strive to become just exactly like he?

But, rather than answering, I shall ask in return: Whether one then is not allowed to restrict one's view intentionally to the great and contemplation-worthy spirit of a single man, in order to examine his particular excellences for themselves in their own context? —— and whether one can, indeed, with the presumptuous strictness of a judgeship, so brazenly arrange the artists in sequence and rank according to the quantity and weight of their merits, just as teachers of morality presume to rank virtuous and sinful human beings above and below each other according to precise rules of order?

I believe that one could admire two minds of a very dissimilar nature, both of which have great qualities. The minds of human beings are just as infinitely varied as are the features and shapes of their faces. And do we not just as well call the venerable, wrinkled, wise countenance of the old man b e a u t i f u l   as the unaffected, responsive, enchanting face of the virgin?

But, concerning this pictorial conception, someone might say to me: When the watchword   B e a u t y   sounds, is it not the latter image, the picture of Venus Urania, which presses forth spontaneously from the inner soul in your breast?

And to this I admittedly know of nothing to answer.

With regard to my twofold picture, whoever bears in mind as I do the spirit of the man whom we have just depicted and the spirit of the one whom I tend to call the divine one, will perhaps find material for reflection in this parable. Similar fantasies which enter into our minds often miraculously cast a brighter light upon an object than the conclusions of reason; and, along with the so-called higher powers of perception, there is a magical mirror in our souls, which sometimes shows us these things portrayed, perhaps, most vividly of all.

—————

Descriptions of Two Paintings[12]

—————

A beautiful picture or painting, in my opinion, is actually not to be described; for, the moment one says more than a single word about it, the image flies away from the panel and flits about in the air on its own. For this reason, the old chroniclers of art have seemed to me to be very wise when they merely call a painting a splendid, an incomparable, a most magnificent work; for it seems to me impossible to say   m o r e   about it. Meanwhile, it has occurred to me to describe a few pictures for once in the following manner, two samples of which I want to present for everyone's inspection, strictly for the sake of the specific type, without my considering this type to be something very superior.

—————

First Picture
The Holy Virgin with the Christ-Child, and little John

Mary

Why should I then be so overblessed,
And selected for the highest bliss
That the earth ever can sustain?
I become despondent at this fortune,
And I know not how to give my thanks,
Not with tears, not with purest joy.
Only with a smile and with deep sadness
Can I look upon the godly child,
And my gaze has not the power to rise up
Unto Heaven and to the generous Father.

Never do my eyes grow at all tired,
Of gazing down with deepest joy of heart
Upon the child that plays here on my lap.
Ah! and what unknown, grandiose things,
Which the guiltless child does not suspect,
Shine forth from those clever blue eyes,
And from all the little trickeries!
Alas! I do not know what I should say!
It seems that I'm no longer on this earth,
When I think to myself vividly:
I, I am the mother of this child.

The Infant Jesus

Pretty and colorful is the world around me!
Yet I am not like the other children,
I cannot play rightly,
Nor grasp anything firmly with my hand,
Cannot rejoice by shouting loudly.

Whatever moves
And stirs before my eyes,
Seems like a fleeting shadow
And a clever mirage.
But, inwardly, I am happy,
And I think of more beautiful things,
Which I cannot express.

L i t t l e   J o h n

Ah! how I worship it, the little infant Jesus!
Ah! how sweetly and full of innocence
It plays in its mother's lap! ——
Dear God in Heaven, How I pray secretly to You,
And thank You,
And praise You for Your great goodness,
And implore Your blessing also upon me!

———————

S e c o n d   P i c t u r e
The Adoration of the Three Wise Men from the East

T h e   T h r e e   W i s e   M e n

Behold! from the distant Orient
Come we, guided by the lovely star,
We, three wise men from that far-off region,
Where the sun ascends in all its brilliance.
Many long years we've aspired to wisdom,
And to wisdom's very fountain-head,
We've pondered many things in our minds;
Thereby, the Lord of All Things graciously
Has blessed us with silver-white heads.
Yet, we have now come all this long way,
From the land where the sun ascends,
To lay down all the wisdom of our years,

All our science and our knowledge,
Humbly in the dust right here,
Ah! before You, You wondrous child,
And in our golden kingly robes,
And with our silver-white heads,
To bow reverently before You,
To worship and adore You.
And, as a sign of our deep reverence
We bring you myrrh, gold, and incense,
A worthy offering of our devotion,
Only as we are capable of giving it.

M a r y

Ah! praise the Lord, my soul!
That He has made me so glorious,
So highly exalted over all people!
That I have borne the child
Who is playing in my lap,
Whom the wise men come to worship
From the distant Orient!
Alas! my eye cannot endure it,
And my heart is breaking!
All the deep wisdom of their years they lay down
In the dust before the infant:
Their knees bent down,
Their heads inclined toward the earth,
And on the ground the golden kingly robes.
Gold, and incense, and myrrh
They bring as an offering;
Ah! a great and magnificent offering to the child! ——
Oh, how blissful the mother is inwardly!
Yet I am not able to thank
The wise men for their great kindness,
Nor to raise my eyes toward Heaven.
But magnificent and grand things
Are felt inwardly in the depths of me.

T h e   I n f a n t   J e s u s

That far-off land must be most beautiful,
Where the bright sun ascends;

For, how magnificent these men are!
But how are they so old and splendid?
Ah! that is the deep wisdom,
That they have golden kingly robes
And silver-white hair.
And they have brought to me
Truly wonderful things!
And yet they are kneeling down before me, ——
The men seem strange to me,
And I do not know
What I should rightly call them.

A Few Words
concerning
UNIVERSALITY,
TOLERANCE
and
HUMAN LOVE
in Art

The Creator, who made our earth and everything upon it, encompassed the entire globe with His glance and poured out the river of His blessing upon the whole earthly realm. However, from His mysterious workshop He scattered over our globe thousands of infinitely diverse seeds of things which bear infinitely varied fruits and, in honor of Him, shoot up into the largest, most colorful gardens. In a wondrous way He guides His sun around the earth in precise circles, so that its beams fall upon the earth in thousands of directions and extract and stimulate the essence of the soil for a variety of creations in every region under heaven.

At   o n e   great moment He gazes with impartial eye upon the work of His hands and receives with satisfaction the offerings of all animate and inanimate Nature. The roaring of the lion is as pleasant to Him as the crying of the reindeer; and the aloe smells just as lovely to Him as rose and hyacinth. Man also emanated from His creating hand in thousandfold forms: —— the brothers of o n e house do not know and understand each other; they speak different languages and are amazed at each other; —— but He knows them all and takes pleasure in all; with impartial eye He gazes upon the work of His hands and receives the offering of all Nature.

In many a way He hears the voices of human beings speaking in confusion about heavenly things and knows that all, —— all, even if it were against their knowledge and intention, —— nevertheless mean H i m, the Ineffable One.

In this manner He also hears the inner feelings of people speak different languages in different zones and in different eras and hears how they argue with each other and do not understand one another: but, for the Eternal Spirit, everything dissolves into harmony; He knows that each individual speaks the language which He has created in him, that each expresses his inner feelings as he can and should; —— if in their blindness they argue with each other, then He knows and recognizes that each is, for himself, in the right; He looks with pleasure upon each and all and delights in the variegated mixture.

A r t is to be called the flower of human emotion. In continuously changing form amidst the manifold zones of the earth it rises up towards heaven, and only o n e united perfume comes forth from this seed for the Universal Father, who holds in His hand the earth with all that is upon it.

In each work of art in all the zones of the earth, He sees the trace of the heavenly spark which, having emanated from Him, passed over through the breast of the individual into his little creation, from which it then glows back again to the great Creator. The Gothic temple pleases Him as well as the temple of the Greek and the crude war-music of the uncivilized is for Him just as lovely a sound as artistic choirs and hymns.

And when, through the immeasurable spaces of heaven, I now return to earth from Him, the Infinite One, and look around among my fellowbrothers, —— alas! then I must utter loud laments that they strive so little to resemble their great eternal model in heaven. They quarrel with each other and do not understand each other and fail to see that they are all hastening toward the same goal, because each remains standing firmly upon his own location and does not know how to lift his eyes over all the world.

Stupid people cannot comprehend that there are antipodes on our globe and that they are themselves antipodes. They always conceive of the place where they are standing as the gravitational center of the universe, —— and their minds lack the wings to fly around the entire earth and survey with o n e glance the integrated totality.

And, similarly, they regard their own emotion as the center of everything beautiful in art and they deliver the final judgment concerning everything as if from the tribunal, without considering that no one has appointed them judges and that those who are condemned by them could just as well set themselves up to the same end.

Why do you not condemn the American Indian, that he speaks Indian and not our language? ——

And yet you want to condemn the Middle Ages, that it did not build such temples as did Greece? ——

O, at least feel your way into these unknown souls and observe that you have received the gifts of the spirit from t h e s a m e hand as your misunderstood brothers! Comprehend, moreover, that each creature can only be creative from within himself with the capacities which he has received from heaven and that each person's creative works must be in conformity with his talents. And if you are not capable of f e e l i n g your way into all unfamiliar beings and e x p e r i e n c i n g their works through their mentalities; then try, at least, to reach up to this conviction indirectly through the intellect's chains of reasoning. ——

If the disseminating hand of heaven had let the embryo of your soul fall upon the African sand deserts, then you would have preached to all the world the shining blackness of skin, the large, flat face and the short, curly hair as essential components of the highest beauty and would have laughed at or hated the first white man. If your soul had arisen several hundred miles further to the East, on the soil of India, then you would feel the secret spirit which exists, concealed from our senses, in the little, strangely shaped idols with many arms and, if you were to see the statue of the Venus of Medici, you would not know what you should think of it. And had it pleased that One, under whose power you stood and are standing, to cast you into the multitudes of southern island dwellers, then you would find in every wild drumbeat and in the crude, shrill shocks of the melody a deep significance, of which you now comprehend not a syllable. In any one of these cases, however, would you have received the gift of creativity or the gift of appreciation of art from another source than the eternal and universal One, to whom you are now indebted for all of your treasures? ——

Amidst all the nations of the earth, the multiplication table of reason follows the same laws and is only applied to an infinitely larger field of objects here, to a very small field there. —— In a similar way a r t i s t i c f e e l i n g is only one and the same divine ray of light which, however, is refracted into thousands of different colors by the diversely polished glass of sensuality in various regions.

B e a u t y: a wondrously strange word! First invent new words for each separate artistic feeling, for each individual work of art! A different color plays in each and, for each, separate nerves are provided in the structure of the human being.

But, with talents of the intellect you spin a rigorous s y s t e m from this one word and want to compel all men to feel according to your prescriptions and rules, —— yet you yourselves do not feel.

He who b e l i e v e s a s y s t e m has expelled universal love from his heart! Intolerance of emotion is still more endurable than intolerance of the intellect; —— s u p e r s t i t i o n better than b e l i e f i n a s y s t e m. ——

Can you force one who is melancholy to find playful songs and lively dancing pleasant? Or one who is sanguine to offer his heart joyfully to tragic horrors?

O, rather let every mortal being and every race under the sun keep its belief and its happiness! and rejoice when others are happy, —— even if you yourself do not know how to be happy about that which is dearest and most precious to them.

We, sons of this century, have had fall to our lot the advantage that we stand on the peak of a high mountain and that many countries and many ages lie spread out around us and at our feet, open to our eyes. Therefore, let us make use of this good fortune and wander about through all the ages and peoples with clear vision and always strive to discover t h e h u m a n e l e m e n t in all their manifold sensations and products of sensation.

—— ——

Every creature strives toward that which is the most beautiful: but it cannot transcend itself and sees what is most beautiful only within itself. Just as a different image of the rainbow enters into every mortal eye, so too does the surrounding world reflect for each individual a different imprint of beauty. However, universal, original beauty, which we can n a m e only in moments of ecstatic intuition and are unable to reduce to words, reveals itself unto the One who created the rainbow and the eye that beholds it.

I began my discourse with Him and I return to Him again: —— in the same way as the spirit of art, —— as all spirit goes forth from Him and, as an offering, penetrates through the atmosphere of the earth up to Him again.

———————

A Memorial
to our
venerable ancestor
ALBRECHT DÜRER[13]
By an art-loving friar

———

Nuremberg! you formerly world-renowned city! How I liked to wander through your quaint streets; with what childlike love I gazed at your antiquated houses and churches, upon which the permanent trace of our early native art is imprinted! How deeply I love the structures of that age, which have such a robust, powerful and true language. How they transport me back into that venerable century when you, Nuremberg, were the vibrantly teeming school of native art and a truly fruitful, overflowing spirit of art lived and thrived within your walls: —— when Master Hans Sachs and Adam Kraft, the sculptor, and, above all, A l b r e c h t   D ü r e r with his friend, Wilibaldus Pirkheimer, and so many other highly praised men of honor were still living! How often I have wished that I were back in that age! How often it has appeared before me anew in my thoughts, while I was sitting in a narrow corner in your venerable libraries, Nuremberg, in the twilight of the little, round-paned windows and brooding over the folio volumes of valiant Hans Sachs or over some other old, yellow, worm-eaten paper; —— or while I was walking under the bold arches of your dark churches, where, through colorfully painted windows, the sunlight splendidly illuminates all the objects of art and paintings of the past age! —— ——

You are surprised again and gaze at me, you narrow-minded and fainthearted ones! O, I know them, indeed, the myrtle-forests of Italy, —— I know it, indeed, the divine ardor in the inspired men of the blessed South: —— how you call me hence, where my soul's thoughts are dwelling constantly, where is the native land of the most beautiful hours of my life! —— You, who see boundaries everywhere where there are none! Are not Rome and Germany situated on o n e   e a r t h? Has the heavenly Father not made p a t h w a y s from North to South as from West to East across the globe? Is a human life too brief? Are the Alps insurmountable? —— Then, more than o n e love must also be able to live in the breast of man. —— ——

But now my grieving spirit is wandering about on the consecrated ground before your walls, Nuremberg; on the cemetery where the bones of Albrecht Dürer are resting, who was formerly the embellishment of Germany, indeed, of Europe. Visited by few, his remains rest amidst innumerable tombstones, each of which is marked with a bronze plaque, as the stamp of the early art. Between the graves tall sunflowers spring up in multitudes, which make the cemetery into a lovely garden. In this setting rest the forgotten bones of our old Albrecht Dürer, on account of whom I am glad that I am a German.

Few must have been given the ability to understand the soul in your pictures as well and to enjoy their unique and particular qualities with such fervor as heaven seems to have granted unto me over many others; for, I look around and find few who lingered before you with such an affectionate love, with such emotion as I.

Is it not as if the figures in your pictures were real people who were talking together? Each is etched so distinctly that one would recognize him in a large crowd; each so true to life that he totally fulfills his purpose. Not one is there with half a soul, as people frequently would like to say regarding very ornamental pictures by more modern masters; each is captured in the fullness of life and set down on the panel in this way. Whoever is supposed to lament, laments; whoever is supposed to be angry, is angry; and whoever is supposed to pray, prays. All of the figures speak; they speak openly and with refinement. No arm moves superfluously or merely to please the eyes and fill up space; all of the limbs, everything speaks to us as if with force, so that we comprehend with genuine firmness the meaning and the soul of the entire picture. We believe everything which the artistic man presents to us; and it is never blotted out of our memory.

Why is it that the contemporary artists of our native land seem to me so different from those praiseworthy men of the past and from you, above all, my beloved Dürer? Why is it that I feel as if you all had handled the art of painting far more seriously, more importantly and more worthily than these ornamental artists of our days? I imagine that I see you, how you stand meditating before the picture you have begun, —— how the conception that you want to make visible hovers very animatedly before your soul, —— how you prudently consider what expressions and positions might affect the viewer the most powerfully and most surely and stir his soul the most forcefully while he is looking at them, —— and you then accurately and painstakingly convey to the panel the beings allied with your lively imagination. —— But the more recent artists do not seem to want one to participate seriously in that which they portray for us; they work for aristocratic gentlemen, who do not want to be moved and ennobled by art but dazzled and titillated to the highest degree; they strive to make their paintings specimens of many lovely and deceiving colors; they test their cleverness in the scattering of light and shadow; —— however, the human figures frequently seem to be in the picture merely for the sake of the colors and the light, I would indeed like to say, as a necessary evil.

I must cry out woe upon our age, that it practices art merely as a frivolous plaything of the senses, while it is actually something very serious and exalted. Do people no longer pay heed to the human being, that they neglect him in art and find pretty colors and all sorts of tricks with highlights more worthy of contemplation? ——

In the writings of M a r t i n L u t h e r, who was very highly esteemed and defended by our Albrecht, in which, as I willingly admit, I have done some reading out of intellectual curiosity and in which much good material may be hidden, I found a remarkable passage concerning the importance of art, which now comes vividly to mind. For this man maintains somewhere very daringly and explicitly that, after theology, music occupies the first place among all the sciences and arts of the human spirit. And I must open-heartedly confess that this bold claim attracted my attention very much to this excellent man. For the soul from which such a claim could come had to feel precisely that deep veneration for art which, from whence I know not, dwells in so few minds and which is, nevertheless, seemingly so very natural and so significant.

Now, if art (I mean its principal and essential part) is really of such importance, then it is very unworthy and foolish to turn away from the expressive and instructive human figures of our old Albrecht Dürer because they are not endowed with the glistening external beauty which the world of today considers to be the sole and highest aspect of art. It does not give evidence of an entirely healthy and untroubled disposition, if someone closes his ears to an intellectual reflection which is, in itself, convincing and penetrating, only because the speaker does not arrange his words in fine order or because he has an incorrect, foreign accent or an unattractive motion of his hands. But do not similar thoughts prevent me from appreciating and admiring for its merits this external and, so to speak, merely physical beauty of art where I come upon it?

This is also charged against you as a crude fault, my beloved Albrecht Dürer, that you merely place your human figures so conveniently next to each other, without intermingling them so that they form a methodical group. I love you in your unaffected simplicity and I spontaneously fix my eye first of all upon the s o u l and deep s i g n i f i c a n c e of your human beings, without such censoriousness even entering my mind. However, many people seem so disturbed by this, as by an evil, tormenting spirit, that they become aroused to despise and to mock before they are able to observe serenely, —— and they are least of all capable of transporting themselves beyond the boundaries of the present into past ages. I am quite willing to admit to you, you eager neophytes, that a young pupil might nowadays speak more cleverly and learnedly about colors, light, and arrangement of figures than old Dürer knew how to; but is it the youth's own intellect which is speaking, or is it not, instead, the artistic wisdom and experience of the past ages? Only individual, chosen mentalities comprehend the actual inner soul of art s u d d e n l y, even if their handling of the paintbrush may still be very imperfect; all the external aspects of art, on the other hand, are brought to perfection little by little through invention, practice, and reflection. It is, however, a base and deplorable vanity which sets the gain of the a g e s upon its own weak head as a crown and wants to conceal its nothingness under borrowed splendor. Away, you wise youths, from the old artist of Nuremberg! —— and may no one venture to judge him with mockery who can still childishly turn up his nose over the fact that he did not have Titian or Correggio as teachers or that, in his day, people wore such odd Old-Franconian clothing.

For, on this account as well, today's teachers do not want to call him, as well as many another good painter of his century, beautiful and noble, because they clothe the history of all peoples and even the sacred stories of our religion in the dress of their own times. But, I consider thereby how e v e r y artist who lets the spirit of past centuries enter into his heart must enliven this with the spirit and breath of h i s o w n age; and how it is, indeed, appropriate and natural that the creative power of the human being lovingly attract to itself everything strange and distant, even the heavenly beings as well, and envelop all in the well-known and beloved forms of i t s world and i t s mental horizon.

When Albrecht was wielding the paintbrush, the German was at that time still a unique and an excellent character of firm constancy in the arena of our continent; and this serious, upright and powerful nature of the German is imprinted in h i s pictures accurately and clearly, not only in the facial structure and the whole external appearance but also in the inner spirit. This firmly determined German character and German art as well have disappeared in our times. The young German learns the languages of all the peoples of Europe and, examining and evaluating, is expected to draw sustenance from the spirit of all nations; —— and the student of art is taught how he should imitate the expressiveness of Raphael and the colors of the Venetian School and the realism of the Dutch and the enchanting highlights of Correggio, all simultaneously, and should in this way arrive at the perfection which surpasses all. —— O, wretched sophistry! O, blind belief of this age that one could combine every type of beauty and every excellence of all the great painters of the earth and, through the scrutinizing of all and the begging of their numerous great gifts, could unite the spirit of all in oneself and transcend them all! —— The period of individual vigor is over; people wish to simulate the talent which has faded away by means of impoverished imitation and shrewd compilation, and cold, immaculate, insipid works are the fruit. —— German art was a pious youth, raised in simplicity within the walls of a small city amidst intimate

115

friends; —— now that it is older, it has become a universal man of the world who, along with his provincial manners, simultaneously wiped away the emotion and the unique character from his soul.

I would not wish for all the world that the enchanting Correggio or the magnificent Paolo Veronese or the mighty Buonarotti had painted in the very same way as R a p h a e l. And I also do not agree in the least with the utterances of those who say: "If Albrecht Dürer had only lived in Rome for a while and learned true beauty and the ideal from Raphael, then he would have become a great painter; one has to pity him and marvel that he, nevertheless, achieved so much in his position." I find nothing to pity here; rather, I rejoice that in this man Fate has granted to German soil a truly native painter. He would not have remained himself; his blood was not Italian blood. He was not born for the perfection and the lofty grandeur of a Raphael; he took his pleasure i n t h i s, depicting for us human beings as they actually were in his surroundings, and he succeeded most admirably.

But, nevertheless, when I for the first time saw paintings by Raphael as well as by you, my beloved Dürer, in a magnificent art gallery during my younger years, it occurred to me most amazingly that, of all the other painters whom I knew, these two had a particularly close affinity to my heart. It pleased me very much that they both present to our eyes so clearly and distinctly mankind in the fullness of soul, so simply and straightforwardly, without the ornamental digressions of other painters. At that time, however, I did not dare to reveal my opinion to anyone, for I believed that everyone would laugh at me and I well knew that the majority perceive nothing other than something very stiff and dull in this early German painter. On the day when I had seen that art gallery I was, however, so filled with this new thought that I fell asleep therewith and, in the night, a delightful vision appeared before me which confirmed me even more firmly in my belief. It seemed to me, namely, that after midnight I had gone with a torch out of the room of the castle in which I was sleeping. Totally alone I walked through the dark halls of the building toward the art gallery. When I arrived at the door, I heard a soft murmuring within; —— I opened it, —— and suddenly I started back in surprise, for the entire large hall was illuminated by a strange light and in front of numerous pictures were standing their venerable masters in living form and in their old-fashioned dress, just as I had seen them in portraits. One of them, whom I did not know, told me that they descended from heaven on many a night and, in the nocturnal stillness, wandered about in picture galleries here and there on earth and viewed the still beloved works of their hands. I recognized many Italian painters; from the Netherlands I saw very few. Full of reverence I passed between them; —— and behold! there, apart from all the others, R a p h a e l and A l b r e c h t D ü r e r were standing hand in hand in the flesh before my eyes and were silently gazing in friendly tranquillity at their paintings,

116

hanging side by side. I did not have the courage to address the divine Raphael; a mysterious, reverential fear sealed my lips. However, I was just about to greet my Albrecht and pour out my love to him; —— but, at that moment, everything became disarranged before my eyes with a great din and I awoke with a violent start.

This vision had given my heart deep joy and the joy became even more complete when, shortly thereafter, I read in old Vasari how, without knowing each other, these two magnificent artists had also really been friends during their lifetimes through their works and how the sincere and life-like products of the early German had been regarded with satisfaction by Raphael and he had considered them not unworthy of his love.

But, to be sure, I cannot conceal the fact that afterwards I always felt just as in that dream regarding the works of the two painters; in the case of those by Albrecht Dürer, namely, I sometimes attempted to explain their true merit to someone and dared to speak expansively concerning their excellencies; but, with the works of Raphael, I always became so surfeited and afflicted in the presence of this heavenly beauty that I was not able to speak about it nor to analyze clearly for someone the source of the divine essence which shone forth for me everywhere.

However, I do not want to turn my attention from you now, my Albrecht. Comparison is a dangerous enemy of enjoyment; even the highest beauty of art exerts its full force upon us only then, as it should, when our eye is not simultaneously looking aside at other beauty. Heaven has distributed its gifts among the great artists of the earth in such a way that we are absolutely compelled to stop before each one and offer up to each his share of our adoration.

True art sprouts forth not only under Italian sky, under majestic domes and Corinthian columns, —— but also under pointed arches, intricately ornamented buildings, and Gothic towers.

Peace be with your remains, my Albrecht Dürer! and may you know how I love you and hear how I am the herald of your name in the world of today, unfamiliar to you. —— Blessed be to me your golden age, Nuremberg! the only age when Germany could boast of having its own native art. —— But the beautiful eras pass away across the earth and disappear, just as shining clouds drift away across the arch of the sky. They are over and are no longer thought of; only a few, out of deep love, call them back to mind from dust-covered books and enduring works of art.

———————

Concerning
T W O   W O N D E R F U L
L A N G U A G E S
and
t h e i r   m y s t e r i o u s   p o w e r

The language of words is a great gift of heaven and it was a perpetual blessing of the Creator that He enabled the first human being to speak, so that he could name all the things which the Highest One had placed around him in the world and all the spiritual images which He had implanted in his soul and could exercise his mind in the diverse play with this abundance of names. We rule over the entire globe by means of words; with easy effort we acquire for ourselves through trade all the treasures of the earth by means of words. Only t h e   i n v i s i b l e   f o r c e   w h i c h   h o v e r s   o v e r   u s   i s   not drawn down into our hearts by words.

We have the earthly things in our hand when we speak their names; —— but when we hear the infinite goodness of God mentioned, or the virtue of the saints, which are indeed subjects that ought to grip our whole being, then our ears alone become filled with empty sounds and our spirit is not elevated as it should be.

However, I know of   t w o   w o n d e r f u l   l a n g u a g e s   through which the Creator has permitted human beings to perceive and to comprehend heavenly things in their full force, as far as this (in order not to speak presumptuously) is possible, namely, for mortal creatures. They enter into our souls through entirely different ways than through the aid of words; they move our entire being   s u d d e n l y,   in a wondrous manner, and they press their way into every nerve and every drop of blood which belongs to us.   G o d   alone speaks the first of these wonderful languages; the second is spoken only by a few Chosen Ones among men, whom He has anointed as His favorites. I mean: N a t u r e   a n d   A r t.   ——

Since my early youth, when I first became acquainted with the God of mankind from the ancient holy books of our religion,   N a t u r e   always seemed to me the most fundamental and the clearest book of explanation concerning His being and His attributes. The rustling in the treetops of the forest and the rolling of the thunder told me mysterious things about Him which I cannot set down in words. A beautiful valley surrounded by fantastic cliff formations or a calm river in which leaning trees are reflected or a pleasant green meadow, shone upon by the blue sky, —— ah! these things have inspired more marvelous emotions deep within me, have filled my spirit more fervently with the omnipotence and infinite goodness of God, and have purified and elevated my entire soul far more than the language of words was ever capable of doing. It is, in my opinion, an all too earthly and clumsy instrument to handle the spiritual as well as the physical realm with it.

I find here a great inducement to praise the power and goodness of the Creator. Around us human beings He placed an infinite number of things, each of which has a different nature and none of which we can understand and comprehend. We do not know what a tree is; nor what a meadow nor what a cliff is; we cannot communicate with them in our language; we only understand e a c h o t h e r. And, nevertheless, the Creator has placed in the human heart such a marvelous sympathy for these things that they bring to it by unknown pathways emotions or sentiments, or whatever one may call them, which we never acquire through the most measured words.

Out of a zeal for the truth which is in itself laudable, the philosophers have gone astray; they have wanted to uncover the mysteries of heaven and place them amidst the things of earth in earthly illumination and have expelled the d i m i n t u i t i o n s of the same from their breasts with bold advocacy of their right. —— Is the weak human being capable of clarifying the mysteries of heaven? Does he rashly think that he can bring to light what God has hidden with His own hand? May he, indeed, arrogantly dismiss the d i m i n t u i t i o n s which descend to us like veiled angels? —— I honor them in deep humility; for it is a great benevolence of God that He send down to us these genuine witnesses of the truth. I fold my hands and worship. ——

A r t is a language of a totally different type than Nature; but, through similar dark and mysterious ways, it also has a marvelous power over the heart of man. It speaks through pictures of human beings and, therefore, makes use of a hieroglyphic script, whose symbols we know and understand in their external aspect. But it fuses spiritual and supersensual qualities into the visible shapes in such a touching and admirable manner that, in response, our entire being and everything about us is stirred and affected deeply. Many a painting of the Passion of Christ or of our Holy Virgin or from the history of the saints has, I may indeed say it, cleansed my mind more and inspired my inner consciousness with more blessedly virtuous convictions than systems of morality and spiritual meditations. Among others, I still think with fervor about a most magnificently painted picture of our Saint Sebastian, how he stands naked and bound to a tree, how an angel draws the arrow out of his breast and a second angel brings a floral wreath from heaven for his head. I am indebted to this painting for very penetrating and tenacious Christian convictions and I now can scarcely bring the same vividly back to mind without having tears well up in my eyes.

The teachings of the philosophers set only our brains in motion, only the one half of our beings; but the two wonderful languages whose power I am proclaiming here affect our senses as well as our minds; or, rather (I cannot express it differently), they seem thereby to fuse all the parts of our nature (incomprehensible to us) into one single new organ, which perceives and comprehends the heavenly miracles in this twofold way.

One of the languages, which the Highest One Himself continues to speak from eternity to eternity, continuously active, infinite N a t u r e, leads us through the vast expanses of the atmosphere directly to the godhead. A r t, however, which, by means of clever mixtures of colored earth and some moisture, copies the human form in narrow, restricted space, striving for inner perfection (a type of creation as was granted to mortal beings to produce), —— it discloses for us the treasures in the human breast, turns our eyes towards our inner selves, and shows us the invisible part, I mean everything that is noble, grand, and divine, in human form. ——

Whenever I walk out of the consecrated temple of our monastery into the open air after the contemplation of Christ on the Cross and the sunshine from the blue sky embraces me warmly and vibrantly and the beautiful landscape with mountains, waters, and trees strikes my eye, then I see a special world of God arise before me and feel great things surge up in my soul in a special way. —— And when I go from the open air into the temple again and reflect upon the painting of Christ on the Cross with seriousness and fervor, then I once again see another entirely different world of God before me and feel great things rise up in my soul in another special way.

Art represents for us the highest human perfection. Nature, to the extent that a mortal eye sees it, resembles fragmentary oracular decrees from the mouth of the deity. However, if it is permissible to speak thusly of such things, then one would perhaps like to say that God may, indeed, look upon all of Nature or the entire world in a manner similar to the manner in which we look upon a work of art.

———

Concerning the Peculiarities
of the
old painter
PIERO DI COSIMO,
of the Florentine School

Nature, the eternally diligent working woman, manufactures millions of creatures of every species with constantly occupied hands and tosses them into earthly existence. With light, playful jesting she, without watching, mixes the ingredients together in various ways, however they might fit at the moment, and abandons each creature that falls from her hand to his own pleasure and affliction. And just as sometimes, in the inanimate realm, she mischievously tosses peculiar and monstrous forms into the crowd, so too does she bring forth amidst mankind several curiosities in every century, which she hides between thousands of the usual type. But these strange souls pass away just as the most commonplace do: knowledge-seeking later generations collect from various documents the individual, stammered sounds which are supposed to depict them for us; but we obtain no intelligible picture and never learn to understand them fully. Even those who saw them with their own eyes, however, were not able to understand them fully; indeed, they scarcely understood themselves. We can only contemplate them, as in the end everything in the world, merely with e m p t y a d m i r a t i o n. ——

These thoughts were stirred up within me when I hit upon the wonderful P i e r o d i C o s i m o in the histories of the old artists. Nature had filled his soul with a continuously seething fantasy and had covered his mind with heavy and dark storm clouds, so that his spirit was constantly in restless toil and moved about amidst extravagant pictures, without ever being reflected in simple and serene beauty. Everything about him was extraordinary and unusual; the writers of the past do not know how to heap up enough powerful words to give us a conception of the intemperance and the atrocity in his entire being. And yet, we find only a few, individual, in part seemingly irrelevant traits noted down in their writings, which do not acquaint us at all thoroughly with the abyss of his soul, nor do they blend into a complete, harmonious picture. But we can, nevertheless, approximately surmise from them that which lies deeper.

In his youth Piero di Cosimo already bore within himself an alert, constantly active mind and an overstocked imagination, by means of which he excelled over his classmates early. His soul was never content to rest quietly upon o n e thought or o n e picture; a host of unusual, strange ideas constantly passed through his brain and carried him away from the present. Sometimes, when he was sitting at his work and was thereby at the same time relating or explaining something, his fantasy, always romping about for itself alone, had unobservedly carried him off to such distant heights that he suddenly stopped short; the relationship of the things present became entangled before his eyes; and he then had to commence his discourse from the beginning again. Human society was loathsome to him; he enjoyed himself best of all in a gloomy solitude, in which, withdrawn into himself, he followed his roaming fancies wherever they led him. He was always alone in a locked room and had a very peculiar pattern of living. He always nourished himself with the same monotonous food, which he prepared for himself at any time of day when he was so inclined. He did not tolerate having his room cleaned; in addition, he opposed the pruning of the fruit trees and vines in his garden; for he wanted to see wild, rough and unkempt Nature everywhere and found pleasure in that which is offensive to other dispositions. Thus, he also had a mysterious inclination to linger a long while with all monsters in physical Nature, with all misshapen animals and plants; he gazed at them with fixed attentiveness in order to enjoy their ugliness to the fullest; afterwards he continually recaptured their images in his thoughts and, however repulsive this was to him as well in the end, he was not able to banish them from his head. Little by little, he had with the strictest diligence sketched together an entire book of such misshapen things. He also frequently fixed his eyes rigidly on old, patched, many-colored walls or on the clouds in the sky and, from all such workings of Nature, his imagination seized various fantastic ideas about wild battles with horses or about huge mountain landscapes with strange villages. —— He felt great joy in a very violent market-square rainfall, which plunged down with a rustling from the roofs onto the pavement; —— on the other hand, he feared thunder like a child and, whenever a thunderstorm raged in the skies, he wrapped himself up tightly in his coat, locked the windows, and crept into a corner of the house until it was over. The screaming of little children, the ringing of bells, and the singing of the monks made him half crazy. —— In his conversation he was colorful and unusual; indeed, he occasionally said such splendidly amusing things that those who heard them were not able to restrain their laughter. In short, he was so constituted that the people of his age passed him off as a highly confused and almost insane mentality.

His spirit, which boiled unceasingly like water simmering in the kettle and drove up froth and bubbles, had a very excellent opportunity to reveal itself with all sorts of new and strange inventions at the masquerades and wanton processions which were held in Florence at carnival-time, so that, through him, this festivity actually became for the first time that which it had never been before. However, amidst all the unusual and greatly admired solemn processions which he arranged, one distinguished itself so particularly and so uniquely that we want to set down a brief story about it. The arrangements for it were made in secret and, therefore, all of Florence was surprised and shocked by it in the extreme.

On the very night, namely, during which the populace rejoicingly thronged the streets of the city, abandoned to the most unrestrained gaiety, —— the crowd suddenly scattered out of fright and looked around in alarm and astonishment. In the early morning light a black, terrifying wagon approached ponderously and slowly, drawn by four black buffalo and marked with the bones of the dead and with white crosses, —— and on the wagon there strutted an immensely huge victor-figure of d e a t h, armed with the dreadful scythe, at whose feet were sitting on the wagon nothing but coffins. However, the slow procession stopped: —— and, accompanied by the muffled rumbling of strange horns, the anxious, horrible sound of which cut through to the marrow, —— and by the bewitching light of distant torches, —— there rose forth, —— whereby all of the people were gripped by a silent horror, —— slowly out of the opening coffins white skeletons with half a body. They sat down on the coffins and filled the air with ominous, hollow singing which, intermingled with the sounds of the horns, caused the blood to curdle in the people's veins. They sang therein about the horrors of death and that all who were now looking at each other alive would also soon be such skeletons as they. A large, disorderly crowd of dead people pressed in all around and behind the wagon with masks resembling skulls on their heads, draped in black marked with white bones and white crosses and sitting on lean horses, —— and each one had a retinue of four other black riders with torches and a huge black flag marked with skulls and bones and white crosses; —— in addition, ten large black flags trailed down from the wagon; —— and, during the slowly creeping procession, the entire army of the dead chanted a psalm of David with hollowly trembling voices. ——

It is very remarkable that this unanticipated procession of the dead, despite the terror that it spread at the beginning, was nevertheless regarded by all of Florence with the greatest pleasure. Painful and unpleasant sensations reach into the soul with force, cling to it firmly, and c o m p e l it, as it were, to participation and to enjoyment; and if they also assail and excite the fantasy with a certain p o e t i c v e r v e, then they can keep one's emotions in sublime and inspired tension. Moreover, I should also like to say that a marvelous secret power seems to be implanted by heaven in such excellent souls as this Piero di Cosimo, enabling them to capture the minds even of the common masses by means of the strange and extraordinary things that they do. ——

Although Piero was unceasingly provoked, driven about, and fatigued by his restless, ominous fantasy, nevertheless, heaven had apportioned to him a long life; indeed, as he approached his eightieth year, his mind was pursued by wilder and wilder visions. Despite the great physical weakness and all the wretchedness of old age, he always drudged for himself alone and violently refused all social contact and sympathetic help. At that time he still wanted to work and, yet, could not because his hands were crippled and trembled continuously; then he fell into the most extreme ill-nature and wanted to do violence to his hands; but while he muttered to himself in anger, the spatula or even the paintbrush fell from him onto the ground again, which was a lamentable sight to behold. He could quarrel with his shadow and go into a rage over a fly. That he was close to his end, he still did not want to believe. He talked a great deal about what a misfortune it is when a slow disease consumes the body, little by little, with a thousand agonies, so that one drop of blood after the other dies away. He called down curses upon doctors, apothecaries, and orderlies and described how terrible it is when one is not permitted food, nor sleep; when one has to draw up his will; when one sees the relatives weeping around the bed. On the other hand, he considered that person fortunate who departs from the world with o n e blow at the execution block; and thought how beautiful it would be to ascend to the angels in paradise in the presence of so many people and amidst the consolations and prayers of the priest and the solicitude of thousands. He raved on with such thoughts unceasingly: —— until finally, one morning, he was found totally unexpectedly, lying dead at the bottom of the staircase in his house. ——

These are the peculiar traits in the personality of this artist, which I have conscientiously repeated from G i o r g i o V a s a r i. With regard to him as an artist, the same author informs us that he liked best of all to paint wild bacchanalia and orgies, frightful monsters, and other such dreadful images; nevertheless, he praises him on account of the highly industrious and self-willed diligence in his pictures. Just as the same Vasari makes the comment in the biography of another similarly moody painter that such serious and melancholic souls often tended to distinguish themselves by exceptional, indefatigable patience and assiduity in their work.

Let him think what he wishes, nevertheless, I cannot believe that this P i e r o d i C o s i m o was truly a genuine artist. To be sure, I find a certain resemblance between him and the great L e o n a r d o d a V i n c i (whom the former also took as his model in the art of painting), for both were driven about by a continuously lively mind with many inclinations, —— the former, however, into dark, cloudy regions of the sky, ——

the latter into the midst of all substantial Nature and the whole swarming multitude of earth.

In my opinion, the artistic spirit should only be a useful instrument to receive all of Nature within oneself and give birth to it again, beautifully transformed, animated with the spirit of man. If, however, out of inner instinct and excess wild and exuberant energy, the artistic spirit is constantly on its own in restless activity, then it is not always an adept instrument, —— rather, one would like to call it itself a sort of art work of Creation.

Heaven is not reflected in the raging and foaming sea; —— it is the serene river in which trees and cliffs and the drifting clouds and all the stars of the firmament behold themselves with satisfaction. ——

How and in what Manner
one actually must regard
and use
the
WORKS OF THE GREAT
ARTISTS OF
EARTH
for the Well-Being of his Soul

I continually hear the childish and frivolous world complain that God has placed only s o   f e w   truly great artists on the earth; the ordinary soul impatiently stares into the future, wondering whether the Father of Mankind will not soon let a new race of outstanding masters rise up. But I say to you, the earth has not borne too few excellent masters; indeed, some of these are so constituted that a mortal being has in one alone ample to gaze upon and contemplate throughout his entire lifetime; but indeed, far, far too few are the ones who are capable of understanding deeply and (what is essentially the same) venerating earnestly the works of these beings (fashioned from more noble clay).

Art galleries are regarded as annual fairs, where one evaluates, praises, and disdains new products in passing by; and they ought to be temples where, in peaceful and silent humility and in heart-lifting solitude, one might admire the great artists as the most lofty among mortals and, with long, uninterrupted contemplation of their works, might warm oneself in the sunshine of the most charming thoughts and sensations.

I compare the enjoyment of the more noble works of art to p r a y e r. That one is not pleasing unto heaven who speaks thereto only in order to be rid of the daily obligation, enumerates words without thoughts, and boastfully gauges his piety according to the beads of his rosary. That one is, however, a favorite of heaven who waits with humble longing for the chosen hours when the gentle, heavenly beam comes down to him voluntarily, splits open the shell of earthly insignificance with which the mortal spirit is generally covered, and releases and displays his more noble inner self; then he kneels down, turns his open heart toward the brilliance of heaven in silent rapture, and saturates it with the ethereal light; thereupon he stands up, happier and more melancholy, with a fuller and lighter heart, and applies his hand to a large, good enterprise. —— I hold this to be the true meaning of prayer.

One would, in my opinion, have to act in just this way with the masterpieces of art in order to use them worthily for the salvation of his soul. It is to be called sacrilegious, when someone reels away from the ringing laughter of his friends in an earthly hour in order, out of habit, to communicate with God for a few minutes in a nearby church. In such an hour it is a similar sacrilege to cross the threshold of the house where the most admirable creations which could be brought forth by the hands of m e n are preserved for eternity, as a quiet declaration of the dignity of this species. Wait, as with prayer, for the blessed hours when the grace of heaven illuminates your soul with higher revelation; only then will your soul be united with the works of the artists in one entity. Their enchanting figures are mute and uncommunicative when you look upon them coldly; your hearts must f i r s t address them intensely, if they are to be able to speak to you and exercise all their power upon you.

Works of art fit into the ordinary flow of life just as little in their own way as does the thought of God; they transcend the ordinary and the usual and we must lift ourselves up to them wholeheartedly in order to make them in our eyes, which are all too often clouded over by the fog of the atmosphere, what in their exalted nature they are.

Everyone can learn how to read alphabetical letters; everyone can let himself be told by learned histories the stories of past ages and retell them; everyone can also study the system of a scientific discipline and comprehend theorems and truths; —— for letters are only there so that the eye might recognize their form; and principles and facts are only an object of our concern as long as the eye of the mind works upon them, to grasp and understand them; as soon as they are our own, the activity of our mind is at an end and we then merely indulge, as often as it pleases us, in a lazy and unfruitful survey of our treasures. —— Not so with the works of magnificent artists. They are not there for that reason, so that the eye might see them, but so that one might penetrate into them with a receptive heart and live and breathe in them. A precious painting is not a paragraph of a textbook which, when with a brief effort I have extracted the meaning of the words, I then set aside as a useless shell: rather, in superior works of art the enjoyment continues on and on without ceasing. We believe that we are penetrating deeper and deeper into them and, nevertheless, they continuously arouse our sense anew and we foresee no boundary at which our soul would have exhausted them. There is aflame within them an eternally burning oil of life, which is never extinguished before our eyes.

With impatience I fly beyond the first viewing; for the surprise of newness, which many souls who snatch at constantly changing pleasures wish to expound as the principal merit of art, has always seemed to me a necessary evil of the first viewing. True enjoyment requires a silent and peaceful frame of mind and is not expressed by outcries and the clapping of hands, but solely by inner emotions. It is a sacred holiday for me, when I devote myself to the contemplation of precious art works with seriousness and with a prepared heart; I return to them frequently and endlessly; they remain firmly impressed upon my mind and, as long as I shall walk the earth, I shall carry them about with me in my imagination, as spiritual amulets, as it were, for the consolation and the inspiration of my soul and shall take them with me into the grave.

He whose finer nerves are once active and receptive to the secret charm which lies hidden in art is often deeply moved in his soul where another passes by indifferently; he shares in the good fortune of finding in his life more frequent occasions for a salutary agitation and excitement of his inner self. I am aware that frequently when (occupied with other thoughts) I passed through some beautiful and grand, pillared portal, the mighty, majestic columns with their lovely stateliness attracted my gaze involuntarily to themselves and filled my spirit with a special sensation, so that I bowed down inwardly before them and passed on with opened heart and with richer soul.

The most important factor is that one not venture to soar with rash courage beyond the spirit of exalted artists and, looking down upon them, judge them: a foolish attempt of the vain pride of men: A r t   i s   a b o v e the human being: we can only admire and esteem the magnificent works of its consecrated ones and open our entire soul before them for the liberating and cleansing of all our emotions.

The Greatness
of
MICHEL' ANGELO
BUONAROTTI

Doubtless every human being who bears a feeling and loving heart within his breast has some particular favorite object in the realm of art; and so I, too, have mine, toward which my mind often turns spontaneously, like the sunflower to the sun. For frequently, when I am sitting there contemplatively in my solitude, then it is as if a good angel were standing behind me, who fortuitously lets the centuries of old painters of Italy rise up before my eyes, like an immense, fertile epic poem with a crowded throng of lively figures. This magnificent vision always presents itself to me anew and my blood is always warmed anew thereby most fervently. It is, indeed, a precious gift which heaven has bestowed upon us, that of loving and cherishing; this feeling alters our entire nature completely and brings the true gold out into the daylight.

This time my eye falls upon the great M i c h e l' A n g e l o B u o n a r o t t i, a man concerning whom so many a one has already expressed his helpless admiration or his impertinent disdain and criticism. I, however, cannot begin to speak of him with a more overflowing heart than his friend and fellow countryman G i o r g i o V a s a r i has done in the introduction to his biography, which reads literally as follows:

"While so many clever and excellent minds strove, according to the precepts of the renowned Giotto and his successors, to reveal to the world samples of the talent which was engendered in their inner selves by the beneficial influence of the stars and the fortunate complexion of their mental powers, and while all made great efforts to copy the magnificence of Nature by means of the excellence of art, in order to attain as far as possible the highest peak of knowledge, which one may well exclusively call 'Perception,' although all their striving was in vain; —— meanwhile, the benevolent Ruler of all things turned His eye condescendingly toward the earth and, in perceiving all the vain exertion of so infinitely many toilsome attempts, the unceasingly eager desire to learn without the slightest fruits, and the presumptuous opinions of human beings, as far away from the truth as darkness from the light; —— then He, in order to tear us away from such errors, resolved to send down to the earth a soul who, through his own capability, should become absolutely master of all art in every aspect. He should set up for the world a model of what perfection is in the art of sketching, of contours, and of highlights and shadows (which give the pictures their refinement); and how, as a sculptor, one must work with discernment and in what way one has to give buildings durability, comfort, lovely proportions, charm, and richness in all sorts of architectural embellishments. Beyond this, however, heaven wanted to give him true moral wisdom as a companion and the sweet art of the Muses as an adornment, in order that the world should admire him above all others and choose him as a mirror and model in life, in works, in sanctity of manners, indeed, in all earthly behavior, and in order that he might be regarded by us more as a heavenly than an earthly being. And because God observed that in those particular arts, namely, the arts of painting, sculpture, and architecture, as in matters requiring much diligence and practice, the natives of the Tuscan area have excelled above all others since time immemorial and have become masterly (for, above all the other Italian States, they are particularly inclined to exertion and intellectual effort of every type); —— therefore, He wanted to designate as his native home F l o r e n c e, as the most worthy city, so that the deserved crown of all virtues could be placed upon his head by a fellow-citizen." ——

Old Vasari speaks of the great Michel' Angelo with such veneration and, at the end, he condenses his general admiration into an affectionate, patriotic emotion in a beautiful and human way and rejoices deeply that this man, whom he honors like a Hercules amidst the heroes of art, had the same little area of earth as he for his homeland. He describes the life of Buonarotti most extensively and frequently acts very happily proud that he enjoyed his most intimate friendship.

However, we do not want to content ourselves merely with marveling about this great man but, instead, we want to penetrate into his inner spirit and press close to the unique character of his works. It is not sufficient to say in praise of a work of art: "It is b e a u t i f u l   and e x c e l l e n t," for these general phrases apply to the most varied works; —— we must be able to surrender ourselves to every great artist, look upon and comprehend the things of Nature with h i s senses, and speak in h i s   s o u l: "The work is c o r r e c t and t r u e in its way."

Painting is a poetry with pictures of human beings. Just as poets animate their objects with totally different emotions, in accordance with the different moods inspired within them by the Creator; so also in painting. Some poets animate all of their works inwardly with a silent and secret poetic soul; with others, however, the overflowing exuberant poetic force breaks through in every phase of the creation.

I find this same dissimilarity between the divine Raphael and the great

Buonarotti: I should like to call the former the artist of the New Testament, the latter of the Old; for the silent, divine spirit of Christ, —— I dare to express the bold thought, —— rests upon the former, —— upon the latter the spirit of the inspired prophets, of Moses and the other poets of the East. There is nothing to p r a i s e and to c r i t i c i z e here; rather, each one is what he is.

Just as the inspired Oriental poets were driven to extraordinary fantasies by the forcefully stirring, internal divine power and out of an inner compulsion forced, so to speak, the words and expressions of the earthly language into lofty regions by means of nothing but fiery images; so, too, the extraordinary and the monstrous always gripped the soul of Michel' Angelo with might and expressed an excited, superhuman power in his figures. He liked to experiment with exalted, fruitful objects; he ventured the boldest and wildest positions and gestures in his pictures; he crowded muscles upon muscles and wanted to stamp into every nerve of his figures the sublime poetic power with which he was filled. He explored the interior gear mechanism of the human machine all the way to its most hidden operations; he spied out the most severe difficulties in the mechanics of the human body in order to combat them and to give vent to and satisfy the sumptuous fullness of his intellectual capacities in the physical parts of art as well: —— just as poets in whom an inextinguishable lyrical fire is burning are not content with great and mighty i d e a s, but also strive particularly to imprint their bold and wild strength in the visible, sensual instrument of their art, in expression and words. The effect is grand and magnificent in both realms: the inner spirit of the totality shines forth then from each of the individual external parts. ——

Buonarotti, upon whom much judgment has been passed, appears to me thusly and whoever regards him in this way amidst the older painters may well ask with astonishment and admiration: Whoever painted before him as he does? Where did he acquire the totally new greatness which no eye before him ever knew? And who led him onto these previously unknown paths?

In the world of artists there is no loftier object, more worthy of reverence, than: —— a true Original! —— To work with diligent assiduity, faithful imitation, clever judgment —— is h u m a n; —— but to see through the entire substance of art with totally new eyes, to take hold of it, as it were, with a totally new grip —— is d i v i n e.

However, it is the fate of the Originals that they elicit a wretched troop of blind followers and Michel' Angelo prophesied this of himself, just as it came about once again. An Original suddenly vaults with one bold leap up to the boundary of the artistic realm, stands there daringly and firmly, and displays that which is extraordinary and marvelous. But, for the weak mind of the human being, there is almost nothing extraordinary and marvelous, the boundary of which does not lie very close to madness and bad taste. The pitiable followers, who lack the independent capacity for a firm position, wander about blindly and what they imitate is a distorted exaggeration, if it happens to be more than a weak copy.

The age of Michel' Angelo, the initial epoch of Italian painting, is really the only age of original artists. Who painted like Correggio prior to Correggio? like Raphael prior to Raphael? —— But it is as if all too generous Nature had impoverished herself of artistic genius with her gifts during this epoch; for the best subsequent masters up to the most recent times have almost all had no other goal than to imitate one or another of the first original and standard-setting artists or even several together. And they also have not become great with ease in any other way than by i m i t a t i n g e x c e l l e n t l y. Even the lofty and well-deserved fame which the Reformer School of Caracci earned is founded upon no other merit than that, through worthy examples, they elevated once again the art of imitating those venerable forefathers, which had fallen into decay. And whom did those forefathers themselves imitate? They created this entire new magnificence from within themselves.

———

L e t t e r
of a
Y O U N G   G E R M A N
P A I N T E R
i n   R o m e
to his friend in Nuremberg

———

D e a r   B r o t h e r   a n d   C o l l e a g u e,

I have not written to you, as I well know, for a long time, although I have thought of you frequently with deep affection; for there are hours in life when everything external progresses too slowly for one's winged thoughts, when the soul wears itself out with ideas and, precisely for this reason, nothing happens outwardly. I have just experienced such an epoch and, now that I am again somewhat at peace internally, I am immediately taking up the pen in order to report to you, the dearest friend of my youth, beloved Sebastian, how I have been and what has been happening with me.

Shall I write to you in detail about how the praised land of Italy is constituted and pour my heart out in disconnected eulogies? The words do not find their appropriate place, for how can I, so entirely ignorant of language, worthily depict for you the clear sky, the vast delightful views through which invigorating air blows playfully? Why, I scarcely know how to seek out colors and lines in my own particular craft, in order to sketch down on the canvas what I see and comprehend inwardly.

But, however different everything may be here as far as sky and earth are concerned, nevertheless, it can still be more readily imagined and believed than that which I have to tell you about art. You may be diligently painting together there in Germany, dear Sebastian, you and our dearest teacher, Albrecht Dürer; but if you were suddenly transported to this place, you would truly be like two deceased ones who do not yet know their way around in heaven. In my thoughts I see the artistic Master Albrecht, sitting on his stool, carving upon a fine little piece of wood with childlike, almost touching industry, as he considers thoroughly the idea and the execution and observes the initiated art object repeatedly; I see his large, tiled room and the round windowpanes and you in front of a copy with untiring, faithful diligence and how the younger pupils go to and fro and the old Master Dürer lets drop many a clever and many an amusing word; then I see our landlady[14] enter, or the well-spoken Wilibald Pirkheimer, who looks at the paintings and sketches and begins a lively dispute with Albrecht; —— and when I picture all this to myself in my thoughts, then I really cannot rightly understand how I happen to have come here and why everything here is so different.

Do you still remember the time when we were first apprenticed to our Master and we could not understand at all that a face or a tree should emerge from the colors which we were grinding? With what surprise we then observed Master Albrecht, who always knew how to apply everything so well and never became embarrassed over the execution of his most magnificent works! I was often as if in a dream when I left the artist's workroom in order to buy wine or bread for him, and in many hours, when all the other inartistic people, artisans or peasants, went past me, then I even thought that he must indeed be a magician, since at his beckoning inanimate things put themselves into the right place and became, as it were, alive.

But what would I have said or felt, if one had at that time held before my childish eyes the radiant countenances of Raphael? Ah, dear Sebastian, if I had understood them, then I certainly would have fallen to my knees and dissolved my entire young soul in devotion, tears, and admiration; for one still finds the earthly element in our great Dürer; one understands how an artistic and well-practiced man was able to hit upon these faces and devices; —— if we actually bore into the painting with our eyes, then we can almost drive the painted figures away again and discover the empty, plain board underneath: —— but with this master, my cherished one, everything is so marvelously arranged that you totally forget that there are paints and an art of painting and only submit yourself inwardly to the heavenly, and yet so sincerely human forms with the warmest love and dedicate your heart and your soul to them. —— Do not think that I am exaggerating out of youthful zeal; you cannot conceive of and comprehend it, if you do not come yourself and see.

On the whole, dear Sebastian, this earth is a very splendid and lovely abode because of art; just now I have felt for the first time how an invisible being dwells in our hearts, a being which is mightily attracted by the great works of art. —— And if I am to admit everything to you, my dear friend of my youth (as I must, for I feel myself forcefully drawn to it), I now love a girl who means more to my heart than everything else, and I am loved by her in return. My senses reel about in an eternal brilliance of springtime and, in many an hour of delight, I would like to say that the world and the sun of heaven were borrowing their radiance from me, if it were not too impudent to want to express one's joy in this manner. For a long time now I have been fervently seeking out her features in the best paintings and have always found them in my favorite masters. I am engaged to her, and in a few days we shall celebrate our wedding; you can see, therefore, that I do not desire to return to our Germany, however I hope to embrace you soon here in Rome.

I cannot describe to you how Maria's heart was constantly anxious about the welfare of my soul, when she heard that I, too, was devoted to the new doctrine. She often implored me fervently to return to the old, true faith and her loving speeches frequently threw my entire fantasy and all that I held to be my convictions into confusion. —— Mention nothing of this which I shall now write to you to our deeply beloved Master Dürer; for I know that it would only grieve his heart and it could profit neither himself nor myself further.

I went into the rotunda recently, because there was a huge festival and splendid Latin music was to be played or, actually in the beginning, only in order to see my loved one again there amidst the worshiping crowd and to improve myself upon her heavenly devotion. The magnificent temple, the teeming crowd of people which pressed in little by little and surrounded me more and more tightly, the splendid preparations, all this disposed my spirit to wonderful attentiveness. I felt very solemn and, even if I was not thinking anything clearly and vividly, as tends to be the case for one in such a tumult, nevertheless, there was a fomenting of such a strange kind within me, as if something extraordinary also were about to occur in me myself. Suddenly everything became quieter and, above us, the mighty music commenced in slow, full, extended strains, as if an invisible wind were blowing over our heads: like an ocean it rolled along in larger and larger waves and the sounds drew my soul completely out of its body. My heart was pounding and I felt a powerful longing for something great and exalted which I could embrace. The sonorous Latin singing which penetrated through the swelling sounds of the music, rising and falling just like ships which sail through the waves of the sea, lifted my soul higher and higher. And, since the music had penetrated my whole being in this manner and was flowing through all my veins, —— then I lifted my eyes, which had been turned inward, and looked around myself, —— and the entire temple came alive before my eyes, so delirious the music had made me. At that moment it stopped; a priest stepped up to the altar, lifted the Host with an enraptured gesture, and showed it to all the people, —— and all the people fell to their knees and trumpets and I myself know not what sort of all-powerful sounds roared and boomed an exalted devotion through everyone's frame. Everything right around me sank down and a mysterious, wonderful force also drew me irresistibly to the ground and I could not have held myself erect with all my strength. And as I now knelt with bowed head and my heart pounded in my breast, then an unknown force lifted my eyes again; I looked around and it most clearly seemed to me as if all the Catholics, men and women, who were down upon their knees and, with their eyes now directed within themselves, now towards heaven, were crossing themselves fervently and tapping their breasts and moving their praying lips, as if all were praying to the Father in heaven for the salvation of my soul, as if all the hundreds around me were pleading for the lost one in their midst and, in their quiet devotion, were drawing me over to their faith with irresistible force. Then I looked over to the side at Maria; her glance met mine, and I saw a big, holy tear press out of her blue eye. I did not know how I felt; I could not bear her gaze; I turned my head to the side, my eyes hit upon an altar, and a painting of Christ on the Cross looked at me with inexpressible sympathy, —— and the mighty pillars of the temple arose before my eyes, worthy of adoration like apostles and saints, and looked down upon me with their capitals, full of majesty, —— and the endless arch of the cupola curved down over me like all-embracing heaven and blessed my pious decisions.

I could not leave the temple after the ceremony was concluded; I threw myself down in a corner and wept and then walked along with contrite heart past all of the saints, past all of the paintings, and it seemed to me as if I were now permitted for the first time truly to observe and venerate them.

I could not resist the force within me: —— I have now, dear Sebastian, gone over to that faith and my heart feels gay and carefree. Art drew me over almightily and I may truly say that I now for the first time rightly understand and inwardly comprehend art. If you can name that which has transformed me so, which has spoken to my soul as if with angelic voices, then give it a name and enlighten me concerning myself; I am merely following my inner spirit, my blood, every drop of which now seems to me more purified.

Ah! did I not in the past already believe the holy legends and the miraculous works, which seem to us incomprehensible? Can you truly understand a sublime picture and regard it with holy devotion without at that moment b e l i e v i n g the presentation? And what more is it, then, if this poetry of divine art produces its effect longer with me?

Your heart certainly will not turn away from mine, that is not possible, Sebastian, and therefore let us then pray to the same God that He enlighten our spirits more and more in the future and pour true piety down upon us: is it not true, friend of my youth, the rest should not and cannot separate us?

Fare very well and greet our Master affectionately. Even if you do not share my opinion, this letter will, nevertheless, certainly please you, for you will learn that I am happy.

THE PORTRAITS OF THE ARTISTS

T h e   M u s e   enters the picture gallery
with a y o u n g A r t i s t

T h e   M u s e

Wander here in silent, joyous earnest,
With the great masters in friendly contact,
Who do fill your bosom full of love:
Repose here, after their precious works,
In the contemplation of their heads.

T h e   Y o u t h

How I feel myself attracted!
How my heart beats
Toward those sweet, comforting glances!

Alas! how you humble me,
That you all look toward me,
So seriously, as toward a central point.
How related I feel to you,
And how estranged!
Boldly I'd now like to grasp the brush,
And sketch magnificent, huge figures
With a firm hand, with daring colors: ——
And, yet, I scarcely dare
To look the great forefathers here in the eye.
I am held firmly as if amidst ghosts, ——
And wondrous lights are falling
From all the pictures here
Into my awakening, expectant senses. ——
What was this old man's name,
Who, with friendly eyes heavy with thought,
Rests in his own greatness?

The Muse

These precious, long, silver locks,
Which fall so gracefully into the beard,
Formerly adorned the old, wise painter
From Tuscany, my   L e o n a r d o,
Who is the founder of the famed school there.

The Youth

Praised be the hand which has with zealous effort
Preserved this precious head for us.
It is he! I see him, how he meditates,
And looks with friendliness at great, vast Nature,
And how he restlessly strives again
For a new perception. ——
But who is this man,
Almost the same as he in appearance and bearing,
Yet grave and more deeply withdrawn into himself?

136

The Muse

A l b r e c h t   D ü r e r, who devoted himself to me,
Pressed in upon me, praying solemnly,
When no one in the distant, barren North
Esteemed me and my art: pious and
Simple was his way of life, like children.
And all his pictures are like he himself.

The Youth

Yes, I recognize the quiet zeal,
The holy humility of the highly praised one,
The inner effort of the active mind. ——
But tell me the name of this one,
Before whose wild gaze I shudder
Secretly within, when my eye meets it!

The Muse

This one is the pride of the fatherland,
Loveliest gem of Tuscany, —— Wonder
Of later generations: behold the power of the great
M i c h e l' A n g e l o B u o n a r o t t i.

The Youth

Ha! the mighty one, strong as a lion!
Who played with sublimities, with horror. ——
But desire urges me further and further, ——
Restlessly I cast my eye about,
And never find what I am seeking.
No forehead is noble and so inspired,
No eye earnest enough and deeply inquiring: ——
To the side and alone, with a long beard,
With a wondrous halo around gray locks,
Hangs, perhaps, the divine R a p h a e l.

The Muse

This youth here was R a p h a e l.

The Youth

This youth? —— Incomprehensible, God!
Are Thy ways,
Incomprehensible the deep wonders of art!
These gay, ingenuous eyes
Looked upon self-created pictures of Christ,
Madonnas, saints, and apostles,
And old wise men and wild battles! ——
Alas! he does not seem older than I myself.
He seems to be thinking of little, happy games,
And the thinking also seems to him a game.
How close I feel to him, ah! how very intimate!
How no severity, no lofty pride of age
Holds me, poor one, away, —— how I should like to
Sink down upon his breast in tears and dissolve in joy!
Ah! he would willingly take me into his arms,
And seek to comfort me in a friendly way
About my admiration, about my bliss. ——
No, I shall let the tears flow; ——
In the most beautiful form divine art
Has revealed itself to mortal men in you. ——

THE CHRONICLE OF ARTISTS[15]

When, in my youth, I moved about here and there with restless spirit and looked up eagerly everywhere, where something was to be seen of art objects, I suddenly found myself in an unfamiliar castle belonging to a count, where for three entire days I could not take my eyes off the many paintings. I wanted to learn them all by heart and excited my blood so greatly thereby that the thousands of varied pictures confused my mind totally. On the third day an old man arrived at the castle, a travelling Italian priest whose name I have not discovered up to this very hour; I also have never heard from him again since that day. He was a highly learned man and had so many things in his head that I was amazed; in external appearance he resembled a philosopher from the sixteenth century. Although I was then still so young, he entered into conversation with me in a most friendly way (for he must have found something in me that pleased him) and walked about with me the whole day in the picture galleries.

Since he perceived my great zeal in contemplation of the paintings, he asked me: Whether I also knew how to name the masters who had done this or that piece? I answered that I did, indeed, know the most famous ones. Thereupon he asked me again: Whether I did not know more about them than the names? When he noticed that I really did not know much more, he began to speak and said to me:

"Up until now, my dear son, you have gazed at the beautiful pictures as if they were miraculous works which had fallen down to earth from heaven. However, consider that all this is the product of human hands, —— that many artists had brought very excellent things into existence at your age. What do you think now? Should you not feel a desire to learn something more about the men who have distinguished themselves in the art of painting? Wonderful thoughts are inspired within us when we observe how their works shine in ever the same eternal magnificence; but the creators of these works, in life and death, were human beings just as we others, except that there burned within them a special heavenly fire, as long as they were living. Considerations of this sort put us into a melancholy and musing mood, in which all sorts of good ideas always tend to pass through our minds."

I still remember the words of this dear, loquacious, old man very precisely and with the most sincere pleasure; for this reason I want to attempt to put down even more of them.

When he saw that I was listening quietly and eagerly, he continued approximately as follows:

"I have observed with joy, my son, that your heart is very much attracted to the admirable R a p h a e l. If you are now standing there in front of a truly magnificent picture by his hands, observing each of his brush-strokes with reverence, and thinking: If I had only seen the holy man in his lifetime, how I would have wanted to worship him! —— and if you were then to hear the old biographers of the artists tell about him in the following manner: —— This Raphael Sanzio was the only child of his parents; the father loved him deeply and desired explicitly that the mother raise him only with her own milk, so that he would not take a place amidst the common people; and while he was growing up, as a tender youth, he helped his father with the work and the father was happy that he did his tasks so well; however, in order to have him learn something suitable, he made an agreement with Master Pietro of Perugia that he take him as an apprentice. With great delight he himself took him to Perugia, where Pietro received him in a most friendly manner; but the mother had wept many tears at the departure and was scarcely able to tear herself away from the child, for she also loved him deeply: —— —— tell me, how will you feel if you hear this? Do you not feel pleased and happy when you learn these things? —— —— And this was the very same person, who, after a brief thirty-seven years, lay cold and pale in the coffin, mourned by all the world. —— The corpse lay in his workroom and an exquisite funeral poem, the divine painting of the Transfiguration, was on the easel next to the coffin. —— This painting, in which we still today see the misery of earth, the solace of noble men, and the glory of the kingdom of heaven portrayed in such magnificent union, —— and the master by whom it was conceived and carried out cold and pale beside it." ——

These things excited me extraordinarily and I asked the strange man to tell me still more about Raphael.

"The nicest thing that I can tell you about him," he answered, "is that as a human being he was just as noble and charming as he was as an artist. He had nothing of the morose and proud nature of other artists, who sometimes intentionally assume all sorts of peculiarities; his entire living and moving on earth was simple, gentle, and serene, like a flowing stream. His willingness to oblige extended so far that when unfamiliar and entirely unrenowned painters implored him for drawings from his hand, he laid aside his own work and satisfied them first. In this way he assisted a great many and advised them like a father, very lovingly. His excellence in art caused a crowd of painters to gather around him who were eager to be his pupils, although they themselves had, in part, already outgrown the years of apprenticeship. Whenever he went to the court, they accompanied him from his house and comprised a large retinue. So many painters of different temperaments certainly could not have lived with each other without disagreement and dissension, however, if the spirit of their great Master had not shone upon them in an enchanting way like a sun of peace and erased all the stains from their souls. In this way they were conquered by his spirit as well as by his paintbrush. —— In the life of Raphael there is also a beautiful, miraculous story, which is this one. He painted an excellent Christ bearing the Cross, with many figures, which was intended for a monastery in Palermo. But the ship in which the picture was to be brought there suffered a violent gale and shipwreck; men and goods were destroyed; —— only this painting, —— it was a special dispensation of Providence, —— this painting was carried by kind waves all the way to the port of Genoa, where it was taken from its crate completely undamaged. Thus, even the raging elements showed the holy man their reverence. Thereupon, the picture was brought to Palermo and there, as the old Vasari expresses himself, it is regarded as just as great a treasure of the island of Sicily as Mount Aetna."

I rejoiced in the magnificent stories more and more deeply, pressed the priest's hands, and asked very eagerly: But where hast Thou learned all these things?

"Understand, my son," he answered, "several deserving men have kept chronicles of the history of art and have described the lives of the artists extensively, the oldest and, simultaneously, the most eminent of whom is named G i o r g i o   V a s a r i. Few people read these books nowadays, although a great deal of wit and human wisdom lies hidden within them. Consider how lovely it is to become acquainted with those men, whom you know according to their various ways of guiding the paintbrush, now according to their various characters and manners as well. Both will then flow together for you into   o n e   conception: and when you comprehend the stories, told in very dull words, with the proper inner feeling, then a magnificent vision, namely   t h e   c h a r a c t e r   o f   t h e   a r t i s t, will rise up before you, which, as it displays itself so multifariously in the thousands of different individual people, will afford you an entirely new, delightful drama. Each character will be a separate painting for you and you will have collected about you a magnificent gallery of portraits for the reflection of your spirit."

At that time I did not yet understand this very well, although subsequently, since I have read the books mentioned, it has become completely my own view. —— In the meantime, I entreated the good old priest most urgently to tell me even more lovely stories from the chronicles of artists. "'I shall think it over," he said with smiling lips; "I like to talk about the old stories of artists." And then he, indeed, told me a great number of the loveliest stories; for he had read all of the books which have ever been written about art frequently and knew the best parts of them from memory. His narratives impressed me so deeply that I have retained them up to the present time almost with his very words, and I wish to re-tell a part of them for pleasure.

When, in the art gallery where we were, we came upon a painting by the excellent   D o m e n i c h i n o,   he said to me that this artist furnished a remarkable example of passionate zeal in art and, in order to demonstrate this, he continued as follows:

"Before this master began a painting, he thought about it for a long time beforehand and sometimes remained alone in his room for days, until the picture was completed in all its most minute parts within his soul. Then he was pleased and said: Now half of the work is done. And once he had reached for the paintbrush, then he again remained the entire day affixed to the easel and was scarcely willing to interrupt his work a few minutes for a meal. He painted with the greatest industry and perfection and put in deep expressiveness everywhere. When one sought to persuade him at one time not to torment himself in this way, but to assume the easier style of other artists, he answered very abruptly: I work merely for myself and the perfection of art. He could not understand how other artists could execute the greatest and most significant things with so little involvement that they were able to chatter with their friends constantly during the painting. For this reason he also considered these to be mere craftsmen who were not acquainted with the inner sanctuary of art. Whenever he painted, he himself was always immersed in his object with such an active soul that he felt within himself the emotions and dispositions which he wanted to portray and involuntarily behaved accordingly. Sometimes, when he had a mourning figure in mind, he was heard lamenting in his workroom with a stifled, moaning voice; or when it was supposed to be a joyful face, then he was lively and talked to himself cheerfully. Therefore he painted in a remote chamber and did not admit anyone, not even any of his pupils, in order not to be disturbed in his raptures and laughed at as eccentric. In his younger years he was, at one time, in such an hour of rapture when a very touching drama took place. The admirable Annibale Carracci came to visit him just then: but as he opened the door, he saw him standing in front of the easel, totally provoked, full of rage and anger, and with a threatening demeanor. He quietly remained at the door and perceived that his friend was occupied with the picture of the martyrdom of Saint Andrew and was just then painting a defiant mercenary, who is threatening the apostle. With deep joy and admiration he gazed at him for a long while and did not move; —— but, at last, he could not restrain himself any longer: —— 'I thank you!' he called out, rushed up to him, and embraced him with pounding heart." ——

This A n n i b a l e C a r r a c c i was himself a very magnificent, powerful man who felt the s i l e n t g r e a t n e s s of art very deeply and regarded it as better to produce magnificent works himself than to dally about near splendid works of art with pretty, superficial words. In contrast, his brother A g o s t i n o was, in addition to his art, a cultivated man of the world, a writer and composer of sonnets, who liked to talk at length about artistic matters. When the two of them had returned from Rome and were sitting and working again in their academy in Bologna, this Agostino began at one time to describe the remarkable antique group of Laocoon in the greatest detail and to emphasize all of the separate beauties with very pretty speeches. Since his brother Annibale was standing there next to him, quite unmoved and lost in a dream, as if he were not comprehending, the former became indignant and asked whether he then felt nothing of this? Inwardly this irritated Annibale; he silently took a piece of charcoal, went up to the wall, and quickly sketched the outlines of the entire Laocoon group from memory so accurately and correctly that one believed he was seeing it before his own eyes. Then he smilingly stepped back from the wall, —— but all those present were amazed and Agostino acknowledged his defeat and recognized him as the victor in the competition." ——

When the strange man had told these stories, I proceeded to speak with him about other matters and asked him, among other things, whether he did not also know stories about boys who had had a particular inclination toward the art of painting from their early youth?

"O, yes," the strange man said smilingly, "we are told about numerous boys who were born and raised in very poor conditions and, as it were, called by heaven out of there to the art of painting. Several examples of this occur to me. One of the very earliest painters of Italy, G i o t t o, was in his youth nothing more than a shepherd boy, who watched over the sheep.[16] He amused himself by sketching his sheep on rocks or in the sand; Cimabue, the fore-father of all artists, once came upon him by surprise while he was doing this and took him along with him, whereupon the boy soon surpassed his teacher. If I am not mistaken, very similar stories are told us about D o m i n i c o B e c c a f u m i and about the adept sculptor C o n d u c c i, who as a boy copied in clay the livestock that he had to tend. The well-known P o l i d o r o   d a   C a r a v a g g i o was also at the beginning nothing more than a lad who carried cement for the bricklayers at the Vat-ican; thereby, however, he zealously watched the pupils of Raphael who were working right there, developed an irresistible desire to paint, and learned very quickly and eagerly. ——Indeed, yet another charming example occurs to me, that of the old French painter, J a c o b   C a l l o t; as a youth he had heard a great deal about the magnificent things in Italy and, since he loved drawing above all else, he developed a mania to see the splendid land. As a boy of eleven years, he secretly ran away from his father without a farth-ing in his pocket and intended to go straight to Rome. He soon had to resort to begging and, when he met up with a troop of gypsies on his route, he at-tached himself to them and travelled with them as far as Florence, where he actually became apprenticed to a painter. Then he went to Rome; here, how-ever, he was seen by French merchants from his native town, who knew of the distress and anxiety of his parents concerning him and forcibly took him back with them. When his father had him again, he wanted to compel him to stick industriously to his academic studies; but all that was effort in vain. In his fourteenth year he ran away to Italy for the second time; but his unlucky star ordained that he should meet his older brother on the street in Turin, who dragged him back to their father once again. At last the father realized that no measure was helping and, of his own accord, gave him permission to go to Italy for the third time, where he then developed into a proficient artist. In all his youthful excursions he had always stayed out of danger and had retained all of his innocence of soul; for he must have stood under the special protection of heaven. Another striking feature about him is that, as a boy, he always prayed to God for two things; namely, that he might become what he wished, might distinguish himself above all others in his accomplishments; —— and then, that he would not become more than forty-three years old. And the miraculous thing is, he actually died in his forty-third year." ——

The old priest had told these stories with a great deal of enthusiasm. Then he walked up and down contemplatively and I observed that he was wandering about in pleasant daydreams, amidst the crowd of artists of the past. I willingly left him in his reflections and was pleased that he would recollect still more things, for the memories seemed to become more and more vivid to him. And after a little while he, indeed, began again as follows:

"I recall a few more lovely anecdotes which prove in two different ways what sort of mighty deity art is for the artist and with what force it governs him. —— There was once an old Florentine painter, M a r i o t t o A l b e r t i n e l l i by name, a zealous artist, but a very restless and sensuous human being. He was finally totally tired of the dubious and wearisome study of the mechanical aspects of art and the hateful animosities and persecutions of the fellow-artists and, since he liked to live well, he decided to take up a gayer occupation and established an inn. When the business was in full swing, he was heartily pleased and frequently said to his friends: 'See! This is a better trade! Now I no longer torment myself over the muscles of p a i n t e d people, but feed and strengthen l i v i n g ones and, what is best of all, I am protected from the detestable displaying of enmity and slandering as long as I have good wine in the keg.' —— But what happened? When he had led this life for awhile, the divine exaltation of art suddenly presented itself to his eyes again so vividly that he abruptly abandoned his inn and passionately threw himself into the arms of art again as a convert." ——

The other story is this. As a young man, the well-known and famous P a r m e g g i a n o painted very excellent things for the Pope in Rome and, to be sure, right at the time when the German emperor, Charles the Fifth, was besieging the city. His troops now broke open the gates and sacked all the houses, of the great as well as the humble. But Parmeggiano paid attention to nothing less than to the din of war and the uproar and remained quietly at work. Suddenly several soldiers break into the room, and behold! he still remains steadfastly and industriously at his easel. Thereupon these wild men, who had not even spared temples and altars, were so very amazed at the great spirit of the man that they dared not touch him, as if he were a saint, and they even protected him from the rage of others." ——

"How marvelous all this is," I cried; "but now I ask you for one thing more," I continued to the dear strange man, —— "Tell me whether what I once heard is true, that the earliest painters of Italy were such God-fearing men and always painted the holy legends with true piety? Several people whom I questioned about this ridiculed me and said that this was vain imagination and a politely invented fairy tale.'

"No, my son," the dear man replied, to my consolation. "That is not a poetic invention but, as I can prove to you from the old books, the honest truth. These venerable men, several of whom were themselves priests and friars, also dedicated the God-given skill of their hands solely to divine and sacred stories and brought to their works of art just such a serious and holy mind and such humble simplicity as is appropriate for consecrated objects. They made the art of painting into a faithful servant of religion and knew nothing about the empty display of colors of today's artists: in chapels and on altars their pictures inspired the holiest sentiments in the one who knelt down and prayed before them. One of the men of old, L i p p o D a l m a s i o, was renowned on account of his magnificent Madonnas, of which Pope Gregory the Thirteenth had a superior one with him in his chamber for private devotions. Another, F r a G i o v a n n i A n g e l i c o d a F i e s o l e, artist and Dominican monk in Florence, was especially famous because of his strict and pious life. He did not concern himself with the world at all, even declined the office of archbishop which the Pope offered to him, and always lived quietly, peacefully, humbly and in solitude. He used to pray every time, just before he began to paint; then he set to work and carried it out as heaven had presented it to him, without pondering over it and criticizing it further. For him, painting was a holy penance; and, sometimes, when he was painting the sufferings of Christ on the Cross, big tears were seen streaming down his face during the work. —— All this is not a beautiful fairy tale, but the genuine truth." ——

The priest concluded with a very strange story, which also falls into that early period of religious painting.

"In his old age, one of the earliest artists," he related, "who is known to us as S p i n e l l o, painted for the church St. Agnolo of Arezzo a very large altar piece, upon which he depicted Lucifer and the Fall of the Evil Angels: in the sky the angel Michael, as he fights with the seven-headed dragon and, down below, Lucifer in the shape of a hideous monster. His mind was so taken up by this horrible figure of the devil that, as is reported, the evil spirit appeared before him in a dream precisely in this shape and asked him frightfully: why he had presented him in this abominable, bestial form and at what place he had seen him in this deformity? The artist awoke from his dream trembling in all his limbs, —— he wanted to call for help and, out of fright, could not bring forth a sound. From that time on he was always

half out of his wits and had a vacant look; moreover, he died not long thereafter. But the wondrous painting is still to be seen today in its original
location." —— ——

Soon afterwards the strange priest went away and travelled onward, before I could even bid him farewell. I felt as if in a dream when I had heard
all the lovely stories: —— I had been introduced to a totally new, marvelous
world. I eagerly inquired everywhere in order to get all the books of life
stories of artists, particularly the work of Giorgio Vasari as well; I read them
with love and zeal and, behold! I found recorded in these books all the stories
which the strange priest had told. It was this man, for me unforgettable, who
directed me to the study of the h i s t o r y   o f   a r t i s t s,   which
provides so much nourishment for the intellect, the heart, and the fantasy,
and I therefore am indebted to him for a great many happy hours.

The strange musical Life
of the
M u s i c a l   A r t i s t
J O S E P H   B E R G L I N G E R
In two Parts

F i r s t   P a r t

Again and again I have turned my eyes to the past and gathered up the
treasures of the art history of past centuries for my own enjoyment; but now
my spirit urges me to linger at the present times for once and try my hand
on the history of an artist whom I knew since his early boyhood and who
was my closest friend. Alas, you unfortunately passed away from the earth
so soon, my Joseph! and I shall not find one such as you so easily again. However, I want to comfort myself by tracing in my thoughts the history of your
spirit from the beginning on, just as you frequently have told me about it in
detail during beautiful hours and just as I myself have become intimately
acquainted with you, and by telling your story to those who find pleasure
in it. ——

146

J o s e p h   B e r g l i n g e r   was born in a little town in southern Germany. His mother departed from the world while placing him into it; his father, already a rather elderly man, was a doctor of medicine and in impoverished financial circumstances. Fortune had turned its back upon him; and it cost him the bitter sweat of his brow to support himself and six children (for Joseph had five sisters), particularly since he was now lacking a prudent housekeeper.

This father was originally a gentle and very goodhearted man who liked to do nothing better than to help, counsel, and give alms, as much as his means allowed; who, after a good deed, slept better than usually; who could sustain himself for a long while upon the good fruits of his heart, with sincere compassion and thanks unto God; and who liked best of all to nourish his mind with touching sentiments. One must, indeed, be deeply stirred by profound melancholy and sincere love whenever one observes the enviable simplicity of these souls, who find such an inexhaustible abyss of magnificence in the ordinary utterances of the good heart that this is completely their heaven on earth, through which they are reconciled with the entire world and always maintained in contented well-being. Joseph had exactly this sensation whenever he observed his father; —— but heaven had endowed   h i m   in such a way that he always aspired to something   e v e n   h i g h e r;   mere h e a l t h   of the soul did not satisfy him, and that it perform its ordinary functions on earth, such as working and doing good; —— he also desired that it should dance about in exuberant high spirits and shout up to heaven, as if to its point of origin.

But the temperament of his father was also constructed out of other things. He was an industrious and conscientious doctor who, throughout his lifetime, had taken pleasure in nothing but in the knowledge of strange things which lie hidden within the human body and in the vast science of all woeful human infirmities and illnesses. As frequently tends to happen, this industrious studying had become for him a secret, nerve-deadening poison, which penetrated all his veins and ate away at many resonant strings of the human heart within him. In addition, there was the despondency over the wretchedness of his poverty and, finally, old age. All this gnawed at the original kindness of his spirit; for, in souls which are not strong, everything with which the human being has trouble passes over into his blood and transforms his inner self, without his knowing it himself.

The children of the old doctor grew up in his household like weeds in a neglected garden. Joseph's sisters were in part sickly, in part feeble-minded, and led a miserably lonely life in their dark little room.

No one could fit into this family less than   J o s e p h,   who was always existing in a realm of beautiful fantasy and divine dreams. His soul resembled a delicate little tree, whose grain of seed a bird had let fall into a wall or ruins, where it sprouts forth modestly between hard stones. He was always alone and quietly withdrawn and delighted only in his inner fantasies; for this reason the father considered him also slightly perverse and of weak mind. He loved his father and his sisters sincerely; but he valued his own inner soul above all else and kept it concealed and hidden from others. One keeps a little treasure chest hidden in this way, whose key one entrusts to no other person's hands.

From his earliest years his principal pleasure had been m u s i c. Now and then he heard someone playing on the piano and also played a bit himself. Little by little, through this frequently repeated enjoyment, he educated himself in such a unique way that his inner being turned completely to music and his mind, attracted by this art, roamed about constantly in the labyrinths of poetic feeling.

An excellent epoch in his life was that of a trip to the episcopal residence, to which he was taken for several weeks by a wealthy relative who lived there and who had become fond of the boy. Here he truly lived in heaven: his spirit was enchanted by beautiful music in thousands of forms and fluttered about not unlike a butterfly in warm breezes.

He primarily visited the churches and heard the holy oratorios, cantilenas, and choirs resound under the lofty arches with full-voiced ringing and the peal of trumpets, whereby, out of inner piety, he often remained humbly on his knees. Before the music started, when he was standing in the dense, softly murmuring crowd of people, it seemed to him as if he were hearing the ordinary and commonplace life of men, bustling unmelodiously amidst each other and all around him like a large annual fair; his brain became stupefied by empty, earthly trivialities. He expectantly awaited the first sound of the instruments; —— and when it now broke forth out of the heavy stillness, mighty and sustained, like the blowing of a wind from heaven, and the full force of the sounds passed over his head, —— then it seemed to him as if suddenly huge wings were stretched forth from his soul, as if he were being lifted up from a barren heath, the gloomy curtain of clouds disappearing before his mortal eyes, and he floating up to the luminous heaven. Then he kept his body quiet and motionless and fixed his eyes steadily upon the ground. The present faded away before him; his inner self was cleansed of all the earthly trivialities, which are the true dust on the lustre of the soul; the music penetrated his nerves with gentle tremors and, as it changed, it caused various pictures to rise up before him. Thus, during many gay and heart-lifting songs in praise of God, it very distinctly seemed to him as if he were seeing King David dance along in front of the Ark of the Covenant singing praises, in his long royal cloak, the crown upon his head; he observed his complete enchantment and all his movements and his heart skipped within his breast. Thousands of dormant sensations were abruptly awakened in his heart and became marvelously intermingled. Indeed, at many a point in the music a particular beam of light seemed to fall into his soul; it seemed to him as if he suddenly became far more clever thereby and looked down upon the entire teeming world with sharper eyes and a certain exalted and peaceful melancholy.

So much is certain, that, when the music had ended and he left the church, he appeared to himself purer and more ennobled. His entire being was still glowing from the spiritual wine which had intoxicated him and he observed all who passed by with different eyes. If he then saw a few people perhaps standing together and laughing on the walkway or exchanging news, this made a very unique, unfavorable impression upon him. He thought: you must remain for life unceasingly in this beautiful poetic intoxication and your entire life must be one musical composition.

But, when he then went to his relative's home for the noonday meal and enjoyed the food in ordinary, gay and jovial company, —— then he was dissatisfied that he had descended into prosaic life so soon again and that his ecstasy had vanished like a shining cloud.

This bitter dissension between his innate ethereal enthusiasm and the worldly segment in the life of every human being, which forcefully pulls everyone down from his raptures every day, tormented him throughout his entire life. ——

Whenever Joseph was at a big concert, he seated himself in a corner, without looking at the brilliant gathering of auditors, and listened with the very same reverence as if he were in the church, —— just as quietly and motionlessly and with his eyes fixed upon the ground before him in the same way. Not the slightest tone escaped him and, at the end, he was very weak and fatigued from the intense attentiveness. His continuously active soul was entirely a medley of sounds; —— it was as if it were detached from his body and were flitting about more freely, or as if his body had become a part of his soul, —— his entire being was embraced so freely and easily by the beautiful harmonies and the slightest convolutions and innuendoes of the sounds imprinted themselves in his gentle soul. —— During gay and charming symphonies by the full orchestra, which he loved particularly, it often seemed to him as if he were watching a lively throng of boys and girls dancing on a lovely meadow, watching how they hopped forwards and backwards and how individual couples occasionally spoke to each other by pantomime and then merged into the happy crowd again. Many places in the music were for him so clear and penetrating that the sounds seemed to him to be w o r d s. At other times the sounds caused a wonderful mixture of gaiety and sadness in his heart, so that he was on the verge of both smiling and weeping; a sensation which we so often encounter on our way through life and which no art is more capable of expressing than music. And with what delight and

149

astonishment he listened to such a piece, which begins with a lively and gay melody, like a Bach, but gradually moves along, imperceptibly and wondrously, in sadder and sadder strains and, finally, breaks out into violent, open sobbing or thunders away as if through wild, rocky crags with an alarming din. —— All these manifold sensations always brought forth corresponding sensual images and new thoughts in his soul: —— a wonderful gift of music, —— which art, indeed, affects us the more powerfully and tosses all the forces of our bodies the more generally into tumult, the deeper and more mysterious its language is. ——

The beautiful days which Joseph had spent in the episcopal residence were finally over and he had to return to his native city and the house of his father. How sad the return trip was! How miserable and dejected he felt to be again in a family whose entire living and activity revolved solely around the meager satisfaction of the most necessary physical needs and with a father who was so little in tune with his inclinations! This father despised and abhorred all the arts as servants of unrestrained desires and passions and flatterers of the aristocratic world. From the beginning he had regarded with displeasure the fact that his Joseph had become so very fond of music; and now, since this love was growing greater and greater in the boy, he was making a persistent and serious attempt to convert him from this ruinous inclination toward an art, the practice of which was not much better than indolence and which merely satisfied the desire of the senses, to medicine as the most beneficiary and, for the human race, most universally useful discipline. He took great pains to instruct him in the elementary rudiments himself and put into his hands books of reference.

This was a very distressing and painful situation for poor Joseph. He secretly repressed his enthusiasm within his breast in order not to provoke his father and intended to force himself to see if he could not learn a useful discipline on the side. However, this created an eternal conflict in his soul. He read one page in his textbooks ten times, without comprehending what he was reading; —— inwardly, his soul constantly sang its melodic fantasies further. The father was deeply concerned about him.

Silently his violent love of music took the upper hand more and more. If no musical strain had reached his ears for several weeks, then he became truly sick at heart; he noticed that his emotions shriveled up; and emptiness arose within him and he had a genuine longing to let himself be enthused by the sounds again. Then even crude players at festivities and annual fairs could, with their wind-instruments, inspire in him feelings about which they themselves had no idea. And whenever any beautiful, grand music was to be heard in the neighboring towns, then he ran out with passionate desire in the most severe snow, storming, and rain.

Almost every day he recollected in his thoughts with melancholy the magnificent time in the episcopal residence and reconstructed in his mind the precious things which he had heard there. Frequently he recited to himself the very lovely and touching words, retained by heart, of the spiritual oratorio, which had been the first thing that he had heard and which had made a particularly deep impression upon him:

Stabat Mater dolorosa
Iuxta crucem lacrymosa,
 Dum pendebat filius:
Cuius animam gementem,
Contristantem et dolentem
 Pertransivit gladius.

O quam tristis et afflicta
Fuit illa benedicta
 Mater unigeniti:
Quae moerebat et dolebat
Et tremebat, cum videbat
 Nati poenas inclyti.

And as it continues on.

Alas, however! —— whenever such an enchanted hour, when he was dwelling in ethereal dreams or when he had just returned, totally intoxicated, from the enjoyment of some magnificent music, was interrupted for him because his sisters were quarreling over a new dress or because his father was not able to give the oldest one sufficient money for the household or the father was telling about a truly wretched, pitiable sick person or because an old, totally hunchbacked beggarwoman came to the door, who could not protect herself from the winter frost in her rags; —— alas! there is no emotion in the world so terribly bitter, so heart-rending as the one by which Joseph was then torn. He thought: "Dear God! is t h i s the world as it is? and is it really Thy Will that I should intermingle thus with the distress of the masses and take part in the base wretchedness? And yet, it appears to be so and my father always preaches that it is the duty and calling of the human being to intermingle in this and give counsel and alms and bind up loathsome wounds and heal odious illnesses! But, nevertheless, an inner voice calls to me again very loudly: "No! no! you are born for a loftier, more noble end!" —— He frequently tormented himself for long periods of time with such thoughts and could not find any escape; but before he anticipated it, the hostile images which seemed to be pulling him forcibly down into the sludge of this earth were wiped out of his soul and his spirit roamed about again in the breezes, undisturbed.

Gradually he became thoroughly convinced that he had been placed into the world by God for this reason: in order to become a truly superior musical artist. Occasionally he thought, indeed, that heaven would draw him forth out of the gloomy and confined poverty in which he had to spend his youth to all the higher brilliance. Although it is pure truth, many will consider it to be a fantastic and unnatural fabrication, when I say that frequently, in his solitude, he fell upon his knees because of the ardent drive of his heart and begged God that He might guide him, so that he might one day become a truly magnificent artist in the eyes of heaven and earth. During this time, when his blood, oppressed by the continuous fixation of his ideas upon the same spot, was often violently agitated, he wrote down numerous little poems, which depicted his condition or the glory of the musical art, and which he most joyously set to music in his childishly tender way, without knowing the rules. The following prayer is a sample of these songs, which he addressed to that one of the saints who is revered as protectress of the musical art:

> Behold how I weep despairingly
> In my chamber solitarily,
>   Holiest Cecilia! ——
> See how I flee from all the world,
> To kneel before you here unheard:
>   Ah! pray, from me be not far!
>
> Ah! the wonder of your melody,
> To which I'm a slave enchantedly,
>   It has disarranged my soul.
> But release the senses' trembling, ——
> Let me flow away with singing,
>   Which delights my heart so well.
>
> Would you like to guide on harp strings
> My weak fingers, so that there springs
>   Feeling forth from out of it;
> That my playing both inspires
> In thousand hearts sweet pains and fires,
>   And stills again all that was lit.
>
> Once I should like dedicating
> To you and all saints with loud ringing
>   An exalted Gloria
> In the temple's crowded hall,
> To delight thousand Christians all:
>   Holiest Cecilia!

For me the minds of men uncover,
So that I, through music's power,
    Master of their souls might be;
That my soul the world infiltrate,
Sympathetically penetrate,
    Intoxicate in fantasy! ——

For more than a year poor Joseph tormented himself and brooded in solitude about a step which he wanted to take. An irresistible force was attracting his spirit back to the magnificent city which he regarded as a paradise for himself; for he was burning with the desire to learn his art from the rudiments on. His relationship with his father, however, was oppressing his heart. The latter had, indeed, noticed that Joseph no longer wanted to apply himself at all with seriousness and zeal in his science, had already half given up and had withdrawn into his despondency, which became more and more intense with advancing age. He concerned himself little more with the boy. Meanwhile, Joseph did not lose his childish emotion on this account; he struggled incessantly with his inclination and he could never gather the courage to utter in his father's presence that which he had to disclose to him. He tormented himself for entire days, weighing all things against each other, however he could not emerge from the horrible abyss of doubts; all his fervent praying bore no fruits: this very nearly broke his heart. The following lines, which I found among his papers, also bear witness to the most troubled and painful situation in which he was at that time:

Ah, what is it that so much oppresses,
Holds me in hot arms with tight embraces,
That I should go with it far from here,
Should my father's home no longer share?
Alas, what enticement and martyrdom
I must endure, though no wrong I have done!

Son of God! for your own wounds' sake
Can you not still my anxious heartache?
Can you not give me revelation,
What should be my inner consideration?
Can you not show me the right course?
Not guide my heart to the right choice?

If you do not rescue me now soon,
Or lay me down to rest in the earth's womb,
I must give myself to this strange might,

Must live just as it wishes, though with fright;
Of this which draws me from my father's side,
Of unknown powers the booty and the pride! ——

His anxiety became greater and greater, —— the temptation to escape to the magnificent city increasingly strong. Will heaven, then, not come to your assistance, he thought? will it give you no sign at all? —— His passion finally reached the highest peak when, during a domestic disagreement, his father once let fly at him in a manner totally different from usual and, since that time, always treated him in a repulsing way. Now it was decided; from now on he dismissed all doubts and scruples; he absolutely did not want to think about it any longer. The Easter holiday was near; he wanted to celebrate that at home, but as soon as it would be over, —— out into the wide world.

It was over. He awaited the first beautiful morning, when the bright sunshine seemed to attract him enchantedly; then he ran out of the house early, as he, indeed, customarily did, —— only this time he did not return again. With delight and with pounding heart he rushed through the narrow streets of the little town; —— he felt as if he wanted to leap over everything which he saw around himself into the open sky. An old relative met him at a corner: —— "In such a hurry, cousin?" she asked, —— "does he want to fetch greens from the marketplace again for the household?" —— "Yes, yes!" Joseph called distractedly and ran out of the gate, trembling with joy.

However, when he had gone a short stretch on the field and looked around, hot tears poured forth from him. Shall I turn around, he thought? But he ran further, as if his heels were burning, and wept continuously, and he ran as if he wanted to escape his tears. So it went through many an unfamiliar village and past many strange faces: —— the sight of the strange world gave him courage again and he felt free and strong, —— he came closer and closer —— and, finally, —— benevolent heaven! what rapture! —— at last he saw the towers of the magnificent city lying before him. —— —— ——

Second Part

I return now to my Joseph as, several years after we left him, he has become conductor of the orchestra in the episcopal residence and is living in great splendor. His relative, who received him very graciously, had become the originator of his happiness and had enabled him to be given the most thorough instruction in the art of music, had also gradually pacified Joseph's father quite well about his step. With the most active industry Joseph had worked himself up and had finally arrived at the highest level of good fortune which he had ever been able to desire.

But the things of the world change before our eyes. At one time, when he had been orchestra conductor for a few years, he wrote me the following letter:

"D e a r   F a t h e r,"

"It is a wretched life that I am leading: —— the more Thou wishest to console me, the more bitterly I feel it." ——

"When I think back to the dreams of my youth, —— how happy I was in these dreams! — I thought that I wanted to dream on ceaselessly and pour out my full heart in works of art, —— but how strange and austere the very first years of apprenticeship seemed to me. How I felt when I stepped behind the curtain! That all the melodies (even if they had produced the most heterogeneous and often the most wonderful sensations in me), all were based upon a single compelling mathematical law! That, instead of flying freely, I first had to learn to climb about in the awkward scaffolding and cage of the grammar of art! How I had to torment myself in order first to produce a correct work with the ordinary, scientific, mechanical understanding, before I could think of adding my emotion to the musical notes! —— It was a tedious mechanical effort. —— Yet, even so! I still had youthful elasticity and hoped for the magnificent future! And now? —— The splendid future has become a miserable present." ——

"What happy hours I enjoyed in the huge concert hall as a boy! When I sat in the corner quietly and unobserved and all the splendor and magnificence enchanted me and I so ardently wished that some day these listeners might gather together for the sake   o f   m y   works, might surrender their emotions   t o   m e. —— Now I sit in this same hall very frequently and also conduct my own works; however, I truly feel very differently. —— That I could imagine that this audience, strutting about in gold and silver, had gathered together to enjoy a work of art, to warm their hearts, to offer their emotions to the artist! If these souls are not capable of becoming excited even in the majestic cathedral, on the most sacred holy day, while everything great and beautiful which art and religion possess comes in upon them forcefully, if they cannot become excited even then, how are they supposed to in the concert hall? —— The feeling and the inclination for art have gone out of style and become indecorous; —— to feel in response to a work of art would be just as strange and ridiculous as suddenly to speak in verses at a social gathering, when one ordinarily makes do in all aspects of his life with rational and commonly understood prose. And for these souls I am wearing out my mind! For these I am inflaming myself, in order to make it possible that one should be able to feel something thereby! That is the lofty calling for which I believed that I was born!"

"And whenever anyone who has a sort of half-emotion wants to praise me and extols critically and submits critical questions to me, —— then I should always like to request of him that he not exert himself so much to learn feeling out of books. Heaven knows how it is, —— whenever I have just enjoyed a musical composition or any other work of art which delights me, then I should like very much to paint my emotion upon a panel with o n e brushstroke, if a color could only express it. —— It is not possible for me to praise with artificial words; I cannot produce anything sensible." ——

"To be sure, the thought is a bit consoling that perhaps, in some little corner of Germany to which this or that work by my hand comes some day, even if long after my death, there lives one or another person in whom heaven has placed such a sympathy with my soul that he feels in my melodies precisely that which I felt while writing them down and what I wanted so very much to implant in them. A lovely idea, with which one can, indeed, pleasantly deceive oneself for awhile!" ——

"But most abominable of all are the many other situations in which the artist becomes involved. Concerning all the disgusting envy and spitefulness, all the repugnantly petty customs and encounters, all the subordination of art to the will of the court; —— I cannot bear to utter o n e word about this, —— it is all so disgraceful and so degrading to the human soul that I cannot bring across my tongue o n e syllable of it. A triple misfortune for music that, in this art, such a crowd of hands is necessary just so that the work exists! I concentrate and elevate my entire soul in order to create a great work; —— and hundreds of insensitive and empty heads want to have their say and demand this and that."

"In my youth I intended to escape earthly misery and have now entered into the mire more than ever. It is unfortunately a certainty; with all the exertion of our spiritual wings one cannot escape the earth; it draws us back forcefully and we again fall into the midst of the most commonplace crowd of mortals." ——

"These are pitiable artists whom I see around me. Even the most noble so petty that they do not know how to control themselves because of arrogance, when once their work has become a universal favorite. —— Dear Heaven! do we not owe the one half of our merits to the divinity of art, the eternal harmony of Nature, and the other half to the benevolent Creator, who gave us the capacity to make use of this treasure? All the thousandfold pretty melodies which produce the most varied emotions within us, have they not arisen from the single, wonderful triad which Nature established an eternity ago? The melancholic, half sweet and half painful sensations which music infuses in us, we do not know how, what are they, then, other than the mysterious effect of the alternating major and minor keys? And must we not thank the Creator, when He has given us precisely the skill to arrange these musical tones, which have been invested with a sympathy for the human heart from the beginning, in such a way that they move the heart? —— —— Truly, it is a r t which one must venerate, not the artist; —— he is nothing more than a weak instrument."

"Thou beholdeth that my zeal and my love for music is not weaker than usual. I am only for this reason so unhappy in this —— —— but I want to drop the matter and not vex Thee with the description of all the offensiveness around me. Enough, I am living in very impure air. How much more ideally I lived at that time, when in unconstrained youth and quiet solitude I still merely e n j o y e d art; than now, since I practice it amidst the most blinding splendor of the world, surrounded by nothing but silk clothes, stars, and crosses, nothing but cultivated and refined people! —— What would I like? —— I would like to leave all this culture in the lurch and take refuge with the simple Swiss shepherd in the mountains and play his Alpine songs with him, according to which he becomes homesick everywhere." —— —— ——

The condition in which Joseph was in his situation can be seen, in part, from this fragmentarily written letter. He felt abandoned and isolated amidst the buzzing of so many inharmonious souls around him; —— his art became deeply debased by the fact that, as far as he knew, it did not make a vivid impression upon a single individual, since it seemed to him to be created only to move the human heart. In many a dark hour he despaired totally and thought: "How strange and singular art is! Has it such mysterious power only for me alone and is it for all other people merely an entertainment of the senses and a pleasant pastime? What is it, truly and in actuality, if it is Nothing for all people and only Something for me alone? Is it not the most unhappy idea to make this art one's entire purpose and principal occupation and imagine to oneself thousands of beautiful things concerning its grand effects upon human hearts? This art, which has no other role in real, earthly life than card-playing or every other pastime?"

When he hit upon such thoughts, then he considered himself to have been the greatest dreamer, that he had striven so hard to become a practicing artist for the world. He turned to the idea that an artist must only be an artist for himself alone, for the elevation of his own heart, and for one or a few persons who understand him. And I cannot call this idea totally wrong. ——

But I want to sum up the rest of my Joseph's life briefly, for the memories of it are very sad for me.

For several years he lived on as conductor of the orchestra and his discontentedness and the uncomfortable awareness that, with all his deep feeling and his inner artistic sense, he was of no use to the world and far less effective than every craftsman, —— increased more and more. He frequently thought back melancholically to the pure, idealistic enthusiasm of his boyhood and, along with this, to his father, how he had taken the trouble to educate him as a doctor, so that he might alleviate the misery of people, heal unfortunate ones, and in this way be of use to the world. Perhaps it would have been better, he thought in many an hour.

Meanwhile, his father had become very weak in his old age. Joseph always wrote to his eldest sister and sent her means of support for the father. He could not bring himself to visit him himself; he felt that this was impossible for him to do. He became more dejected; —— his life was on the wane.

On one occasion he had conducted in the concert hall a new musical piece which he himself had composed: it seemed to be the first time that he had had some effect upon the hearts of the audience. General amazement, silent applause, which is far more beautiful than loud, caused him to rejoice in the idea that he had perhaps practiced his art worthily this time; he again gathered courage for new work. When he went out into the street, a very wretchedly clothed girl crept up to him and wanted to speak with him. He did not know what he should say; he looked at her; —— God! he cried out: —— it was his youngest sister in the most pitiful condition. She had run on foot from home to bring him the news that his father was deathly ill and wanted very urgently to speak with him once again before his end. All the singing in his breast was broken up again; in gloomy stupefaction he got ready and travelled hastily to his native city.

I do not wish to depict the scenes which took place at his father's deathbed. One ought not to believe that extensive and sorrowful mutual confessions occurred; they understood each other very deeply without many words; —— just as Nature generally seems to mock us greatly, in that human beings truly understand each other for the first time in such critical final moments. Nevertheless, Joseph was most deeply broken up by everything. His sisters were in the most miserable condition; two of them had lived disreputably and had run away; the eldest, to whom he had always sent money, had squandered most of it and had let the father starve; in the end he saw the latter die wretchedly before his eyes: —— alas! it was horrible, how his poor heart was wounded and pierced through and through. He took care of his sisters as well as he could and went back, because business obligations called him away.

He was supposed to compose new Passional music for the approaching Easter celebration, about which his envious competitors were very curious.

However, hot streams of tears poured forth from him whenever he was about to sit down to the work; he could not save himself from his broken heart. He was deeply depressed and buried under the scum of this earth. Suddenly he flung himself open forcefully and stretched his arms up toward heaven with the most intense longing; he filled his spirit with the highest poetry, with loud, jubilant singing and, in a marvelous state of enthusiasm, but with continuous, violent swings of emotion, he wrote down a Passional composition which, with its penetrating melodies that embrace all the pains of suffering, will eternally be a masterpiece. His soul was like a sick man who, in a wonderful paroxysm, shows greater strength than a healthy one.

However, after he had conducted the oratorio in the cathedral on that holy day with the most intense exertion and excitement, he felt extremely fatigued and enervated. A nervous debility overtook his entire system, like a harmful dew. —— He was ailing for a short time and, thereupon, he died in the springtime of his years. —— ——

I have bestowed many tears upon him and I feel strange whenever I review his life. Why did heaven wish that, throughout his entire lifetime, the battle between his ethereal enthusiasm and the base wretchedness of this earth should make him so unhappy and, finally, tear apart his dual essence of spirit and body!

We do not comprehend the ways of heaven. —— But let us once again admire the variety of exalted spirits which heaven has placed into the world for the service of art.

A Raphael produced in all innocence and naïveté the most highly spiritual works, in which we behold all of heaven; —— a Guido Reni, who led such a wild gambler's life, created the gentlest and holiest pictures; —— an Albrecht Dürer, an unpretentious Nuremberg citizen, prepared very tender works of art with assiduous, mechanical diligence in the very same room in which his ill-tempered wife quarreled with him daily; —— and Joseph, in whose harmonious works such mysterious beauty lies, was different from all of these!

Alas! that it had to be precisely his l o f t y f a n t a s y that destroyed him! —— Shall I say that he was perhaps created more to e n j o y art than to p r a c t i c e it? —— Are those perhaps fashioned more fortunately, in whom art works silently and secretly like a veiled spirit and does not disturb them in their activities upon earth? And must the constantly enthused one perhaps also boldly and strongly interweave his lofty fantasies into this earthly life as a firm woof, if he wants to be a true artist? —— Yes, is not this incomprehensible power of creativity perhaps something totally different and —— as it now seems to me —— something still more wondrous, still more divine than the power of fantasy? ——

The artistic spirit is and remains an eternal mystery to the human being; he grows dizzy whenever he seeks to probe its depths; —— but it remains eternally an object for the highest admiration: just as this is to be said concerning everything great in the world. —— ——

After these reminiscences about my Joseph, however, I can write nothing more. —— I am concluding my book, —— and should only like to wish that it might be useful to one or another person for the awakening of good thoughts. ——

———————

I Raphael: The Sistine Madonna (circa 1514). *Reproduction permission granted by the Staatliche Kunstsammlungen Dresden.*

II Raphael: Saint Cecilia (circa 1515). *Reproduction permission granted by the Pinacoteca Nazionale, Bologna.*

WILHELM HEINRICH WACKENRODER

Contributions
to the
Fantasies on Art
for Friends of Art

Together with
Ludwig Tieck's Preface

Hamburg
Published by Friedrich Perthes
1799

Ludwig Tieck's Preface[1]

I submit these pages to the public partly with confidence, partly with anxiety. A segment of these essays is a legacy of my deceased friend W. H. W a c k e n r o d e r. He completed the last of these shortly before his illness and communicated to me that they were intended to be a continuation of the book: *Confessions from the Heart of an Art-Loving Friar*. For this reason the reader again encounters the name J o s e p h B e r g l i n g e r here, as well as the tone of that book in general. My friend had a particular fondness for the essays on music and he wished very much, with the lovely vivacity characteristic of him, to see them printed. Now for the first time I am able to fulfill his wish and the reader will thank me for the transmission of these essays, in which one meets with an even bolder type of imagination and a more polished language. His style is more compact and more powerful in these essays; one is frequently compelled to admire the singularity, boldness, and truth in his images; and every sensitive reader will mourn with me the beautiful promise which German literature has lost through his early death.

With a great deal of timidity I have added the pages which are from my hand. All of these ideas originated in conversations with my friend and we had decided to form an entity, so to speak, out of the individual essays; —— however, since I have now been lacking his advice and his assistance in the working out of this, I have therefore also lacked the courage which would have inspired me in his company.

In the first section, the first and fifth items are written by Wackenroder; among Berglinger's essays the four last ones belong to me. I have omitted an unfinished essay of my friend on R u b e n s, as well as a c a n t a t a with which he himself was dissatisfied.

—— From the beginning it was his desire to be able to live for art; his fondest hope was one day to be named amidst the artists; even if the latter is denied him, certainly no one who knew him, who had only a slight feeling

163

for his noble and charming originality, and who respected his deep love for all art, will ever be able to forget him.

A Portrayal
of how the early German artists lived: in which are introduced as examples ALBRECHT DÜRER, along with his father Albrecht Dürer the Elder[2]

It is a delightful matter to re-create in one's mind an artist deceased long ago from the works which he left behind and, from amidst all the various lustrous beams, find the focal point to which they lead back or, rather, the heavenly star from which they emanated. Then we have before us the World-Soul[3] of all his creations, — a poem of our imagination, from which the actual life of the man is completely excluded.

But it is almost more delightful if in our thoughts we embody this shimmering phantom with flesh and limb, — if we can imagine him as one of us, as our friend and brother, and how he too was a member of the great chain of humanity, resembling all his lesser brothers in external constitution. Then the thought comes to us, how even this most beautiful human soul first had to emerge from the egg of ignorant childhood, — how father and mother brought a child into the world without a notion of his future high genius. We imagine the magnificent artist to ourselves in all the scenes of life: we see him as a boy, how he venerates and loves his old father, — as a man, how he maintains his friendship with brother, sister, and relations, how he takes a wife and becomes a father himself, — in brief, how he too experiences from birth to death all the fortunes which are characteristic of mankind.

This contemplation becomes particularly touching, invigorating, and instructive for me when such an artist, although he possessed an extraordinary mind and rare skill, nevertheless conducted his life as a very modest and

164

simple man in the manner which was generally customary among our German forebears of the past centuries and which, because it so deeply pleases my heart, I wish to portray here in a few words.

In former times it was, you see, the custom to look at life as a beautiful craft or trade, to which all men profess allegiance. God was regarded as the master-workman, baptism as the apprentice's indenture, our earthly pilgrimage as the travelling-time of journeymen. R e l i g i o n was to these men the beautiful book of explanation by means of which they learned to understand and comprehend life rightly, its purpose, and the precepts and regulations according to which they could most easily and securely carry out life's work. Without religion life seemed to them only a wild, crude game, —— an aimless darting back and forth of weavers' shuttles from which no fabric comes into being. In all events, large and small, religion was constantly their staff and their sustainer; it gave to every otherwise little esteemed occurrence a deep significance for them; it was a miracle-tincture in which they could dissolve all things of the world; it cast a mild, uniform, harmonious light over all the confused destinies of their existence, —— a gift which may indeed be called the most precious for mortal beings. Its soft varnish broke off the sharp point of the glaring color of unrestrained wantoness, —— but it also cast a shining lustre upon the dry, black, earthen color of misfortune. —— —— Thus, these people continued on through the hours of their lives, slowly and prudently, step by step, and ever mindful of the beneficial present. Every moment was precious and important to them; they conducted the labor of life faithfully and industriously and kept it free of mistakes, because they could not justify it to their conscience to damage by impious carelessness such a praiseworthy and honorable calling as had been imparted to them. They did what was right, not for the sake of a reward, but merely from the never-diminishing feeling of gratitude toward the one who alone understood the art of weaving the first threads of their existence into the evanescent void. —— At the end, when the great Master called them from the workshop, they, dissolved in holy thoughts, serenely commended themselves and all their daily accomplishments into His hands. Then the PERSONALIA[4] of the one who had passed away were written up as a brief chronicle or, in the presence of the relatives weeping beside the coffin, a funeral oration was delivered, which originally had the significance of a testimonial to the faithfully and honestly completed life's work and served as a model for the young people. But the unknown God in heaven thereupon employed this completed life's work to His grand, mysterious purpose: for out of all the millions of lives departing from the earth, He builds a new, more beautiful world beyond that blue firmament, nearer to His throne, where every good person will find his place. —— ——

The people were of this disposition in earlier, pious times. Why must I say: they w e r e? Why, —— if a mortal being may ask, —— why have You let the world become debased, all-bountiful Heaven?

Woe unto the foolish, contemporary wise ones who, from inner poverty and sickness of spirit, regard the world of humanity as a worthless swarm of insects and who, by observing the brevity and transitoriness of the thousands of teeming lives on this earth, let themselves be misled into a weary, morose depression or into insolent despair, in which they think that they will attain the highest goal if they wantonly strive to crush and squash their life like an empty pod. Whoever thus despises life, despises all virtue and perfection of which mankind has an idea, the stage and drill-ground for which is life alone. —— There is a great difference between whether one himself despises his occupation or whether one modestly evaluates his work as worth little but loves his occupation, indeed, seems to work merely for his own pleasure. —— To be sure, we are only drops in the ocean; to be sure, we all, a teeming roundelay, dance into the arms of death after a brief existence: however, our spirit surmounts the narrow boundaries, in it dwell the ineffable powers, incomprehensible to us ourselves, which are capable of transplanting heaven and the entire earth, time and eternity into the narrow space between birth and the grave. —— Our life is a flimsy bridge, stretched out from one dark region to another: as long as we walk upon it, we see the entire heavenly firmament mirrored in the water. ——

In the days of our German forebears, however, —— for that portrayal is based primarily on the calm, serious character of our ancestral nation, —— when, amidst all their gaiety, these people nevertheless piously, seriously, and slowly constructed the tower of life from hours and days piled up one upon the other; which of those people can offer to our retrospective imagination a more magnificent and more worthy image than the a r t i s t s who lived in that way? For to them their art, —— for they, too, carried it on not primarily as a hobby and because of boredom (as tends to happen now), but with industrious application, like a craft —— to them it must unconsciously have been a mysterious symbol of their life. Indeed, in these artists art and life were molded together into a product of o n e casting and, with this inner strengthening union, their existence progressed along an all the more firm and secure path through the transitory surrounding world. In peaceful, modest tranquillity, without many sharp words, they painted or shaped their human figures and faithfully gave them the same nature which the mysteriously wondrous living original revealed to them: and precisely in this way they molded their lives very obediently according to the excellent heavenly precepts of religion. Moreover, by no means did they think of subtle questions concerning why the human body was fashioned precisely in this way and not differently or for what purpose they were copying it, and it occurred to them just as little to inquire about the reason why religion existed or about the

166

purpose for which they themselves had been created. They did not find doubts and riddles anywhere; they carried out their work as seemed natural and necessary to them and joined together their lifetime most dispassionately out of nothing but correct, orderly activities, just as they incorporated into their painted figures the appropriate bones and muscles out of which the human body happens to be constructed.

It is a great, heartfelt joy for me when, with my thoughts collected, I observe these workers, faithful in art as in life, which the German past and, above all, that fruitful sixteenth century has brought forth. However, in order to introduce a few examples, I wish to illustrate my preceding general description with several individual features from the history of my dear A l b r e c h t   D ü r e r   and his father, who is the goldsmith, A l b r e c h t   D ü r e r   t h e   E l d e r. For even if these small features may seem insignificant in themselves, nevertheless I believe that, following the complex picture which I outlined above, one will better understand the correct meaning of these features and their true significance.

In the work of the noble Joachim von Sandrart[5] (in which the same, with praiseworthy zeal, would like to grasp the whole realm of art with his two hands), we find in the "Life of Albrecht Dürer" a short essay written by this artist himself in which, as a memento to himself and his descendants, he recorded with few, but faithful and pious words several accounts of his life and of his family. In those times it was not unusual for one to reflect upon the completed course of his life and evaluate it by a precise recording; and in such a description one never separated oneself from all other people, rather, one always looked upon himself only as a member and brother of the vast human race, in that one put down his entire genealogical table and modestly assigned to himself his appropriate place on one of the side branches of the old, venerable family tree and did not make himself alone the principal trunk of the world. The delightfully intertwined chain of kinship was a holy bond: several friends related by blood constituted, as it were, a single, subdivided life and each felt himself to be the richer in vital power, in the more other hearts the same ancestral blood was beating: —— the totality of relatives, finally, was the holy, small forecourt to the grand concept of humanity. Out of a beautiful, spontaneous instinct the early ancestors, whom heaven had appointed as instruments for giving life to their prolific descendants and, indirectly, all the excellences of life (I mean, virtue and a pious way of thinking) were not mentioned other than with grateful respect. In his youth the son eagerly listened to his old father whenever the latter told about his fortunes or those of his father; he avidly assimilated all things in his memory as if they were important articles of faith, for he too was supposed to carry out the work of life which his ancestors had already completed so laudably.

These are the thoughts which surge up in me when I read Albrecht

Dürer's account of his father and his ancestors, which he begins with the following introductory words:

> I, Albrecht Dürer the younger, have compiled from the writings of my father where he comes from, how he came here and remained and ended blessedly: May God be gracious to him and to us. Amen.

Thereupon he relates: his father's father, called Antoni Dürer, had come as a boy into a little town in Hungary to a goldsmith and there he had learned this craft. Then he had married a young girl by the name of Elisabeth and with her he had begotten four children and the first son, Albrecht Dürer, had been his dear father and had also become a goldsmith. This his dear father had later stayed for a long time with the great artists in the Netherlands and, in the year 1455, he had come to Nuremberg, on the very day when Philipp Pirkheimer had celebrated his wedding at the citadel and a magnificent dance had been held under the huge linden tree.

Right at the beginning Albrecht Dürer expresses the whole nature of his father very forcefully and concisely in two words, when he says: he had been an a r t i s t i c and a p u r e man. And at the close he adds the following characteristics, which depict him very vividly before our eyes. He had scantily fed himself along with his wife and children by means of the work of his hands and had carried on his life amidst many troubles, vexations, and grievances. Among all those who knew him, he had had great praise, for he had been a pious man, patient, gentle, honorable, and always full of gratitude toward God. Furthermore, he had been of few words, had lived at all times in tranquillity and seclusion and had indulged in very few worldly pleasures. His greatest desire had been to raise his children as an honor to God; to this end he had spent a great deal of energy on them and had spoken to them daily about the love of God. Finally, in his illness, when he saw his death before him, he had willingly commended himself unto it, had ordered his children to live piously, and had passed away in a Christian manner before midnight after St. Matthew's Eve of the 1502nd year.[6]

To lead such a quiet, d e p e n d e n t life, during which one at no point forgets that one is nothing other than a w o r k e r o f G o d, this is to walk the surest path to happiness. But he who worships no God, that means in other words, he who wants to make himself God and Ruler of the universe, finds himself in distressing derangement and enjoys only the sad, false happiness of a foolish, mad beggar, who thinks he is a crowned emperor. ——

We also find in the place mentioned above another document left behind by the elder Dürer, a register of all his children, eighteen in number, which he carefully recorded in his own handwriting in a special book, according to first names and day and hour of birth. This good citizen and goldsmith of

Nuremberg, Dürer the Elder, may certainly have had numerous clever thoughts often throughout his lifetime; but it doubtless did not occur to him to write down many of them, indeed, this may perhaps have seemed strange to him: it was far more natural for him to keep a precise register of all the children which heaven had bestowed upon him. But, of all these eighteen children, we now after a few centuries remember none but the beloved Albrecht and all of the others have been committed to oblivion. To be sure, the father could foresee nothing of this at his birth, rather, he uses similar words as for the others and records him without distinction as follows:

> Also, in the year 1471 after the birth of Christ, during the sixth hour of St. Prudentia's Day, on a Friday during Rogation Week, my wife Barbara gave birth to my second son, who was named Albrecht after me.

After our Albrecht Dürer the Younger had inserted this register concerning all his brothers and sisters from his father's book, then he adds: "Now almost all of these my brothers and sisters, the children of my dear father, have died, several in their youth, the others when they were grown up; only we three brothers are still living, as long as God is willing, namely I Albrecht, likewise my brother Hans and my brother Andreas." —— As long as God is willing! A beautiful maxim! A childlike feeling that we mortals, hanging in the precious bonds of God's love, let ourselves be rocked back and forth by Him amidst the scents of flowers on this green earth, as long as He thinks is useful for us.

For him, our esteemed Albrecht Dürer, He considered the age of 57 useful; however, therewith He also endowed him generously, so that in art he might become a far greater man than his father. At the beginning the latter instructed him in the goldsmith trade and wanted to transplant the craft of the grandfather to the grandson. For, in the Germany of past times, if this craft had once been implanted in the stock of a family, then the branches which sprang up later were usually also enriched and the bond of kinship was gilded, as it were, by the hereditary virtue of this art. Various noble families of artisans originating in the flourishing old cities of southern Germany furnish an example of this. —— Thus, the young Albrecht practiced the work of a goldsmith under his father's direction and (as Sandrart relates), progressed so far that he constructed the seven instances of the suffering of Christ in chased work. At that time it seemed to each individual without reflection most appropriate and natural to initiate himself into the art with h o l y objects and, by means of a performance which would be pleasing, show his gratitude to heaven for the first youthful skill which he had acquired. —— But Dürer harbored inwardly a far greater inclination toward painting and, although the father would have liked very much to keep him as a son of his craft, he nevertheless gave in and, —— says Albrecht Dürer, —— "on St.

Andrew's Day of the year 1486 my father consigned me into the apprenticeship of Michael Wohlgemuth, to serve him for three years; during this time
God granted me diligence, so that I learned well, but I had to suffer much
from his servants; and when I had served out my time, my father sent me
away, and I stayed away for four years, until my father sent for me again." In
this simple tone he enumerates the circumstances of his life: without looking
to the right or to the left, he proceeds along his straight path and acts as if
everything which he meets had to be thus and not otherwise.

In his paintings, copper foils, and wood engravings, which contain for
the most part religious representations, our Dürer reveals a faithful, workman-
like assiduity. That spirit which infused in him the aspiration toward the
perfection, carried out in fine lines, which one sees so openly and unpre-
tentiously in his works and which drove him to investigate carefully the best
and most proper proportions of the human body and to preserve them in a
book which, translated into all languages, later served as a canon for all people
who engaged in drawing; this was the very same spirit which also enjoined
him to pursue the right and the good everywhere in his life and in his actions.
To be sure, the trumpet of Fama proclaimed and glorified his name far and
wide in the best nations of Europe (that is to say, in addition to the German
Empire, in Italy, France, Spain, Holland and England), so that he received
from the most famous painters of that time as well as from emperors and
kings the greatest honors, which his father, the honorable goldsmith, had by
no means encountered. But despite all this, the precious man did not deviate
at all from his father's way of living but calmly and prudently carried on the
pilgrim's staff of his earthly journey, step by step, in the same manner and
was an a r t i s t i c and a p u r e man.

From such examples one will perceive that where a r t and
r e l i g i o n unite, the most beautiful river of life flows forth out of the
converging streams.

But just as these two grand, divine realities, r e l i g i o n and
a r t, are man's best directresses for his external, real life, so too t h e i r
treasures are the most abundant and most precious funds of thoughts and
feelings for the inner spiritual life of the human soul and it seems to me
a very significant and mysterious idea when I compare them to two magical
concave mirrors, which r e f l e c t for me s y m b o l i c a l l y
a l l t h i n g s o f t h e w o r l d, through whose magic images
I l e a r n t o p e r c e i v e a n d u n d e r s t a n d t h e
t r u e n a t u r e o f a l l t h i n g s. ――

―――――――

The Church of Peter[7]

Exalted miracle of the World! My spirit soars in holy intoxication when I gaze upon your boundless magnificence. With your mute infinity you awaken thought upon thought and do not let the admiring mind come to rest.

An entire century has gathered at your stony grandeur, and you have risen to this lofty height upon innumerable human lives! ——

Your homeland is in naked quarries, you mighty walls and pillars! There many a rough hand has for a meager income forced away from defiant, untamed Nature her cliffs of marble, unconcerned about what might ever become of the unshapen clump; the sole thought of the worker was only his iron tool, his instrument, until he then took it into his hand for the last time and died.

How many a one, concerned with nothing else in the world but firmly piling these stones one on top of the other for a meager wage, has departed from the world while doing this. How many a one, whose occupation it was to carve out these columns and entablatures with all sorts of little decorations in free, pure lines and who could be inwardly very proud of a beautiful capital, has closed his eyes. The capital is now lost in the total structure and perhaps no eye in the world has again observed it attentively, since the last time that he looked upon it with delight.

A whole succession of masters of architecture have participated in the creation of this colossus: it was they who directed all the hundreds of rough hands with drawings and models of minute proportions and who conjured the unshapen children of the cliffs into beautiful forms. And it was the greatest of these masters who, with a sterile web of numbers and crooked lines on low-grade paper, prescribed for the huge dome the law of dauntlessly mounting the burden of the walls and maintaining itself suspended high in the breezes.

Then too, a whole succession of keepers of the Holy See, who by means of pitiful little pieces of metal from their lifeless, inert treasure chambers which they scattered in the world like electrical sparks, bringing forth to the light of day out of the sleeping energy of rough hands, the sleeping art of the sculptors, the beautifully dreaming visions of the architects, a united, visible reality, —— who exchanged for the millionfold repeated, wretched uniformity of these insignificant pieces of metal such a miraculous, sublime achievement of such inexhaustible beauty and grandeur for the world and for human dignity: —— these, too, have long ago stood up from their magnificent See and humbly sunk their feet into that same dark region which the millions who worshipped them as deputies of the Lord have entered.

What a diversity of human traces speaks forth from all your stones! How many people have been dashed to pieces in your creation! And you stand there, an immortal construction, supported by your mighty walls, and look out fearlessly into long centuries. ——

The thousands of individual stones of the cliffs, the clumsy masses which resembled mutilated limbs have become fused into columns, whose exalted shape the eye embraces with a loving gaze, or into the dome, on whose graceful, immense curvature one's glance floats up triumphantly. The innumerable mutilated parts have disappeared: a totality of walls and columns stands there, as if during the construction of the world it had been shaped by giants out of rich clay or cast from molten cliffs in immense molds. —— And on what does the astonishing reality of this incredible dream which frightens the imagination rest but on a few hasty words and pen-lines of those triply crowned heads?

But you are resplendent in your existence and retain nothing more of your origin. Human beings created you and you are of a higher nature than the species of your creators, you cause the mortal multitudes of long centuries to kneel down under your dome and you envelop them with the deity, which eternally speaks out of your walls.

Praise unto mortal man, that he can create immortality! Praise unto the weak and unhallowed one, that he can bring forth exalted holiness, before which he himself kneels down! Under the heaven of devout art the mortal procreative power produces a golden fruit, more noble than stem and root; the root may perish, the golden fruit holds locked within itself divine powers. —— The men are only the portals through which, since the earth's creation, the divine powers have been reaching the earth and appearing visibly to us in religion and enduring art.

It is a magnificently bold thought to take the forms of beauty which please us in small, transitory objects and to build them up for eternity, majestically, with boulders in immense spaces. It is a very noble art which, despising all human form and language (the object of all the other arts), takes pride only in placing before our eyes a magnificent symbol of beautiful uniformity, of stability and purposefulness, these cardinal virtues and universal archetypes and ideals in the human soul. Like the harmonious fund of wisdom in the soul of the wise individual, the products of this art are a beautiful, firmly unified harmony of parts which support and are supported, of columns and walls striving boldly upwards, and of ceilings and arches motionlessly suspended, protecting, and gazing downward. Her products are out in the open under the heavens of the Lord and are rooted directly in the earth, the arena of all things; they do not let themselves be governed by hands, as do the products of the other arts; the generation which brought them into being becomes contained within them, feels itself embraced by them, and they are the noble containers which preserve in their expanses all other art and science, indeed, the most exalted activity of the world.

For what greater object are they able to preserve and enclose than the striving of mankind toward God? O, for this their walls must expand and their domes must rise up as far as they can, in order to encompass an immense area, in order to gather many, many children of the earth into One maternal womb, so that the solitarily straying devotion of thousands, assembled under this dome and enveloped by the eternal embrace of these holy walls, may burn together in One united flame, so that God may receive a worthy offering. These holy walls have initiated innumerable crowds to prayer in the past and they longingly anticipate embracing in their arms countless ones in the future.

I hear them, indeed, those rational wise men who scornfully say: "What does this inanimate, barren luxury mean to the world? Man prays just as piously in a narrow, unembellished space —— and we could have fed and clothed many needy ones, as well as widows and orphans, with these stony treasures." —— I know well that people bitterly reproach both art and religion when they exalt themselves before the world in rich, regal magnificence. These may be very well-founded thoughts of human reason, but nevertheless they are not the thoughts of creative caution.

These wise men want to create our earth anew according to a uniformity calculated by human reason and a rigid intellectual order of things. But what is the earth other than o n e sound audible to us from the hidden harmony of the spheres? —— o n e fleeting flash of lightning visible to us from the concealed dark clouds of the universe and what are w e? —— —— That vigorous surging up and down of earthly things, —— so that the lofty associates with the lofty and the level expanses and the depths waste away in neglect, —— seems to me no different from the particular, mysterious pulsation, the frightful, incomprehensible respiration of the earthly creature. If the earth wants to bring great and exalted things into real, physical existence, nevertheless her striving always remains e a r t h l y, and for magnificence and dignity she knows no more worthy companions than earthly treasures. —— Thus, even inanimate Nature, acting completely in the earthly sense, has prodigally rewarded the marvelous beauty of her mountain ranges with a subterranean profusion of precious metals, while endless barren wildernesses languish away under her miserly hand.

Therefore be silent, human wit, and let yourselves be enchanted, you pious senses, by the exalted, presumptuous splendor. —— ——

But alas! how even this marvel of the world disappears in the t i n y infinity of the things of this earth! —— It shrinks up when one's eye departs from it for a short stretch of time and it does not exist for all the rest of the world. Entire continents have never heard of it and even thousands who do see it have more important things to think about and walk past with indifference.

MUSICAL ESSAYS
BY
JOSEPH BERGLINGER

Introductory Remembrance

My beloved J o s e p h B e r g l i n g e r, whose touching life-story you have read in the *Confessions from the Heart of an Art-Loving Friar,* wrote down various fantasies on the art of music, primarily during the time of his apprenticeship in the episcopal residence, several of which I want to append to my book herewith. —— His views on art agreed with mine most extraordinarily and, through frequent mutual confessions of our hearts, our feelings became more and more intimately allied. Furthermore, in these little essays, which are the flowers of isolated beautiful hours, one will joyfully find that melodic harmony which we unfortunately miss with such bitter sorrow, when we survey the over-all tenor of his real life.

A Wondrous
ORIENTAL TALE
of a Naked Saint[8]

The Orient is the home of everything wondrous. Amidst the antiquity and childlike simplicity of attitudes there, one also finds very strange signs and puzzles which present a problem to the mind that considers itself to be more clever. Strange beings often dwell in the wildernesses there, beings whom we would call insane, who are however worshipped there as supernatural beings. The oriental mind regards these naked saints as the wondrous receptacles of a higher spirit which strayed away from the realm of the firmament into a human form and now does not know how to conduct itself in a human manner. Indeed, all things in the world are colored according to the way that we look at them; the intellect of the human being is a miraculous tincture, by means of which everything that exists becomes transformed according to our preference.

It happened that one of these naked saints was living in a remote cliff grotto, past which a little river rushed.[9] No one could say how he had come to be there; he had been noticed there for several years: a caravan had first discovered him and, since then, frequent pilgrimages had been made to his solitary abode.

Day and night this wondrous creature had no rest in his dwelling-place; it always seemed to him as if he were hearing the W h e e l   o f   T i m e make its howling revolution unceasingly in his ears. In the face of this uproar he could do nothing, undertake nothing. The violent anguish which fatigued him with endless toil prevented him from seeing or hearing anything but how the frightful wheel turned and turned again with a raging and a violent heavy-gale howling which reached to the stars and beyond. Like a waterfall of thousands of roaring torrents which plunged down from the sky, eternally, eternally poured forth without a momentary pause, without a second's peace, thus it sounded in his ears and all his senses were intently focused solely on this. His laboring anguish became more and more caught up and carried away in the whirlpool of this wild confusion; the monotonous sounds grew more and more ferociously wild; he was not able to rest but was seen day and night in the most strained, most intense activity, like that of a man who is struggling to turn an enormous wheel. From his disjointed, wild utterances it was discovered that he felt as if he were being dragged along by the wheel, that he wanted to assist the wild, darting revolution with the full force of his body, so that there would be no danger of time standing still even for a moment. Whenever one asked him what he was doing, then, as if in a fit, he shrieked out the words: "You wretched ones! Don't you hear the roaring Wheel of Time?"[10] and then he again struggled and turned still more violently, so that his perspiration flowed down onto the ground and with distorted gestures he placed his hand on his beating heart, as if he wanted to feel whether the great wheel mechanism were in its eternal motion. He became enraged whenever he saw that the travelers who had pilgrimaged to him were standing very calmly and watching him or walking back and forth and speaking with each other. He shook in vehemence and pointed out to them the incessant rotating of the eternal wheel, the monotonous, measured progression of time; he gnashed his teeth that they didn't feel or notice anything about this motion, in which they would also become entangled and dragged along; he flung them away from himself when they came too close to him in his frenzy. If they did not want to place themselves in danger, then they had to imitate vigorously his strenuous movement. But his frenzy became much more wild and dangerous whenever it happened that any physical labor was undertaken in his surroundings, for example, whenever a person who didn't know him gathered herbs and felled wood near his cave. Then he tended to burst out laughing hysterically over the fact that someone was still able to think of these trivial earthly concerns amidst the frightful rolling on of time; at such moments he bounded from his cave in a single, tiger-like leap and, if he could snatch the unfortunate one, he smashed him to the ground dead in a single motion. He then jumped quickly back into his cave and turned the Wheel of Time more violently than before; however, he raged on for a long time and scorned in disjointed utterances how it was possible for human beings to work at something else, to undertake a t a c t l e s s occupation.

He was not capable of stretching out his arm toward any object or reaching for anything with his hand; he couldn't take a step with his feet like other people. A trembling anguish flew through all his nerves whenever he wanted to try to interrupt the giddy whirlwind even a single time. But once in a while during beautiful nights, when the moon suddenly appeared before the entrance to his dark cave, he stopped abruptly, sank to the ground, threw himself in all directions and whimpered in despair; he also cried bitterly like a child that the rushing of the mighty Wheel of Time did not leave him the peace to do anything else on earth, to act, to be effective, and to create. Then he felt an all-consuming longing for unknown beautiful things; he endeavored to raise himself upright and bring his hands and feet into tranquil and composed movement, but in vain! He sought something d e f i n i t e , u n k n o w n, which he could seize and to which he could cling; he wanted to rescue himself from himself outside or in himself, but in vain! His crying and his despair rose to the highest pitch; with a loud roar he leapt up from the ground and again turned the violently rushing Wheel of Time. This persisted day and night for several years.[11]

There was once, however, a beautiful, moonlit summer night and the saint was again lying on the floor of his cave, crying and wringing his hands. The night was enchanting: the stars twinkled in the deep-blue firmament like golden embellishments on a widely arched, protecting shield and, from the bright cheeks of its countenance, the moon radiated tender light, in which the green earth bathed itself. The trees were hanging on their trunks like floating clouds in this bewitching light and the dwellings of the people were transformed into dark shapes of rock and dimly lit ghost palaces. No longer blinded by the sun's brilliance, the inhabitants were living with their eyes on the firmament and their souls were reflected in the heavenly luster of the moonlit night.

Two lovers, who on this night wanted to surrender themselves totally to the charms of nocturnal solitude, came floating in a light skiff up the river which rushed past the cliff grotto of the saint. The penetrating moonbeam had illuminated and opened to the lovers the innermost, darkest depths of their souls. Their most tender feelings flowed forth and surged away united in boundless torrents. Ethereal music floated up from the skiff into the open heavens; sweet bugles and I know not what other enchanting instruments brought forth a floating world of sounds and, in the harmonies which were drifting up and down, the following song was heard:

> Sweetest thrills of expectation
> Flow away o'er field and stream,
> Moonbeams make the preparation
> For the lovers' sensual dream.
> How the waves whisper, o how they call,
> And reflect in their dark depths the heavenly All.
>
> Love high in the firmament,
> Under us in quiet flow,
> Starlight brilliance vainly spent,
> Were love not kindled by its glow:
> Gently fanned by heaven's breath,
> Smiled upon by sea and earth.
>
> O'er all the flowers moonlight glows,
> And all the palms are slumb'ring now,
> In forest sanctuaries flows
> The song of love and lovers' vow:
> In all the sounds which drift above,
> In the palms and the blooms lurks the beauty of love.

At the first sound of this music and singing the roaring Wheel of Time had vanished from the naked saint. These were the first harmonies which had drifted into this desolate place; the unfamiliar longing was stilled, t h e s p e l l   b r o k e n, the lost spirit released from its earthly shell. The body of the saint had disappeared; an angelically beautiful phantom, woven of light vapors, floated out of the cave, stretched its slender arms longingly towards heaven, and ascended in a dancing movement from the ground into the sky, in rhythm with the sounds of the music. The luminous phantom floated higher and higher into the air, lifted up by the gently swelling sounds of the horns and the singing; —— with heavenly gaiety the figure danced to and fro here and there on the white clouds which were floating in the heavens; with

177

dancing feet it vaulted higher and higher into the sky and finally flew around between the stars in serpentine turns; then all the stars sounded and droned through the air an intensely radiating heavenly chord, until the spirit disappeared into the infinite firmament.

Traveling caravans gazed upon this wondrous nocturnal apparition in amazement and the lovers thought that they were seeing the spirit of love and of music.

The Marvels
of the
MUSICAL ART

Whenever I so very fervently enjoy how a beautiful strain of sounds suddenly, in free spontaneity, extricates itself from the empty stillness and rises up like sacrificial incense, floats gently on the breezes, and then silently sinks down to earth again; —— then so many new, beautiful images sprout forth and flock together in my heart that I cannot control myself out of rapture. —— Sometimes music appears to me like a phoenix, which lightly and boldly raises itself for its own pleasure, floats upwards triumphantly for its own gratification, and pleases gods and men by the flapping of its wings. —— At other times it seems to me as if music were like a child lying dead in the grave; —— o n e reddish sunbeam from heaven gently draws its soul away and, transplanted into the heavenly aether, it enjoys golden drops of eternity and embraces the original images of the most beautiful human dreams. —— And sometimes, —— what a magnificent fullness of images! —— sometimes music is for me entirely a picture of our life: —— a touchingly brief joy, which arises out of the void and vanishes into the void, —— which commences and passes away, why one does not know: —— a little, merry, green island, with sunshine, with singing and rejoicing, —— which floats upon the dark, unfathomable ocean.

Ask the virtuoso why he is so heartily gay upon his lyre. "Is not," he will answer, "all of life a beautiful dream? a lovely soap-bubble? My musical piece is the same."

Truly, it is an innocent, touching pleasure to rejoice over sounds, over pure sounds! A childlike joy! —— While others deafen themselves with restless activity and, buzzed by confused thoughts as by an army of strange night birds and evil insects, finally fall to the ground unconscious; —— O, then I submerge my head in the holy, cooling wellspring of sounds and the healing goddess instils the innocence of childhood in me again, so that I regard the world with fresh eyes and melt into universal, joyous reconciliation. —— While others quarrel over invented troubles, or play a desperate game of wit, or brood in solitude misshapen ideas which, like the armor-clad men of the fable, consume themselves in desperation; —— O, then I close my eyes to all the strife of the world —— and withdraw quietly into the land of music, as into the l a n d o f b e l i e f, where all our doubts and our sufferings are lost in a resounding sea, —— where we forget all the croaking of human beings, where no chattering of words and languages, no confusion of letters and monstrous hieroglyphics makes us dizzy but, instead, all the anxiety of our hearts is suddenly healed by the gentle touch. —— And how? Are questions answered for us here? Are secrets revealed to us? —— O, no! but, in the place of all answers and revelations, airy, beautiful cloud formations are shown to us, the sight of which calms us, we do not know how; —— with brave certainty we wander through the unknown land; —— we greet and embrace as friends strange spiritual beings whom we do not know, and all the incomprehensibilities which besiege our souls and which are the disease of the human race disappear before our senses, and our minds become healthy through the contemplation of marvels which are f a r m o r e i n c o m p r e h e n s i b l e and exalted. At that moment the human being seems to want to say: "That is what I mean! Now I have found it! Now I am serene and happy!" ——

Let the others mock and jeer, who race on through life as if on rattling wagons and do not know this land of holy peace in the soul of the human being. Let them take pride in their giddiness and boast, as if they were guiding the world with their reins. There will come times when they will suffer great want.

Happy the one who, when the earthly soil shakes unfaithfully under his feet, can rescue himself serenely on airy tones and, yielding to them, now rocks himself gently, now dances away courageously and forgets his sorrows with such a pleasing diversion!

Happy the one who (weary of the business of splitting ideas more and more finely, which shrinks the soul) surrenders himself to the gentle and powerful currents of desire, which expand the spirit and elevate it to a b e a u t i f u l f a i t h. Such a course is the only way to universal, all-embracing love and only through such love do we come close to divine blessedness. —— ——

This is the most magnificent and the most wonderful picture of the musical art which I can sketch out, —— although most people will consider it to be empty dreaming.

But, from what sort of magic potion does the aroma of this brilliant apparition rise up? —— I look, —— and find nothing but a wretched web of numerical proportions, represented concretely on perforated wood, on constructions of gut strings and brass wire. —— This is almost more wondrous, and I should like to believe that the invisible harp of God sounds along with our notes and contributes the heavenly power to the human web of digits.

And how, then, did man arrive at the marvelous idea of having wood and metal make sounds? How did he arrive at the precious invention of this most exceptional of all arts? —— That is also so remarkable and extraordinary that I want to write down the story briefly, as I conceive of it.

The human being is initially a very innocent creature. While we are still lying in the cradle, our little minds are being nourished and educated by a hundred invisible little spirits and trained in all the polite skills. Thus, little by little, we learn to be happy by smiling; by crying, we learn to be sad; by staring wide-eyed, we learn to worship whatever is exalted. But, just as in childhood we don't yet know how to handle the toy correctly, so too, we don't rightly understand how to play with the things of the heart and, in this school of the emotions, we still mistake and confuse everything.

However, when we have come of age, then we understand how to employ the emotions, whether gaiety or sorrow or any other, very skillfully where they are appropriate; and sometimes we express them very beautifully, to our own satisfaction. Indeed, although these things are actually only an occasional embellishment to the events of our usual lives, yet we find so much pleasure in them that we like to separate these so-called emotions from the complex chaos and mesh of the earthly creature in whom they are entangled and elaborate them particularly into a beautiful memory and preserve them in our individual ways. These feelings which surge up in our hearts sometimes seem to us so magnificent and grand that we lock them up like relics in expensive monstrosities, kneel down before them joyously and, in our exuberance, do not know whether we are worshipping our own human heart or the Creator, from whom all great and magnificent things come.

For this preservation of the emotions, various splendid inventions have been made and, thus, all the fine arts have arisen. But I consider music to be the most marvelous of these inventions, because it portrays human feelings in a superhuman way, because it shows us all the emotions of our soul above our heads in incorporeal form, clothed in golden clouds of airy harmonies, —— because it speaks a language which we do not know in our ordinary life, which we have learned, we do not know where and how, and which one would consider to be solely the language of angels.

It is the only art which reduces the most multifarious and contradictory emotions of our souls to the s a m e beautiful harmonies, which plays with joy and sorrow, with despair and adoration in the same harmonious tones. Therefore, it is also music which infuses in us true s e r e n i t y o f

s o u l, which is the most beautiful jewel that the human being can acquire;
—— I mean that serenity in which everything in the world seems to us natural,
true, and good, in which we find a beautiful cohesion in the wildest throng of
people, in which, with sincere hearts, we feel all creatures to be related and
close to us and, like children, look upon the world as through the twilight of a
lovely dream. —— ——

When, in my simplicity, I feel very blessed under open skies before God,
—— while the golden rays of the sun stretch the lofty, blue tent above me and
the green earth laughs all around me, — then it is fitting that I throw myself
upon the ground and, in loud jubilation, joyously thank heaven for all magnificence. But what does the so-called artist among men do thereupon? He
has observed me and, internally warmed, he goes home in silence, lets his
sympathetic rapture gush forth much more magnificently on a lifeless harp
and preserves it in a language which no one has ever spoken, the native
country of which no one knows, and which grips everyone to the core. ——

When a brother of mine has died and, at such an event of life, I appropriately display deep sorrow, sit weeping in a narrow corner, and ask all the stars
who has ever been more grieved than I, —— then, —— while the mocking future already stands behind my back and laughs about the quickly fleeting pain
of the human being, —— then the virtuoso stands before me and becomes so
moved by all this woeful wringing of the hands, that he recreates this beautiful
pain on his instrument at home and beautifies and adorns the human grief with
desire and love. Thus, he produces a work which arouses in all the world the
deepest compassion. —— But I, after I have long forgotten the anxious wringing of the hands for my dead brother and then happen to hear the product of
his sorrow, —— then I exult like a child over my own so magnificently glorified
heart and nourish and enrich my soul with the wonderful creation. ——

But when the angels of heaven look down upon this entire delightful plaything which we call a r t, —— then they must smile in tender sadness over
the race of children on earth and over the innocent artificiality in this art of
sounds, through which the mortal creature wants to elevate himself to them.
—— ——

Concerning the
VARIOUS GENRES IN
EVERY ART
and especially concerning
Various Types of
Church Music

———

It always seems strange to me when people who profess to love art constantly restrict themselves in literature, in music, or in any other art, to works of o n e genre, o n e coloration, and turn their eyes away from all other types. Even if Nature has for the most part endowed those who are themselves artists in such a way that they only feel entirely at home in one field of their art and only have strength and courage enough to sow and plant in this their native soil, nevertheless I cannot understand why a true l o v e of art should not wander through all its gardens and enjoy all wellsprings. No one is born with only half a soul! —— But, to be sure, —— although I scarcely have the heart to defame all-bountiful Nature in this way, —— many of today's people seem to be so parsimoniously endowed with sparks of love that they can expend these only upon works of one type. Indeed, they are proud in their impoverishment; out of indolent presumption, they despise exercising the mind in the contemplation of other beauties as well; they regard their narrow confinement to certain favorite works as so much the greater virtue and believe that they love these the more nobly and purely, the more other works they despise.

Thus, it happens very frequently that some people seek pleasure solely in gay and comical things, others solely in serious and tragic things. But when I observe the fabric of the world impartially, then I see that Fate needs only to throw its weaving spool in this direction or in that, in order to bring forth a comedy or a tragedy in the same human souls within a moment's time. Therefore, it seems to me natural that, in the realm of a r t, I also willingly deliver myself and my entire being unto its governing Fate. I release myself from all bonds, sail with streaming pennants on the open sea of emotion, and willingly disembark wherever the heavenly breeze from above happens to carry me. ——

If someone desired to raise the question: whether it is lovelier to sit in the

parlor during winter, in the lamplight, amidst a splendid circle of friends, ——
or lovelier to watch the sun shine down upon charming meadows in solitude on
high mountains: —— what should one answer? Whoever preserves in his breast
a heart which feels best when it can warm itself fervently and can pound and
beat the harder, the better, that person will ecstatically seize e v e r y beautiful situation in order to exercise his precious heart in this trembling of su-
preme delight.

The blessed men who are predestined by heaven for the surplice and the
priesthood are to me an excellent model in this. Such a man, for whom that
upon which other mortals cannot bestow enough time (because the Creator
has endowed the substance of the world all too abundantly), is made into a
beautiful occupation, namely to direct his eyes steadily toward the Creator, ——
so that the smaller streams of thankfulness and devotion come together from
all the surrounding people into him as into a river which flows unceasingly
into the sea of eternity. —— such a man finds everywhere in life excellent occasions to honor his God and to thank Him; he erects altars in all places and,
to his rapturous eyes, the wondrous image of the Creator shines forth out of all
the intermingled features in the things of this world. —— And thus, it seems to
me, —— for the glory of art has reduced me into a bold simile, —— thus should
he also be constituted, who would like to kneel down before art with an upright heart and offer to it the homage of an eternal and boundless love. —— ——

In the glorious art which heaven benevolently selected for me at my birth
(for which I shall be thankful thereto as long as I live), it has been the case all
along that the type of music which I am just then hearing seems to me each
time to be the best and most magnificent and causes me to forget all the other
types. Just as I believe, in general, that the true enjoyment and, simultaneously,
the true test of the superiority of an art work occurs when one forgets all other
works because of this o n e and does not even think of comparing it with
another. Hence it happens that I enjoy the most varied genres in the art of music, as, for example, church music and dance music, with the same love. Yet I
cannot deny that the creative power of my soul inclines more to the first type
and restricts itself to the same. I occupy myself most of all with it and, therefore, I now want briefly to express my opinion about it exclusively.

Judging from the subject, religious music is, to be sure, the noblest and
most exalted, just as in the arts of painting and poetry[12] the holy segment dedicated to God must be in this respect the most sacred to man. It is touching to
see how these three arts storm the fortress of heaven from totally different sides
and, in keen rivalry, compete with each other to come closest to the throne of
God. I dare say, however, that the highly rational Muse of the poetic art and,
particularly, the silent and serious Muse of painting regard their third sister[13]
as the most audacious and the most rash in the praise of God, because she dares

to speak about the things of heaven in a foreign, untranslatable language, with loud resonance, with violent movement, and with harmonious union of a whole multitude of living creatures.

But this holy Muse does not speak of the things of heaven continually in one manner alone, but rather derives her pleasure from praising God in highly varied ways, —— and I find that each way is a balsam for the human heart, if one understands its true significance correctly.

Sometimes she moves along in lively, gay notes, lets herself be led by simple and pleasant harmonies or by decorative and elaborate ones into all sorts of delightful, melodious mazes, and praises God in the manner of children who deliver a speech or a dramatic presentation before their good father on his birthday, for the latter is very pleased when they demonstrate to him their gratitude with childlike, unconstrained liveliness and, in the course of thanking, simultaneously give a little sample of their skills and acquired arts. Or one can also say that this type of church music expresses the character of those individuals who like to express themselves with many light and artfully chosen words about the greatness of God, who are full of wonder and rejoice with affectionate smiles that He is so very much greater than they themselves. They know no other elevation of the soul than a gay and graceful one; in their naïveté they know no other and better language for the praise and worship of Him than the one they use toward a noble, mortal benefactor; and they are not embarrassed to pass with light agility from the smallest joys and pleasures of life to the thought of the Father of the universe. —— This type of church music tends to be the most frequent and the most beloved and it seems truly to represent the disposition of the majority of men.

Another exalted type is characteristic of only a few chosen spirits. They do not look upon their art (as most people do) as a mere problem of constructing out of the available notes many different, pleasing edifices of sound according to rules, and the edifice is not their highest goal; —— rather, they use large masses of sounds like wonderful paints, in order to paint for the ear that which is magnificent, exalted, and divine. —— They consider it unworthy to carry the glory of the Creator on the small, fluttering butterfly-wings of childlike gaiety, but beat the air with the wide, powerful pinions of eagles. —— They do not arrange and plant the notes like flowers in small, orderly beds, in which we chiefly admire the skillful hand of the gardener; instead, they create huge peaks and valleys with hallowed palm forests, which elevate our thoughts, above all, to God. —— —— This music moves along in powerful, slow, proud strains and thereby transports our souls to that intensified state of excitement which is generated by exalted thoughts within us and generates such thoughts in return. Or it rolls along more fervently and more magnificently amidst the voices of the full choir, like majestic thunder in the mountains. —— This music resembles those minds which are so filled beyond all measure with the almighty thought of God that they thereby totally forget the frailty of the human race and are audacious enough to announce to the earth in a loud, proud, trumpet-like voice the greatness of the Highest One. In the unconstrained delirium of ecstasy they believe that they have comprehended the being and the magnificence of God to the core; they make all nations acquainted with Him and they praise Him, in that they strive upwards to Him with all their might and exert themselves to resemble Him. ——

But there are also some quiet, humble, constantly penitent souls to whom it seems a sacrilege to address God in the melody of earthly gaiety, to whom it seems rash and presumptuous to absorb His entire sublimity boldly into their mortal beings: —— that gaiety is also incomprehensible to them and they are lacking the courage for this bold self-elevation. These people remain on their knees continuously, with hands folded and eyes lowered, and praise God merely in that they fill and nourish their minds with the constant idea of their frailty and distance from Him and with melancholy longing for the blessings of the pure angels. —— To these belongs that old chorale-like church music which sounds like an eternal "MISERERE MEI DOMINE!," the slow, deep chords of which creep along in deep valleys like pilgrims laden with sin. —— Its contrite Muse rests for long periods on the same chords; but each new change of the chords, even the most simple one, in this serious, weighty progression causes an upheaval in our entire souls and the gently advancing power of the sounds thrills through us with anxious shudders and exhausts the last breath of our taut hearts. Sometimes bitter chords intervene which overwhelm the heart with remorse, whereby our souls shrink up totally before God; but then crystal-clear, transparent sounds loosen the bonds of our hearts again and console and cheer up our inner selves. Finally, at the close, the progression of the music becomes slower than before and gripped by o n e deep, basic tone as by the aroused conscience; inner humility winds around in numerous, intertwined convolutions and cannot separate itself from the beautiful exercise of atonement, —— until it finally exhales its entire, dissolved soul in a deep, softly echoing sigh. —— ——

FRAGMENT
of a
LETTER BY
JOSEPH BERGLINGER

—— Recently, dear Father, on the holiday I enjoyed a delightful evening. It was a warm summer evening and I was going out the gates of the city when gay music in the distance led me on with its enticing strains. I went in pursuit of it through the streets of the suburb and, in the end, was led into a large public garden, which was most elaborately adorned with hedges, avenues, and covered passageways, with grass lawns, basins, fountains, and pyramids of yew in between, and which was enlivened by a crowd of colorfully dressed people. On a green elevation in the middle was an open garden hall, which served as the focal point of the crowd. I walked back and forth in the square before the hall and here my heart was frequented by the happiest and liveliest emotions.

The players were sitting on the green lawn and were bringing forth from their wind instruments the liveliest, gaiest spring melodies, as fresh as the new foliage which is bursting forth from the branches of the trees. They filled the air with the delightful fragrance of their music[14] and all the drops of blood exulted in my veins. Truly, whenever I hear dance music, it occurs to me that this type of music obviously speaks in the most meaningful and most distinct language and that it necessarily must be the most natural, the oldest and p r i m o r d i a l music.

People of all different classes and ages were now walking along beside me on the wide avenues. The merchant had come there from his accounting table, the craftsman from his workshop; and several aristocratic young gentlemen in splendid clothes strolled rashly through between the slower pedestrians. Sometimes a large family came along with children of every size and occupied the entire width of the avenue; and then sometimes a seventy-year-old couple, who smilingly observed how the crowd of children tested their young lives in elated mischievousness on the green grass or how the older youths overheated themselves with lively dances. Each person had left his individual worry at home in his chamber; no worry was identical with the next, —— but here all were in tune with each other in the harmony of pleasure. And, to be sure, even if the music and the colorful scene did not cause everyone to feel as deeply joyful as I, —— nevertheless, for me this entire lively world was dissolved into a shimmer of joy; —— the sounds of the oboes and horns seemed to play around all the faces like bright beams and it seemed to me as if I were seeing everyone crowned with a garland or walking with a halo. —— My spirit, transfigured by the music, penetrated through all of the varied physiognomies into every heart, and the teeming world all around me seemed to me like a drama which I myself had created or a copper-plate which I myself had engraved: so well did I believe that I was seeing what each figure expressed and signified and how each was what it was supposed to be.

These pleasant dreams occupied my attention for a long while, —— until the scene shifted.

The bright warmth of the day gradually emptied itself into the dark chill of night, the colorful crowds went home, the garden became dark, lonely, and still, —— occasionally a tender song from a bugle floated along like a blessed spirit in the soft glow of the moon, —— and the entire, hitherto so lively natural scene was dissolved into a gentle fever of melancholic sadness. The drama of the world was over for this day, —— my actors had gone home, —— the tangle of the dense crowd was loosened. For God had withdrawn from the earth the light half of his huge cloak, decorated with sun, and had covered the house of the world with the other black half, on which moon and stars are embroidered, —— and now all of His creatures were sleeping in peace. Joy, pain, toil and quarrel, everything was now observing a truce, in order to break out again tomorrow anew: —— and thus, on and on, into the most distant mists of the ages, where we can see no end. ——

O! this constant, monotonous succession of thousands of days and nights, —— so that the whole life of the human being and the whole life of the entire world is nothing but an endless, strange game on a board of black and white fields, whereby in the end no one wins but cursed Death, —— this could drive one crazy at many an hour. —— But one must reach with a courageous arm through the heap of debris upon which our life has crumbled and cling tenaciously to a r t, which reaches beyond everything into eternity, —— which offers us its radiant hand from heaven, so that we float above the desolate abyss in a bold position, between Heaven and Earth! —— —— ——

The Characteristic Inner Nature
OF THE MUSICAL ART
and the
Psychology of Today's Instrumental Music[15]

The sound wave or note was originally a crude material in which un-civilized peoples strove to express their undeveloped emotions. When their souls were deeply shaken, they also shook the surrounding air with screaming and the beating of drums, as if to bring the external world into balance with their inner spiritual excitation. However, after incessantly active Nature has, over many centuries, developed the originally stunted powers of the human soul into an extensive web of finer and finer branches, so too, in the more recent centuries, an ingenious system has been built up out of t o n e s, whereby in this material too, just as in the arts of forms and colors, there has been set down a sensual copy of and testimony to the beautiful refinement and harmonious perfection of the human mind of today. The monochrome beam of sound has been broken up into a bright, sparkling fire of art, in which all the colors of the rainbow glitter; this could not have occurred, however, had not many wise men first descended into the oracle caves of the most occult sciences, where Nature, begetter of all things, herself unveiled for them the fundamental laws of sound. Out of these secret vaults they brought to the light of day the new theory, written in profound numbers. In accordance with this, they constructed a fixed, knowledgeable order of multitudinous individual notes, which is the plentiful fountain-head from which the masters draw the most varied tonal combinations.

The s e n s u a l power which the tone has carried within itself from its origin has, through this learned system, acquired a refined diversity.

The dark and indescribable element, however, which lies hidden in the effect of the tone and which is to be found in no other art, has gained a won-derful significance through the system. Between the individual, mathematical, tonal relationships and the individual fibers of the human heart an inexplicable sympathy has revealed itself, through which the musical art has become a comprehensive and flexible mechanism for the portrayal of human emotions.

Thus has the characteristic inner nature of today's music developed. In its present perfection it is the youngest of all the arts. No other is capable of fusing these qualities of profundity, of sensual power, and of dark, visionary significance in such an enigmatical way. This remarkable, close fusion of such apparently contradictory qualities constitutes the whole pride of its superiority; although precisely this same thing has produced many strange confusions in the exercise and in the enjoyment of this art and many a foolish argument between mentalities which can never understand each other.

The scientific profundities of music have attracted many of those speculative minds, who are rigorous and sharp-witted in all of their activities and who do not seek the beautiful for its own sake, out of an open, pure love, but treasure it only because of the coincidence that unusual, strange powers can be aroused by it. Rather than welcoming that which is beautiful, like a friend, on all pathways where it presents itself to us in a friendly manner, they regard their art as a dangerous enemy instead, seek to subdue it in the most perilous ambush, and triumph thereupon over their own strength. The inner machinery of music, like an ingenious weaver's loom for woven cloth, has been developed to a level of perfection worthy of astonishment by these learned men; their individual works of art, however, are often to be regarded no differently from excellent anatomical studies and difficult academic postures in the art of painting.

It is sad to behold, when this fruitful talent has gone astray into an ungainly and emotionally impoverished soul. Then, in a breast foreign to it, the inventive feeling, which is lacking eloquence in sounds, yearns for union, —— while Creation, which wants to exhaust everything, seems to enjoy initiating pitiful attempts with such painful tricks of Nature.

Furthermore, no other art but music has a raw material which is, in and of itself, already impregnated with such divine spirit. Its vibrating material with its ordered wealth of chords comes to meet the creating hands halfway and expresses beautiful emotions, even if we touch it in an elementary, simple way. Thus it is that many musical pieces, whose notes were arranged by their composers like numbers in an accounting or like the pieces in a mosaic, merely according to the rules, but ingeniously and at a fortunate hour, —— speak a magnificent, emotionally rich poetry when they are performed on instruments, although the composer may have little imagined that, in his scholarly work, the enchanted spirit in the realm of music would beat its wings so magnificently for initiated senses.

On the other hand, many internally rigid and immovable minds, who are not unlearned but are born under an unfortunate star, enter clumsily into the realm of tones, pull them out of their proper places, so that one hears in their works only a painful, plaintive outcry of the martyred spirit.

But, whenever benevolent Nature unites these separate souls of art in o n e mortal frame, when the emotion of the one who hears burns even more ardently in the heart of the highly learned master of art, and he dissolves the profound science in these flames, then an inexpressibly beautiful work emerges, in which emotion and scholarship are as firmly and inseparably commingled as stone and colors in a ceramic painting.[16] ——

Those individuals who regard music and all the arts only as institutions to provide their dull and coarse organs with the necessitous sensual nourishment, —— since, after all, sensuality is to be regarded merely as the most powerful, most penetrating, and most human language in which that which is exalted, noble, and beautiful can speak to us, —— these sterile souls are not to be mentioned. If they were capable of it, they ought to worship the deeply founded, immutable h o l i n e s s which is characteristic of this art above all others, that in its works the fixed, oracular law of the system, the natural magnificence of the triad, cannot be destroyed and defiled even by the most infamous hands, —— and that it is n o t   e v e n   c a p a b l e of expressing that which is defiled, base, and ignoble in the human spirit but can, in itself, present no more than c r u d e and h a r s h melodies, to which the quality of baseness must be lent by the earthly thoughts attaching themselves to these melodies.

Now, when the subtle reasoners ask: where, actually, the center of this art is to be found, where its true meaning and its soul lie hidden, where all its varied manifestations are held together? —— then I cannot explain or demonstrate it to them. Whoever wants to discover with the divining-rod of the investigating intellect that which can only be felt from within will perpetually discover only thoughts about emotion and not emotion itself. An eternally hostile chasm is entrenched between the feeling heart and the investigations of research, and the former is an independent, tightly sealed, divine entity, which cannot be unlocked and opened up by the reason. —— Just as every individual work of art can be comprehended and inwardly grasped by emotion: —— just as every individual color, according to the teachings of painters, reveals its true nature when illuminated by light of the same color. —— He who undermines the most beautiful and most holy things in the realm of the spirit with his "Why?" and with relentless searching for Purpose and Cause, is actually not concerned with the beauty and divinity of the things themselves but with the concepts, as the boundaries and husks of the things, with which he sets up his algebra. —— However, he —— to speak boldly, whose heart's desire carries him almightily through the sea of thoughts from childhood on, straight as an arrow like a daring swimmer, up to the magic castle of art, such a one pushes thoughts courageously from his breast like interfering waves and penetrates into the innermost sanctuary and is intensely aware of the secrets which rush in upon him. ——

And, therefore, I venture to express from the depths of my being the true meaning of the musical art and say:

Whenever all the inner vibrations of our heartstrings —— the trembling ones of joy, the tempestuous ones of delight, the rapidly beating pulse of all-consuming adoration, —— when all these burst apart with   o n e   outcry the language of words, as the   g r a v e   of the inner frenzy of heart: —— then they go forth under a strange sky, amidst the vibrations of blessed harp-strings, in transfigured beauty as if in another life beyond this one, and celebrate as angelic figures their resurrection. ——

Hundreds and hundreds of musical works express gaiety and pleasure, but in each one a different spirit sings and toward each of the melodies different fibers of our hearts respond with trembling. —— What do they want, the faint-hearted and doubting reasoners, who require each of the hundreds and hundreds of musical pieces explained in words, and who cannot understand that not every piece has an expressible meaning like a painting? Are they trying to measure the richer language by the poorer and to resolve into words that which disdains words? Or have they never felt without words? Have they filled up their hollow hearts merely with descriptions of feelings? Have they never perceived within themselves the mute singing, the masked dance of invisible spirits? Or do they not believe in fairy tales? ——

A rushing river shall serve as my image. No human art is capable of sketching for the   e y e   with   w o r d s   the flowing of an immense river, following all the thousands of individual smooth and mountainous, plunging and foaming waves. —— Language can only inadequately c o u n t   and   n a m e   the changes, not visibly portray for us the interdependent transformations of the drops. And so it is also with the secret river in the depths of the human soul. Language counts and names and describes its transformations, in a foreign medium; —— the musical art causes it to flow past us ourselves. It reaches spiritedly into the mysterious harp, it strikes certain obscure, marvelous signals in the dark world in a definite succession, —— and the strings of our hearts resound and we understand their ringing.

The human heart becomes acquainted with itself in the mirror of m u s i c a l   s o u n d s;   it is they through which we learn to   f e e l e m o t i o n;   to many spirits, dreaming in hidden crannies of the mind, they give living consciousness, and they enrich our souls with entirely new, bewitching essences of feeling.

And all the resounding emotions are directed and guided by the dry, scientific system of numbers, as by the strange, miraculous incantations of an old, frightful sorcerer. Indeed, in a curious way, the system brings forth many wondrously new changes and transformations of the emotions, so that the mind is astounded by its own nature, —— just as, for instance, the language of words sometimes reflects new thoughts from the expressions and signs of thoughts and directs and governs the dances of reason in their movements. ——

No art portrays the emotions in such an artistic, bold, such a   p o e t i c and, therefore, for cold minds such a forced manner. The essence of all art is the p o e t i z a t i o n of the emotions, wandering around lost in real life, into manifold, fixed masses; it separates what is united, unites firmly what is separated, and, in the narrower, more sharply defined boundaries, there beat higher, more surging waves. And where are the boundaries and leaps sharper, where do the waves beat higher than in the musical art?

However, in actuality, only the pure, f o r m l e s s essence, the motion and the color, and also primarily the thousandfold n u a n c e s of the emotions flow in these waves; ideal, angelically pure art knows in its innocence neither the o r i g i n nor the g o a l of its excitations, does not know the relationship of its emotions to the real world.

And, despite all its innocence, nevertheless, through the overwhelming magic of its s e n s u a l f o r c e, it arouses all the wonderful, teeming hosts of the f a n t a s y, which populate the musical strains with magical images and transform the formless excitations into distinct shapes of human emotions, which draw past our senses like elusive pictures in a magical deception.

There we see the leaping, dancing, breathless gaiety which perfects every little drop of its existence into a harmonious entity of joy.

The gentle, rock-solid contentedness, which spins its entire existence out of one harmonious, limited view of the world, applies its pious convictions to all situations of life, never alters its movement, smooths all roughnesses, and rubs away the color in all nuances.

The masculine, exulting joy, which sometimes passes through the entire labyrinth of musical tones in many a direction, like pulsating blood flows warmly and quickly through the veins, —— sometimes elevates itself to the heights as if in triumph, with noble pride, with verve and elasticity.

The sweet, ardent yearning of love, the ever-alternating swelling and receding of desire, when with gentle boldness the soul suddenly soars out of its tender creeping through nearby musical strains into the heights, and sinks down again, —— turns from one unsatisfied striving to another with lascivious displeasure, rests willingly on gently painful chords, strives eternally for resolution and, in the end, only dissolves in tears.

The deep pain, which sometimes drags along as if in chains, sometimes moans interrupted sighs, then gushes forth in long laments, wanders through all types of pain, lovingly perfects its own suffering and, amidst the dark clouds, only infrequently catches sight of faint shimmers of hope.

The mischievous, liberated, gay mood, like a whirlpool that causes all earnest feelings to be shipwrecked and plays with their fragments in the gay vortex, —— or like a grotesque demon that mocks all human dignity and all human pain with farcical mimicry and delusively mimics itself, —— or like a restlessly floating, airy spirit, that tears all plants out of their firm, terrestrial soil and scatters them into the infinite breezes and would like to curse the entire world.

But who can count and name them all, the ephemeral fantasies which chase the musical strains through our imagination like changing shadows?

And yet, I cannot refrain from extolling, in addition, the latest, highest triumph of musical instruments: I mean those divine, magnificent symphonic pieces (brought forth by inspired spirits), in which not one individual emotion is portrayed, but an entire world, an entire drama of human emotions, is poured forth. I wish to relate in general terms what hovers before my senses.

With easy, playful joy the resounding soul rises forth from its oracular cave, —— like the innocence of childhood, which is practicing a lustful opening dance of life, which unknowingly jests above and beyond the whole world and smiles back only upon its own inner gaiety. —— But soon the images around it acquire firmer contours; it tests its power on stronger emotion; it suddenly dares to plunge itself into the midst of the foaming flood-tides, moves lithely through all heights and depths, and rolls all emotions up and down with spirited delight. ——But alas! it penetrates rashly into wilder labyrinths; with boldly forced impudence it seeks out the horrors of dejection, the bitter torments of pain, in order to quench the thirst of its vital energy; and, with one burst of the trumpet, all frightful horrors of the world, all the armies of misfortune break in violently from all sides like a cloudburst and roll in upon each other in distorted shapes, frightfully, gruesomely, like a mountain range come alive. In the midst of the whirlwinds of despair the soul desires to elevate itself courageously and defiantly obtain for itself proud salvation, —— and is continuously overpowered by the frightful armies. —— All at once the madly bold power is shattered, the figures of horror have dreadfully disappeared, —— the early, distant innocence emerges in painful recollection, hopping sadly like a veiled child, and calls back in vain, —— the fantasy intermingles a host of images in confusion, dismembered as in a feverish dream, —— and with a few gentle sighs the entire, loudly resounding world full of life explodes, like a shining mirage, into the invisible void.

Then, as I sit there listening for a long while in more ominous stillness, then it seems to me as if I had experienced a vision of all the manifold human emotions, how they incorporeally celebrate a strange, indeed, an almost mad pantomimic dance together for their own pleasure, how they dance between each other impudently and wantonly, with a frightful s p o n t a n e i t y, like the unknown, enigmatical sorcerer-goddesses of Fate.

That mad spontaneity, with which joy and pain, nature and artificiality, innocence and wildness, jesting and shuddering, befriend each other in the

soul of the human being and often suddenly extend a hand to each other: ——
what art presents those m y s t e r i e s   o f   t h e   s o u l on its
stage with such dark, secret, gripping significance? ——

Indeed, our hearts fluctuate every moment in response to t h e   v e r y
s a m e   t o n e s, whether the resounding soul will boldly despise all
vanities of the world and strive with noble pride upwards toward heaven,
—— or whether it will despise all heavens and gods and press with shameless striving merely toward one single earthly bliss. And precisely this
m i s c h i e v o u s   i n n o c e n c e, this frightful, oracularly am-
biguous obscurity, makes the musical art truly a divinity for h u m a n
hearts. —— ——

But why do I, foolish one, strive to melt words into tones? It is never as
I feel it. Come, Thou musical strains, draw near and rescue me from this
painful earthly striving for words, envelop me in Thy shining clouds with
Thy thousandfold beams, and raise me up into the old embrace of all-loving
heaven.

———————

A   L e t t e r
by
J O S E P H   B E R G L I N G E R

———————

Alas! my deeply beloved, my venerable Father! I write to Thee[17] this
time with a highly disturbed mind and in the anxiety of an irresolute hour,
which, as Thou well knowest, has come over me frequently in the past and
now will not leave me. My heart is contracted by a painful cramp, my fantasies
flutter into one another in confusion, and all my emotions dissolve into tears.
My lustful enjoyment of art is poisoned deep in the bud; I wander around
with sickly soul and, from time to time, the poison pours through my veins.

What am I? What am I supposed to do, what am I doing in the world?
What sort of evil spirit has driven me so far off from all human beings that
I do not know what I should consider myself to be? So that my eye is totally
lacking the standard of reference for the world, for life, and for the human
spirit? So that I merely roll about on the sea of my inner doubts, now lifted
high above the other human beings on a mighty wave, now plunged into the
deepest abyss? ——

Out of the firmest foundation of my soul, the exclamation presses forth: It is such a divine striving of the human being, to create that which is consumed by no ordinary p u r p o s e and u t i l i t y, —— which, independent of the world, is eternally resplendent in its own brilliance, —— which is driven by no wheel of the great wheel-mechanism and drives none in turn. No flame of the human heart rises up higher and straighter toward heaven than art! No substance so concentrates in itself the intellectual and spiritual power of the human being and makes him to such a degree an autonomous, human god!

But alas! whenever I am standing upon this presumptuous pinnacle and my evil spirit afflicts me with arrogant pride concerning my feeling for art and with a shameless air of superiority over other men, —— then, then there suddenly open up all around me, on all sides, such dangerous, slippery abysses, —— all the holy, lofty images break away from my art and take flight back into the world of other, better men, —— and I lie stretched out, cast off, and, in the service of my goddess, I seem to myself like —— I don't know why —— like a foolish, vain idolator.

Art is a seductive, forbidden fruit; whoever has once tasted its innermost, sweetest juice is irretrievably lost to the active, living world. He creeps further and further into his own self-gratification and his hand totally loses the capacity to extend itself effectively to a fellow creature. —— Art is a misleading, deceptive superstition; in it we think that we have before us the last, innermost essence of humanity itself; and yet, it merely foists upon us a beautiful p r o d u c t of man, in which are set down all of the egotistical, self-satisfying thoughts and emotions which remain sterile and ineffective in the world of action. And I, imbecile, esteem this product more highly than the human being himself, whom God has created.

It is horrible, when I think about it! Throughout my entire life I sit there, a lustful hermit, and merely suck upon beautiful harmonies inwardly each day and strive to enjoy every last morsel of beauty and sweetness. —— And when I now hear the reports: how untiringly the history of the world of mankind rolls along vivaciously right around me, with thousands of important, great events, —— how men affect each other with unceasing activity and how, in the crowded tumult, the c o n s e q u e n c e s, good and evil, follow after every little deed like huge ghosts, —— alas! and then the most shocking thing of all, —— how the highly inventive soldiers of misery torment thousands right around me with thousands of different afflictions in sickness, in grief and poverty, how, in addition to the horrible wars of nations, the bloody war of misfortune rages everywhere on the entire planet and each passing second is a sharp sword that strikes wounds blindly here and there and does not become tired, so that thousands of creatures scream pitiably for help! —— —— And, in the midst of this tumult, I remain sitting peacefully, like a child on his little chair, and blow musical compositions into the air like soap-bubbles: —— although my life will also close just as earnestly with death.

Alas! these cruel emotions are dragging my heart through a despairing anxiety and I am dying of shame because of myself. I feel, I feel bitterly that I don't know how to, don't have the capacity to lead a charitable life, pleasing unto God, —— that men who think very ignobly of art and contemptuously trample its best products with their feet accomplish infinitely more that is good and live in a manner more pleasing to God than I!

In such anxiety I understand how those pious, ascetic martyrs felt who, overwhelmed with sorrow at the sight of the inexpressible sufferings of the world, like despairing children subjected their bodies to the most highly selected mortifications and penances for their entire lifetimes, only in order to come into equilibrium with the dreadful excess of the suffering world.

And whenever the sight of misery now comes across my path and asks for help, whenever suffering individuals, fathers, mothers, and children stand before me, crying together and wringing their hands and screaming violently in pain, —— these are, to be sure, not gay, beautiful chords; this is not the lovely, merry playfulness of music; these are sounds which tear the heart, and the softened spirit of the artist falls into anxiety, does not know how to respond, is ashamed to take flight, and has no power to save. The artist torments himself with pity. —— He observes the entire group involuntarily as a product of his fantasy come alive and, even if he is ashamed of himself at the same moment, he still cannot refrain from extracting out of the wretched misery something which is beautiful and suitable as artistic material.

This is the deadly poison which lies hidden in the innocuous bud of artistic feeling. —— It is this, that art rashly tears human emotions, which have grown firmly in the soul, out of the holiest depths of the maternal soil and carries on outrageous commerce and trade with these emotions, torn away and shaped artificially, and thus wantonly makes a mockery of the original nature of man. It is this, that the artist becomes an actor, who regards every life as a rôle, who looks upon his stage as the genuine model and normal world, as the impermeable core of the world, and regards ordinary, actual life merely as a wretched patchwork imitation, as the inferior, enveloping capsule.[18] ——

What good does it do, however, when I lie sick in the midst of these dreadful doubts about art and about myself, —— and some magnificent music springs up, —— ha! then all these thoughts take flight in tumult; then the lustful tugging of desire begins its old game again, then it calls and calls irresistibly back and the entire childish bliss opens up anew before my eyes. I become frightened when I consider to what foolish thoughts the wanton musical strains can catapult me, with their alluring sirens' voices and with their wild roaring and trumpet blaring. ——

196

I eternally fail to reach firm ground with myself. My thoughts revolve and roll over each other unceasingly and I become dizzy when I want to attain beginning and end and definite peace. Many a time my heart has had this cramp and spontaneously, just as it came, it relaxed again and it was in the end nothing but a deviation of my soul into a painful minor key, which was in the proper place.

Thus I mock myself, —— and even this mockery is merely wretched play.

It is a misfortune that the man who is entirely dissolved in artistic feeling so deeply scorns reason and worldly wisdom, which are supposed to give man such firm tranquillity, and cannot come to grips with them at all. The worldly wise man regards his soul as a systematic book and finds beginning and end and truth and falsehood separated in specific words. The artist regards it as a painting or musical composition, knows no firm conviction, and finds everything beautiful which is in the proper location.

It is as if Creation held all human beings, as well as all quadrupedal animals or birds, imprisoned in fixed species and classes of the natural history of the mind; each sees everything from his own prison and no one can escape his own species. ——

And therefore, as long as I live, my soul will resemble the floating Aeolian harp, in the strings of which a strange, unfamiliar breath blows and changing winds flutter about as they please.[19]

Appendix I

NOTES TO

Confessions From the Heart of an Art-Loving Friar

1. Goethe, Schiller, and the Schlegel brothers all shared this negative view of Friedrich von Ramdohr with Wackenroder and Tieck. For the reserved evaluation of Ramdohr communicated by Goethe and Schiller, see their correspondence (Goethe to Schiller, Sept. 4, 1794, and Schiller to Goethe, Sept. 7, 1794). For the Schlegels' opinion, see the "prize question" (*Preis-Aufgabe*) in the *Athenaeum*, II (Berlin, 1799), p. 333.

2. Wackenroder devotes numerous passages to praise of the works of Raphael (1483–1520), particularly his renowned Madonnas. He frequently deviates from his source in Vasari's *Vite* in order to dramatize specific points related to Raphael's artistic life. Ernst Dessauer was the first critic to point out that Wackenroder employs the technique of contrasting all other artists in the reflection of the "divine" Raphael, repeatedly establishing Raphael as the embodiment of the "highest" level of artistic achievement (cf. Ernst Dessauer, "Wackenroders 'Herzensergiessungen eines kunstliebenden Klosterbruders' in ihrem Verhältnis zu Vasari," III, p. 218ff.).

3. "Art enthusiasm"—"Kunstenthusiasmus"; this term is used by Wackenroder interchangeably with the term "Kunstbegeisterung" to describe the quality of spiritual energy which enables an individual to experience and appreciate works of art. It corresponds closely to K. Ph. Moritz's idea of "Empfindungsvermögen." Wackenroder's use of this concept is even broader than the use Moritz makes of the term "Empfindungsvermögen," however, since, according to Wackenroder, neither true artistic creativity nor true appreciation of art can occur without this "art enthusiasm."

4. Count Baldassare Castiglione (1478–1529), Italian author of *Libro del Cortegiano*, 1518 (trans. into English as *The Courtier*, 1561) is known to have been a friend of Raphael and to have influenced the artist in the creation of several of his art works, among them the famous "School of Athens." The letter referred to in this passage was written to Castiglione in 1514 and contains Raphael's admission that he patterned his "Triumph of Galatea" not after a living model, but after an "image" in his mind. (Cf. Chap. 3 above, particularly n. 17.)

5. Wackenroder uses the name of Donato d'Agnolo Bramante (1444–1514), a High Renaissance Italian architect renowned primarily for his design of the circular Tempietto in the courtyard of San Pietro in Montorio and for his work on other churches of Rome, as a ruse in the fiction of the "dust-covered parchments." The art-loving friar claims to find several sheets "by the hand of Bramante." There is no factual basis for the existence of such sheets.

6. The prose introduction and poem entitled "Longing for Italy" express a widespread yearning for that country and, most particularly, for exposure to its art; this feeling was by no means confined to Tieck, the author of this particular part of the *Confessions*, and to Wackenroder. It recurs among many of their contemporaries, including Goethe, Moritz, Fr. Schlegel, A. W. Schlegel, etc. It is a motif which Tieck developed further in his novel, *Franz Sternbalds Wanderungen* (1798).

7. In narrating the events surrounding the death of Francesco Francia (1450–1517), Wackenroder deviates extensively from his source in Vasari's *Vite* and embellishes Vasari's account with additional details designed to intensify the emotional factors associated with this death. His motive is to dramatize Francia's grief and dismay at the moment of his realization that he is inferior to Raphael as an artist. (Cf. also the discussion of Francesco Francia in Chap. 3 above.)

8. The figure of Saint Cecilia, patron saint of music and of the blind, has provided an inspirational artistic subject for Rubens, Domenichino, and Raphael, as well as numerous other artists. Raphael's portrait of Saint Cecilia in Bologna is generally evaluated as one of his finest works of art. In addition, St. Cecilia has been commemorated in literary tributes such as Chaucer's "Seconde Nonnes Tale" and Dryden's ode: "Alexander's Feast or, the Power of Music; an Ode in Honor of St. Cecilia's Day." (Cf. also Joseph Berglinger's song in praise of St. Cecilia, W.W., pp. 120–121.)

9. In his letter to Raphael, Antonio addresses the esteemed artist with the German pronouns "Ihr," "Euch," and "Euer" in order to give expression to his respect (see Appendix II, n. 17 below). On the other hand, Raphael answers Antonio with the pronouns traditionally used in addressing young people, the intimate pronouns "Du," "Dir," and "Dich."

10. Wackenroder pays a significant compliment to Leonardo da Vinci (1452–1519), when he chooses to say that "if he had lived during mythical times, then he would inevitably have been considered to be a son of Apollo." The manifold virtues and attributes of the Greek Apollo make him a most worthy model for the versatile Leonardo. (Cf. W.W., p. 40: "Kurz, wenn er in den fabelhaften Zeiten gelebt hätte, so wäre er unfehlbar für einen Sohn des Apollo gehalten worden.")

11. Francis I (1494–1547), king of France and patron of the arts, called Leonardo da Vinci to his court in 1516 and visited the aging and sickly artist frequently. Wackenroder recounts the story of Leonardo's death in the arms of Francis I with much drama and emotion, a treatment in striking contrast with Vasari's factual and unemotional report of this event in his *Vite*, which was Wackenroder's source.

12. The authorship of these two descriptions of art works has not been established with certainty. As noted in Part I they do not describe specific works by known artists, but are general poetic descriptions similar to some of the poems in *The Wanderings of Franz Sternbald*. Their unique and new feature lies in the fact that the characters portrayed in the paintings have speaking roles. (Cf. Fr. von der Leyen's edition, II, p. 259.)

13. As indicated in Chap. 1 above, there is considerable scholarly dispute concerning the actual extent of Wackenroder's knowledge of Dürer's works and the motives for his "admiration" of Dürer. As examples of two diametrically opposed interpretations of this issue, Heinz Lippuner bluntly states that Wackenroder seems to have concerned himself very little with the work of the "great Nuremberger" and to have regarded all early German art with classical eyes (cf. H. Lippuner, *Wackenroder / Tieck und die bildende Kunst*, p. 101); on the other hand, Paul R. Proskauer reads Wackenroder's praise of Dürer much more literally and states: "Dürer possessed what Wackenroder does not have, namely simplicity. It is usually the person who is aware of the problematical side of his being who envies the uncomplicated individual."

[A.1]

(Cf. P. R. Proskauer, "The Phenomenon of Alienation in the Work of Karl Philipp Moritz, . . ." p. 176.)

14. The wife of Albrecht Dürer is traditionally described as an ill-tempered and quarrelsome woman who sorely tried the patience of her calm, composed, and long-suffering husband as well as his pupils and friends. Willibald Pirkheimer, one of Dürer's friends, is said to be responsible for the prolific spreading of this legend (cf. the article on Pirkheimer in *Allgemeine Deutsche Biographie*, XXVI [Leipzig, 1888]).

15. Wackenroder mentions Domenichino Zampieri (1581–1641), Annibale Caracci (1560–1609), Agostino Caracci (1557–1602), Giotto di Bondone (ca. 1266–1337), Cimabue (ca. 1240–1302), Domenico Beccafumi (1486–1551), Andrea Conducci (ca. 1460–1529), Polidoro da Caravaggio (1490/1500–1543), Jacques Callot (1592–1635), Parmeggiano (1503–1540), Lippo di Dalmasio (1352–ca. 1410), Fra Giovanni Angelico (1387–1455), and Aretino Spinello (ca. 1346–1410), touching upon each of these artists briefly in the "Chronicle of Artists." Heinz Lippuner has compiled a complete list of all of the Italian, French, and Dutch artists mentioned by either Wackenroder or Tieck in the *Confessions*, the *Fantasies*, *The Wanderings of Franz Sternbald*, and in the travel diaries (cf. H. Lippuner, *Wackenroder/Tieck und die bildende Kunst*, nn. to Chap. 2, pp. 210–211).

16. The motif of the "shepherd boy" peacefully watching over his sheep is introduced here for the first time in the *Confessions*. It was one of the favorite *topoi* of eighteenth-century "sentimental" literature and of Romanticism. As an example in miniature of the gradual change in Wackenroder's tone from the earlier essays to the late Berglinger letter, one should compare this passage with the lines which occur near the close of the second part of the Berglinger chronicle in the *Confessions*: "What would I like? —— I would like to leave all this culture in the lurch and take refuge with the simple Swiss shepherd in the mountains and play his Alpine songs with him, according to which he becomes homesick everywhere." (W.W., p. 127: "Was ich möchte? —— Ich möchte all diese Kultur im Stiche lassen und mich zu dem simplen Schweizerhirten ins Gebirge hinflüchten und seine Alpenlieder, wonach er überall das Heimweh bekömmt, mit ihm spielen.")

[A.I]   201

Appendix II

NOTES TO
Fantasies on Art for Friends of Art

1. Tieck's preface to the *Fantasies* is not only a tribute to his deceased friend, but also an explanation of the reason why the possible "sequel" mentioned in the preface to the *Confessions*, "To the Reader of These Pages," never came into existence in the form Wackenroder had originally intended.

2. The admiration of Albrecht Dürer initiated in the *Confessions* is continued here. The story of the Dürer family is expanded to include Albrecht Dürer the Elder (1427–1502), who settled in Nuremberg shortly after the middle of the fifteenth century and served as an assistant under a master goldsmith of the city, Hieronymus Holper. This essay on Dürer and his father is a further step toward the highly developed "Dürer admiration" (*Dürerbewunderung*) of Tieck's novel, *Franz Sternbalds Wanderungen* (1798).

3. "World-Soul"—"Weltseele"; this term was first coined by the Pythagoreans and Plato (Tim. 34 B). It has been employed with a variety of definitions and implications by the Stoics, Neo-Platonics, Bruno, Herder, Goethe, and so forth. Wackenroder uses it here to signify the "organizing principle" which unites all of an artist's creations into a single totality. In *Von der Weltseele*, published in 1798, Schelling uses the term as the organizing principle which unites all of Nature into a single, harmonious entity; (cf. "Weltseele" in Johannes Hoffmeister, *Wörterbuch der philosophischen Begriffe*, 2d ed. [Hamburg, 1955]).

4. The term "PERSONALIA," which is printed in Wackenroder's original text in capital letters, is derived from the Latin noun *persona*. It refers to all biographical facts concerning the life of an individual.

5. Wackenroder mentions Joachim von Sandrart, *Teutsche Akademie der edlen Bau-, Bild- und Mahlereykünste*, 2 vols. (Nuremberg and Frankfurt, 1675) as his source for information concerning the life of Albrecht Dürer and for the Dürer quotations which the essay contains. Wackenroder probably used the second edition of Sandrart's work, edited by J. J. Volkmann, 2 vols., 1768 and 1775. He may also have referred to Matthes Quad's *Teutscher Nation Herrlichkeit* (Cologne, 1609). His interest in Dürer and his family originated with his visit to Nuremberg (W.W., pp. 497–521) in June, 1793.

6. According to the Roman Catholic calendar, St. Matthew's Day is celebrated on September 21, therefore Albrecht Dürer the Elder died late in the evening on September 20, 1502 (cf. *A Catholic Dictionary*, originally published under the title *The Catholic Encyclopaedic Dictionary*, ed. Donald Attwater, 3d ed. [New York, 1958], p. 315).

7. Never having visited the city of Rome, Wackenroder had no firsthand impression of St. Peter's Cathedral. Paul Koldewey suggests that Wackenroder gained his knowlege of the cathedral secondhand from Karl Philipp Moritz's description of St. Peter's, first printed in his periodical *Italien und Deutschland* (4. Stück, 82ff. and 5. Stück, 28ff.). Koldewey cites resemblances between the essays by Moritz and Wackenroder in support of this contention (cf. Koldewey, *Wackenroder und sein Einfluss auf Tieck*, pp. 64–66). Even more striking to this author are the pages of Moritz's volume, *Die neue Cecilia: Letzte Blätter von Karl Philipp Moritz* (Berlin, 1794), where the buildings of Rome are described in eloquent language closely paralleling that of Wackenroder's essay on the *Peterskirche*, especially pp. 26–27.

8. Klaus Weimar convincingly disputes Werner Kohlschmidt's argument (cf. "Der junge Tieck und Wackenroder," p. 42) that Tieck is the author of the "Wondrous Oriental Tale of a Naked Saint." Weimar points out that Kohlschmidt overlooks the fact that the kernel idea of the tale already occurs in a letter from Wackenroder to Tieck written in late 1792 (W.W., pp. 379–388; particularly p. 385ff.). Weimar also stresses the presence of the same motif in "A Letter by Joseph Berglinger," which is now generally attributed to Wackenroder. (Cf. Klaus Weimar, *Versuch über Voraussetzung und Entstehung der Romantik*, p. 68.)

9. Wackenroder's "Oriental Tale" recalls the fairy tale motif of the hermit in his remote, isolated cave, a motif which also occurs in various other Early Romantic works, most notably in Novalis' *Heinrich von Ofterdingen*. In Wackenroder's tale, however, there is a new, desperately negative and nihilistic tone, for the "naked saint," despite his retreat from the active world, is nevertheless possessed by the compulsive idea that he must unceasingly turn the raging Wheel of Time. For a discussion of this in relation to other German Romantic literature (cf. Walter Wiora, "Die Musik im Weltbild der deutschen Romantik," *Beiträge zur Geschichte der Musikanschauung im 19. Jahrhundert*, ed. Walter Salmen [Regensburg, 1965], pp. 11–50).

10. E. Hertrich corrects Koldewey's interpretation that the preface of Tieck's "Marvelous Love Story of the Beautiful Magelone and Count Peter of Provence" (*Wundersame Liebesgeschichte der schönen Magelone und des Grafen Peter aus der Provence*) stands under the direct influence of Joseph Berglinger's fairy tale. Hertrich points out that the traditional literary image of the Wheel of Fortune includes the up-and-down motion, the alternation of fortune and misfortune, which characterizes Tieck's "Magelone." In contrast, this feature is totally lacking in the image of Berglinger's Wheel of Time. It is not the rise and fall, but the ceaselessness and the monotony of the rushing revolutions of the Wheel that captivate the saint, so that he perceives nothing else and only turns the monstrous wheel (cf. Elmar Hertrich, *Joseph Berglinger: Eine Studie zu Wackenroders Musiker-Dichtung*, p. 174).

11. The consciousness of time—and of its fleeting, transitory quality—entered into European thought during the sixteenth century and became intensified during the Thirty Years War. It is by no means a new thought in the Berglinger fairy tale. As Marianne Thalmann explains in *Romantik und Manierismus* (p. 18): "Schon im 16. und 17. Jahrhundert wird die Welt Eindruck und Erlebnis. Zeitbewusstsein zieht mit den unzähligen Wunderuhren, Weltreisen und Buchdruck in das europäische Denken ein. Was fasziniert, ist die Zeit. Der Raumzusammenhang, wie ihn die Renaissance gepflegt hat, wird in Raumteile aufgelöst. Jede Zentralisation ist aufgegeben." Klaus Weimar interprets the "Oriental Tale of a Naked Saint" as containing three types of experience of time. The pilgrim, the herb gatherer, and the wood cutter all experience time as the totally unproblematic medium of their lives; the naked saint is obsessed with the awareness of passing time to such a degree that time dominates him, becomes wholly problematic for him, and he hears the Wheel of Time raging on incessantly; the third experience of time is that made possible by music, which fills and orders time with its own releasing rhythm (cf. K. Weimar, *Versuch über Voraussetzung und Entstehung der Romantik*, pp. 69–70).

[A.II]

12. "Poetry"—"Poesie"; this translation was selected because of the archaically limited con-notations of the English word "poesy," which would not appropriately convey the wider definition of the German term to include all forms of creative writing. The same selection was made by Ernst Behler and Roman Struc in their translation of Friedrich Schlegel's *Gespräch über die Poesie as Dialogue on Poetry* (University Park & London, 1968).

13. Wackenroder's use of the term "Muse" in this passage follows the tradition of Homer. He simply refers to three Muses, those of poetry, painting, and religious music; however, he does not identify them with specific names.

14. Although Wackenroder does not employ the technique of synesthesia as frequently as do his contemporaries, Tieck, Brentano, Hölderlin, et al., he does use it occasionally, particularly with reference to the description of music. This passage exemplifies his use of the technique, for Berglinger speaks of the musical sounds as if they had a lovely fragrance: "Sie füllten die ganze Luft mit den lieblichen Düften ihres Klanges an" (W.W., p. 215).

15. This essay points directly to Wackenroder's interest in the "psychology" of music, name-ly, the effect of music upon the psyche of the listener. Along with the Berglinger essays, it also demonstrates the point made by Murray H. Abrams that, in the late eighteenth century, "In place of painting, music becomes the art frequently pointed to as having a profound affinity with poetry." (Cf. M. H. Abrams, *The Mirror and the Lamp: Romantic Theory and the Critical Tradition* [New York, 1953], p. 50.)

16. In his English introduction to the *Herzensergiessungen* (1948), A. Gillies suggests that the content of the essay is based to a large extent on the lectures of Johann Nikolaus Forkel (1749–1818). Wackenroder attended the lectures of Forkel at Göttingen. He is known to have read the first volume of Forkel's *Allgemeine Geschichte der Musik* (Leipzig, 1788) and al-though the second volume was not published until 1801, it is probable that he acquired much of its content in lecture form (cf. Gillies' edition of the *Herzensergiessungen*, pp. xxviii–xxix).

17. Berglinger employs the pronouns "Ihr" and "Euch" in addressing the friar, who is called *Pater* in the context of this letter. The English pronouns "Thou" and "Thee" were selected for the translation, since they provided approximately the same tone of respectful veneration in eighteenth-century English.

18. Wackenroder makes direct use of the *theatrum mundi* topos in this passage (cf. Ernst Robert Curtius, *European Literature and the Latin Middle Ages*, pp. 138–144). However, for Wackenroder it is the artist who creates his *own theater* through the aid of his creative imagi-nation. The actors in the "real" world are a mere reflection of those upon his stage.

19. Here Wackenroder makes use of a popular Romantic metaphor, that of the Aeolian lyre. However, he employs it in a new way, as an analogy for the poetic mind. The soul of the individual with artistic feeling resembles the floating Aeolian lyre. (Cf. Shelley, "Defence of Poetry," *Shelley's Literary and Philosophical Criticism*, ed. John Shawcross [Oxford, 1909], p. 121: "Man is an instrument over which a series of external and internal impressions are driven, like the alternations of an ever-changing wind over an Aeolian lyre, which move it by their motion to ever-changing melody.")

[A.II]

Bibliography[1]

1. Editions of Wilhelm Heinrich Wackenroder's Works

1797 *Herzensergiessungen eines kunstliebenden Klosterbruders*. Berlin: Friedrich Unger.
First Edition, actually printed in late 1796.

1799 *Phantasien über die Kunst für Freunde der Kunst*. Edited by Ludwig Tieck. Hamburg: Friedrich Perthes.
First Edition, containing Tieck's contributions along with those of Wackenroder.

1814 *Phantasien über die Kunst, von einem kunstliebenden Klosterbruder*. Edited by Ludwig Tieck. Berlin: Realschulbuchandlung.
Revised version in which Tieck included all of Wackenroder's contributions to the *Herzensergiessungen* and *Phantasien*, but omitted his own.

1818 *Phantasien über die Kunst, von einem kunstliebenden Klosterbruder*. Edited by Ludwig Tieck. Vienna: Leopold Grund.
Revised printing of the 1814 edition.

1864 *Briefe an Ludwig Tieck*. Edited by C. E. von Holtei. Breslau.
First Edition of Wackenroder's correspondence with Tieck.

1886 *Tieck und Wackenroder*. Vol. CXLV of *Deutsche National-Litteratur*. Edited by Jakob Minor. Stuttgart: Union Deutsche Verlagsgesellschaft.
Containing a brief introduction by the editor and the complete text of the 1799 edition, *Phantasien über die Kunst für Freunde der Kunst*.

1904 *Herzensergiessungen eines kunstliebenden Klosterbruders*. Edited by Karl Detlev Jessen. Leipzig: Eugen Diederichs.
Containing a thirty-page introduction by the editor and the complete text of the 1797 edition.

1910 *Werke und Briefe*. Edited by Friedrich von der Leyen. 2 vols. Jena: Eugen Diederichs.
Containing the *Herzensergiessungen* and the *Phantasien* with Tieck's contributions separated from Wackenroder's work and printed in Vol. I, Anhang I. Vol. II contains their correspondence as well as one travel diary: "Bericht Wackenroders über seine Pfingstreise mit Tieck 1793."

[1] There is a vast quantity of critical literature on Wackenroder. This bibliography is not intended to provide a complete listing of that literature. In addition to the studies cited and discussed in the interpretation and notes, I have included all other critical works which were useful in the writing of the present study.

1917 *Herzensergiessungen eines kunstliebenden Klosterbruders*. Edited by Ernst Ludwig Schellenberg. Weimar: Gustav Kiepenheuer.
Containing a ten-page introduction by the editor, five illustrations, and Wackenroder's contributions to the *Herzensergiessungen* and *Phantasien*, but not those of Tieck.

1921 *Herzensergiessungen eines kunstliebenden Klosterbruders*. Edited by Oskar Walzel. Leipzig: Insel.
Containing a forty-one-page introduction by the editor, the complete text of the 1797 edition, and an *Anhang* including a variety of testimonials to Wackenroder and his works.

1931 *Kunstanschauung der Frühromantik*. Vol. III of *Deutsche Literatur, Reihe Romantik*. Edited by Andreas Müller. Leipzig.
Containing the complete text of the *Herzensergiessungen* and excerpts from the *Phantasien*.

1938 *Werke und Briefe von Wilhelm Heinrich Wackenroder*. Berlin: Lambert Schneider.
First composite edition, containing the complete texts of the *Herzensergiessungen* of 1797 and the *Phantasien* of 1799, the preface and table of contents of the 1814 edition, as well as the correspondence, excluding one of the extant "Reiseberichte" and the "Frühe Arbeiten und Versuche."

1938 *Wilhelm Heinrich Wackenroder: Reisebriefe*. Edited by Heinrich Höhn. Berlin: Lambert Schneider.
A special edition of the travel diaries, including all but the then undiscovered "Reise nach Nürnberg und Fürth," and containing an introduction, illustrations, and critical notes by the editor.

1947 *Phantasien über die Kunst für Freunde der Kunst*. Edited by K. F. Riedler. Zürich: Thalwil.
Containing the text of the 1799 edition and an introduction by the editor.

1948 *Welhelm Heinrich Wackenroder and Ludwig Tieck: Herzensergiessungen eines kunstliebenden Klosterbruders* together with Wackenroder's contributions to the *Phantasien über die Kunst für Freunde der Kunst*. Edited by A. Gillies. Oxford: Basil Blackwell.
Containing the complete text of the 1797 edition and the parts of the *Phantasien* generally attributed to Wackenroder as well as an English introduction and notes on Wackenroder's sources; reprinted in 1966.

1949 *Herzensergiessungen eines kunstliebenden Klosterbruders*. Edited by Hans Heinrich Borcherdt. Munich.
Containing the complete text of the 1797 edition as well as Tieck's preface to the 1814 edition and twenty pages of critical notes.

1955 *W. Wackenroder, L. Tieck: Herzensergiessungen eines kunstliebenden Klosterbruders*. Edited by Richard Benz. Stuttgart: Reclam.
Containing the complete text of the 1797 edition and an eleven-page "Nachwort" by the editor; reprinted in 1963.

1967 *Werke und Briefe von Wilhelm Heinrich Wackenroder*. Heidelberg: Lambert Schneider.
Photomechanical reproduction of the composite edition of 1938, with the addition of the recently discovered travel diary: "Reise nach Ansbach und Nürnberg" and an updated bibliography. This edition was selected as the source for all references to Wackenroder's writings in the introductory sections of this study and the critical notes because it is the best readily accessible, complete edition. It is cited with the abbreviation: W.W.

2. Translations of Wilhelm Heinrich Wackenroder's Works

Guglielmo Enrico Wackenroder. *Opere e lettere*. Translated into Italian by Gina Martegiani. Lanciano, 1916.

Wilhelm Heinrich Wackenroder. *Fantaisies sur l'art par un religieux ami de l'art*. Translated into French by Jean Boyer. Paris, Aubier: Éditions Montaigne, 1945. A dual-language edition.

Wilhelm Heinrich Wackenroder. *Geijutsu o Aisuru ichi shûdôsô no shinjô no Hireki*. Translated into Japanese by Eiichi Egawa. Tokyo: Iwanami shoten, 1956.

3. Editions of Literary Works Other Than Those of Wilhelm Heinrich Wackenroder

Athenaeum, I–III (Berlin, 1798–1800). Edited by Friedrich and August Welhelm Schlegel. (Photomechanical reproduction of the original journal, Stuttgart, 1960.)

Charakteristiken. *Die Romantiker in Selbstzeugnissen und Äusserungen ihrer Zeitgenossen*. Vol. I of *Deutsche Literatur. Sammlung literarischer Kunst- und Kulturdenkmäler in Entwicklungsreihen*. Edited by Paul Kluckhohn. Reihe Romantik. Stuttgart, 1950.

Eichendorff, Joseph Freiherr von. *Neue Gesamtausgabe der Werke und Schriften in vier Bänden*. Edited by Gerhart Baumann in cooperation with Siegfried Grosse. Stuttgart, 1957–1958.

Goethe, Johann Wolfgang von. *Werke*, Abt. 1, XLVIII, XLIX, XIX, XXXV. Ed. im Auftrage der Grossherzogin Sophie von Sachsen. Weimar, 1887–1920.

————. *Gedenkausgabe der Werke, Briefe und Gespräche*, IX, XIII, XVIII, XIX, XX. Edited by Ernst Beutler. Zürich, 1948–1962.

Heine, Heinrich. *Sämtliche Werke*, V. Edited by Ernst Elster. Leipzig and Vienna, 1898.

Herder, Johann Gottfried von. *Sämmtliche Werke*, V, VIII, X. Edited by Bernhard Suphan. Berlin, 1877–1913.

————. *Sämmtliche Werke: Zur schönen Literatur und Kunst*, XV. Stuttgart and Tübingen, 1829.

Hölderlin, Friedrich. *Sämtliche Werke* (*Grosse Stuttgarter Ausgabe*), III. Edited by Friedrich Beissner. Stuttgart, 1964–1968.

Humboldt, Wilhelm von. *Gesammelte Werke*, VIII. Ed. von der Königlich Preussischen Akademie der Wissenschaften. Berlin, 1903–1920.

Köpke, Rudolf. *Ludwig Tieck. Erinnerungen aus dem Leben des Dichters nach dessen mündlichen und schriftlichen Mittheilungen*. 2 vols. Leipzig, 1855.

Meyer, Johann Heinrich. *Neu-deutsche religios-patriotische Kunst* (1817). In: Goethe, *Werke*, Abt 1, XLIX. Ed. im Auftrage der Grossherzogin Sophie von Sachsen. Weimar, 1887–1920.

Miller, Johann Martin. *Siegwart. Eine Klostergeschichte*. 2d ed. Karlsruhe, 1782.

Moritz, Karl Philipp, ed. "ΤΝΩΘΙ ΣΑΥΤΟΝ oder Magazin zur Erfahrungsseelenkunde als ein Lesebuch für Gelehrte und Ungelehrte" (Berlin, 1783–1793), I–X.

———. *Die neue Cecilia: Letzte Blätter von Karl Philipp Moritz.* Berlin, 1794. (Photomechanical reprint of the 1st ed., Stuttgart, 1962).

———. *Schriften zur Ästhetik und Poetik.* Edited by Hans Joachim Schrimpf. (= *Neudrucke deutscher Literaturwerke,* Neue Folge 7) Tübingen, 1962.

———. *Anton Reiser. Ein psychologischer Roman* (=*Bibliothek deutscher Romane*) Wiesbaden, 1959.

Novalis. *Schriften. Die Werke Friedrich von Hardenbergs,* I–IV. 2d rev. ed. Edited by Paul Kluckhohn and Richard Samuel. Stuttgart, 1960.

Pierce, F. E. *Fiction and Fantasy of German Romance: Selections from German Romantic Authors, 1790–1830.* New York and Oxford, 1937.

Reichardt, Johann Friedrich, ed. *Deutschland,* I–IV. Berlin, 1796.

———. *Leben des berühmten Tonkünstlers Heinrich Wilhelm Gulden, nachher genannt Guglielmo Enrico Fiorino,* 1. Teil. Berlin, 1779.

Schlegel, August Wilhelm. *Sämmtliche Werke,* X. Edited by E. Böcking. Leipzig, 1847.

———. *Kritische Schriften und Briefe,* I–VI. Edited by Edgar Lohner. (= *Sprache und Literatur*), Stuttgart, 1962–1968.

Schlegel, Friedrich. *Dichtungen,* Abt. 1, V. Edited and introduced by Hans Eichner. (=*Kritische Friedrich-Schlegel-Ausgabe,* ed.; Jean-Jacques Anstett, Ernst Behler, Hans Eichner, et al.) Munich, Paderborn, Vienna, Zürich, 1962.

———. *Dialogue on Poetry and Literary Aphorisms.* Translated, introduced, and annotated by Ernst Behler and Roman Struc. University Park, Pa., 1968.

Schüddekopf, Carl, and Walzel, Oskar. *Goethe und die Romantik. Briefe mit Erläuterungen,* 1. Theil. (= *Schriften der Goethe-Gesellschaft,* XIII) Weimar, 1898.

Shelley, Percy. *Shelley's Literary and Philosophical Criticism.* Edited by John Shawcross. Oxford, 1909.

Tieck, Ludwig. *Schriften.* Berlin, 1828–1854.

———. *Franz Sternbalds Wanderungen. Eine altdeutsche Geschichte.* Vol. I of *Deutsche Literatur. Sammlung literarischer Kunst- und Kulturdenkmäler in Entwicklungsreihen.* Edited by Paul Kluckhohn. Reihe Romantik. Frühromantische Erzählungen. Leipzig, 1933.

4. Critical Works

Abrams, Murray H. *The Mirror and the Lamp: Romantic Theory and the Critical Tradition.* New York, 1953.

A Catholic Dictionary (originally published under the title *The Catholic Encyclopaedic Dictionary*). 3d ed. Edited by Donald Attwater. New York, 1958.

Alewyn, Richard. "Wackenroders Anteil," *Germanic Review*, XIX (1944), 48–58.

Apfelstedt, H. *Selbsterziehung und Selbstbildung in der deutschen Frühromantik. Friedrich Schlegel, Novalis, Wackenroder, Tieck*. Munich, 1958.

Benz, Richard. *Die deutsche Romantik. Geschichte einer geistigen Bewegung*. Leipzig, 1937.

――――. *Goethe und die romantische Kunst*. Munich, 1940.

Brion, Marcel. *L'Allemagne romantique. Kleist, Brentano, Wackenroder, Tieck, Caroline von Günderode*. Paris, 1962.

Catholy, Eckehard. *Karl Philipp Moritz und die Ursprünge der deutschen Theaterleidenschaft*. Tübingen, 1962.

Curtius, Ernst Robert. *European Literature and the Latin Middle Ages*. Translated from German by Willard R. Trask. New York and Evanston, 1953.

Dessauer, Ernst. "Wackenroders 'Herzensergiessungen eines kunstliebenden Klosterbruders' in ihrem Verhältnis zu Vasari." In: *Studien zur vergleichenden Literaturgeschichte*. Berlin, 1906–1907. VI, 245–270 and VII, 204–235.

Dilthey, Wilhelm. *Gesammelte Schriften*, Vols. II, IV, and VI. Leipzig and Berlin, 1914–1924.

――――. *Leben Schleiermachers*. 2d ed. Berlin and Leipzig, 1922.

Eichendorff heute. Edited by Paul Stöcklein. Munich, 1960. (Photomechanical reprint, Darmstadt, 1966).

Eichner, Hans. "The Genesis of German Romanticism," *The Queen's Quarterly*, LXXII (1965), 213–231.

Francke, Kuno. *A History of German Literature as Determined by Social Forces*. New York, 1916. (1st ed. under the title *Social Forces in German Literature*, 1896).

Fricke, Gerhard. "Bemerkungen zu Wilhelm Heinrich Wackenroders Religion der Kunst." In: *Festschrift Paul Kluckhohn und Hermann Schneider gewidmet*. Tübingen, 1948. (Reprinted in G. Fricke, *Studien und Interpretationen*. Frankfurt am Main, 1956.)

Gillies, Alexander. "Wackenroder's Apprenticeship to Literature: His Teachers and Their Influence." In: *German Studies Presented to H. G. Fiedler*. Oxford, 1938.

Goodnight, Scott Holland. *German Literature in American Magazines Prior to 1846*. Madison, Wisc., 1907.

Gülzow, Erich. *Wackenroder. Beiträge zur Lebensgeschichte des Romantikers*. Stralsund, 1930.

Gundolf, Friedrich. *Romantiker*. Neue Folge. Berlin-Wilmersdorf, 1931.

Haertel, M. H. *German Literature in American Magazines, 1846–1880*. Madison, Wisc., 1908.

Hammer, Dorothea. *Die Bedeutung der vergangenen Zeit im Werk Wackenroders unter Berücksichtigung der Beiträge Tiecks*. Frankfurt am Main, 1960.

Hartmann, Hans. *Kunst und Religion bei Wackenroder, Tieck, und Solger*. Erlangen, 1916.

[B]

Haym, Rudolf. *Die romantische Schule. Ein Beitrag zur Geschichte des deutschen Geistes.* 1st ed. Berlin, 1870. (Photomechanical reprint, Darmstadt, 1961).

Henkel, Arthur. "Was ist eigentlich romantisch?" In: *Festschrift für Richard Alewyn.* Cologne, 1967.

Hertrich, Elmar. *Joseph Berglinger, Eine Studie zu Wackenroders Musiker-Dichtung.* Berlin, 1969.

Huch, Ricarda. *Die Romantik,* Vol. I. Leipzig, 1922.

Jost, Walter. *Von Ludwig Tieck zu E. T. A. Hoffmann. Studien zur Entwicklungsgeschichte des romantischen Subjektivismus.* Vol. IV of *Deutsche Forschungen.* Edited by Friedrich Panzer and Julius Petersen. Frankfurt am Main, 1921.

Kahn, Robert L. "Some Recent Definitions of German Romanticism, or The Case against Dialectics," *Rice University Studies,* L (Fall, 1964), 3–19.

Kayser, Wolfgang. *Die Vortragsreise: Studien zur Literatur.* Bern, 1958.

—————. *Das sprachliche Kunstwerk: Eine Einführung in die Literaturwissenschaft.* 6th ed. Bern, 1960.

Kluckhohn, Paul. *Die deutsche Romantik.* Bielefeld and Leipzig, 1924.

Kohlschmidt, Werner. "Nihilismus der Romantik." In: *Form und Innerlichkeit, Beiträge zur Geschichte und Wirkung der deutschen Klassik und Romantik.* Munich, 1955.

—————. "Wackenroder und die Klassik, Versuch einer Präzisierung." In: *Unterscheidung und Bewahrung. Festschrift für H. Kunisch zum 60. Geburtstag.* Berlin, 1961. (Reprinted in W. Kohlschmidt, *Dichter, Tradition und Zeitgeist. Gesammelte Studien zur Literaturgeschichte.* Bern and Munich, 1965.)

—————. "Bemerkungen zu Wackenroders und Tiecks Anteil an den Phantasien über die Kunst." In: *Philologia Deutsch, Festschrift zum 70. Geburtstag von Walter Henzen.* Bern, 1965.

—————. "Der junge Tieck und Wackenroder." In: *Die deutsche Romantik.* Edited by H. Steffen. Göttingen, 1967.

Koldewey, Paul. *Wackenroder und sein Einfluss auf Tieck. Ein Beitrag zur Quellengeschichte der Romantik.* Leipzig, 1904.

Korff, Hermann August. *Geist der Goethezeit,* Vols. I–IV. Leipzig, 1923–1948.

Kreuzer, Helmut. *Die Boheme, Beiträge zu ihrer Beschreibung.* Stuttgart, 1968.

Kröll, Joachim. "Ludwig Tieck und W. H. Wackenroder in Francken," *Archiv für Geschichte und Alterthumskunde von Oberfranken,* XLI (1961), 345–377.

Langen, August. "Verbale Dynamik in der dichterischen Landschaftsschilderung des 18. Jahrhunderts," *Zeitschrift für deutsche Philologie,* LXX (1949), 249–318.

—————. "Deutsche Sprachgeschichte vom Barock bis zur Gegenwart." In Vol. I of *Deutsche Philologie im Aufriss.* Edited by Wolfgang Stammler. Berlin, Bielefeld, and Munich, 1952.

—————. *Der Wortschatz des deutschen Pietismus.* 2d enlarged ed. Tübingen, 1968.

————. "Der Wortschatz des 18. Jahrhunderts." In: *Deutsche Wortgeschichte.* Edited by F. Maurer and F. Stroh. 2d ed. Berlin, 1959–1960.

————. "Karl Philipp Moritz' Weg zur symbolischen Dichtung," *Zeitschrift für deutsche Philologie,* LXXXI (1962), 169–218, 402–440.

————. "Zum Problem der sprachlichen Säkularisation in der deutschen Dichtung des 18. und 19. Jahrhunderts," *Zeitschrift für deutsche Philologie,* LXXXIII (1964), 24–42.

Lippuner, Heinz. *Wackenroder/Tieck und die bildende Kunst. Grundlegung der romantischen Aesthetik.* Zürich, 1965.

Lovejoy, Arthur O. "On the Discrimination of Romanticisms," *PMLA,* XXXIX (1924), 229–253.

Lüdeke, H. *Ludwig Tieck und die Brüder Schlegel.* Frankfurt, 1930.

Mahrholz, Werner. *Deutsche Selbstbekenntnisse. Ein Beitrag zur Geschichte der Selbstbiographie von der Mystik bis zum Pietismus.* Berlin, 1919.

Malsch, Wilfried. *Der Geschichtliche Sinn der Kunstanschauung und der Kritik in der deutschen Klassik.* (In press.)

Markwardt, Bruno. *Geschichte der deutschen Poetik,* Vol. III. Berlin and Leipzig, 1937–1959.

Matenko, Percy. *Ludwig Tieck and America.* Chapel Hill, 1954. (Reprinted by Ams. Press, Inc., New York, 1966.)

Mittner, Ladislao. "Galatea. Die Romantisierung der italienischen Renaissancekunst und -dichtung in der deutschen Frühromantik," *Deutsche Vierteljahrsschrift,* XXVII (1953), 555–581.

Morgan, Bayard Quincy. *A Critical Bibliography of German Literature in English Translation, 1481–1927, with Supplement Embracing the Years 1928–1935.* 2d ed. Stanford, 1938.

Müller, Andreas, ed. *Kunstanschauung der Frühromantik. Deutsche Literatur. Sammlung literarischer Kunst und Kulturdenkmäler in Entwicklungsreihen,* Vol. III. Reihe Romantik. Leipzig, 1931.

Müller-Vollmer, Kurt. *Poesie und Einbildungskraft. Zur Dichtungstheorie Wilhelm von Humboldts.* Stuttgart, 1967.

Nadler, Josef. *Die Berliner Romantiker, 1800–1814: Ein Beitrag zur gemeinvölkischen Frage: Renaissance, Romantik, Restauration.* Berlin, 1921.

Petersen, Julius. *Die Wesensbestimmung der deutschen Romantik. Eine Einführung in die moderne Literaturwissenschaft.* Leipzig, 1926.

Proskauer, Paul R. "The Phenomenon of Alienation in the Work of Karl Philipp Moritz, Wilhelm Heinrich Wackenroder and in 'Nachtwachen' von Bonaventura." Ph.D. dissertation, Columbia University, 1966.

Robson-Scott, W. D. "Wackenroder and the Middle Ages," *Modern Language Review,* L (1955), 156–167.

Rouge, I. "Wackenroder et la genese de l'esthetique romantique." In: *Mélanges Henri Lichtenberger*. Paris, 1934.

Ryan, Lawrence. *Hölderlins "Hyperion." Exzentrische Bahn und Dichterberuf*. Stuttgart, 1965.

Sanford, David Bruce. "Wackenroder and Tieck: The Aesthetic Breakdown of the *Klosterbruder* Ideal." Ph.D. dissertation, University of Minnesota, 1966.

Santoli, Vittorio. "L. Tieck e W. H. Wackenroder (a proposito de concetto dell'arte," *La Cultura. Revista mensile di filosofia, lettere, arte*, V (1925–1926), 63–68.

Scheidig, Walther. *Goethes Preisaufgaben für bildende Künstler, 1799–1805* (= *Schriften der Goethe-Gesellschaft*, LVII). Weimar, 1958.

Schneider, Karl Ludwig. *Klopstock und die Erneuerung der deutschen Dichtersprache im 18. Jahrhundert*. Heidelberg, 1960.

Schöne, Albrecht. *Säkularisation als sprachbildende Kraft. Studien zur Dichtung deutscher Pfarrersöhne* (= *Palaestra*, MMXXVI). Berlin, 1958.

Schoolfield, George C. *The Figure of the Musician in German Literature* (= University of North Carolina Studies in the Germanic Languages and Literatures, XIX). Chapel Hill, 1956.

Schrimpf, Hans Joachim. "W. H. Wackenroder und K. Ph. Moritz. Ein Beitrag zur frühromantischen Selbstkritik," *Zeitschrift für deutsche Philologie*, LXXXIII (1964), 385–411.

Seidlin, Oskar. *Versuche über Eichendorff*. Göttingen, 1965.

Staiger, Emil. "Ludwig Tieck und der Ursprung der deutschen Romantik," *Die neue Rundschau*, LXXI (1960).

Stockley, V. *German Literature as Known in England, 1750–1830*. London, 1929.

Stöcker, Helene. *Zur Kunstanschauung des 18. Jahrhunderts. Von Winckelmann bis zu Wackenroder* (= *Palaestra*, XXVI). Berlin, 1904.

Strich, Fritz. *Deutsche Klassik und Romantik, oder Vollendung und Unendlichkeit: Ein Vergleich*. Munich, 1922.

Strohschneider-Kohrs, Ingrid. *Die romantische Ironie in Theorie und Gestaltung* (= *Hermaea. Germanistische Forschungen*, Neue Folge, VI). Tübingen, 1960.

Tecchi, Bonaventura. *Wilhelm Heinrich Wackenroder*. Florence, 1927. (Translated from Italian to German by Claus Riessner. Bad Homburg v. d. H., 1962).

Thalmann, Marianne. *Romantik und Manierismus*. Stuttgart, 1963.

Thomas, Calvin. *A History of German Literature*. London, 1909.

Thornton, Karin. "Wackenroder's Objective Romanticism," *Germanic Review*, XXXVII (1962), 161–173.

Trainer, James. *Ludwig Tieck. From Gothic to Romantic* (= *Anglica Germanica. British Studies in Germanic Languages and Literatures*, VIII). The Hague, 1964.

[B]

Vasari, Giorgio. *Delle Vite de più eccellenti pittori, scultori ed architettori.* Florence, 1550. (Translated into English and annotated by E. H. and E. W. Blashfield and A. A. Hopkins, *Lives of Seventy of the Most Eminent Painters, Sculptors and Architects.* New York, 1917.) Cited: Vasari, *Lives.*

Walzel, Oskar. *Deutsche Romantik.* 4th ed. Leipzig, 1918. (Translated into English by A. E. Lussky. New York, 1932).

————. "Die Sprache der Kunst." In: *Vom Geistesleben Alter und Neuer Zeit.* Leipzig, 1922. (Reprinted in *Jahrbuch der Goethe-Gesellschaft*, I, 1964).

————. *Grenzen der Poesie und Unpoesie.* Frankfurt, 1937.

Weimar, Klaus. *Versuch über Voraussetzung und Entstehung der Romantik.* Tübingen, 1968.

Wellek, René, and Warren, Austin. *Theory of Literature.* New York, 1949.

Wellek, René, "The Concept of 'Romanticism' in Literary History," *Comparative Literature,* I (1949), 1–23, 147–172.

————. *A History of Modern Criticism: 1750–1950.* Vols. I–IV. New Haven, 1955.

————. *Concepts of Criticism.* New Haven, 1963.

————. *Confrontations: Studies in the Intellectual and Literary Relations between Germany, England, and the United States during the Nineteenth Century.* Princeton, 1965.

Wiora, Walter. "Die Musik im Weltbild der deutschen Romantik." In: *Beiträge zur Geschichte der Musikanschauung im 19. Jahrhundert.* Edited by Walter Salmen. Regensburg, 1965.

Wölfflin, Heinrich. "Die Herzensergiessungen eines kunstliebenden Klosterbruders." In: *Studien zur Literaturgeschichte Michael Bernays gewidmet.* Hamburg, 1893. (Reprinted in Wölfflin's *Kleine Schriften.* Basel, 1946.)

Wörterbuch der philosophischen Begriffe. 2d ed. Edited by Johannes Hoffmeister. Hamburg, 1955.

Wolkan, R. "Ein unbekanntes Tagebuch Wilhelm Wackenroders," *Süddeutsche Monatshefte,* IX (1912).

Zeydel, Edwin H. "The Relation of K. Ph. Moritz's *Anton Reiser* to Romanticism," *Germanic Review*, III (1928), 295–327.

————. *Ludwig Tieck and England: A Study in the Literary Relations of Germany and England during the Early Nineteenth Century.* Princeton, 1931.

————. *Ludwig Tieck, The German Romanticist. A Critical Study.* Princeton, 1935.

————. "The Concepts 'Classic' and 'Romantic': Some Fundamental Observations," *The Germanic Review*, XIX (1944), 161–169.

Index

216

217

218

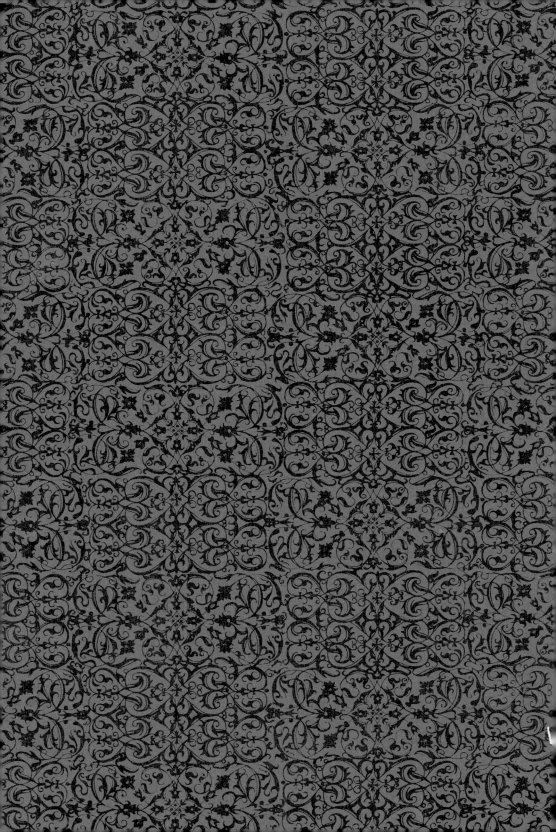

WILHELM HEINRICH WACKENRODER'S

Confessions and Fantasies

WILHELM HEINRICH WACKENRODER'S

Confessions and *Fantasies*

Translated and annotated
with a Critical Introduction
by

MARY HURST SCHUBERT

THE PENNSYLVANIA STATE UNIVERSITY PRESS
University Park and London